Perspectives
for
Reform
in
Teacher Education

Perspectives
for
Reform
in
Teacher Education

edited by
Bruce Joyce and Marsha Weil

Columbia University Teachers College

Prentice-Hall, Inc., Englewood Cliffs, New Jersey

© 1972 by Prentice-Hall, Inc., Englewood Cliffs, New Jersey

13–660696–2

LIBRARY OF CONGRESS CATALOG CARD NUMBER: 71–150714

Current Printing (Last Digit):

10   9   8   7   6   5   4   3   2   1

PRINTED IN THE UNITED STATES OF AMERICA

PRENTICE-HALL INTERNATIONAL, INC., *London*
PRENTICE-HALL OF AUSTRALIA, PTY. LTD., *Sydney*
PRENTICE-HALL OF CANADA, LTD., *Toronto*
PRENTICE-HALL OF INDIA PRIVATE LIMITED, *New Delhi*
PRENTICE-HALL OF JAPAN, INC., *Tokyo*

To
Katie, Rhoada, Clark,
Lucy, and Irene
whose strength and sensitivity
made it happen,
at least in a few places.

Contents

vii

Perspectives
for
Reform
in
Teacher Education

Introduction

To create a better education we must establish truly humane and experimental schools, for we are still ignorant about education and must learn to study it even while carrying it out. Humanistic, experimental schools require teachers who are innovators and who search restlessly for a better way to help their students grow.

In this book we present a collection of papers which are sources of ideas for educating teachers. Most of these papers were written to provide a frame of reference for experimentation in one phase or another of a teacher education program and to conceptualize the entire shape of a program. Most of them were part of a teacher education program which is carried on and studied at Teachers College, Columbia University. The developmental project was funded by the Bureau of Research of the United States Office of Education as part of a larger effort in which ten institutions were funded to develop teacher education programs by applying systematic planning procedures.

The first paper consists of a rationale for the Teachers College program, the central purpose of which is to prepare teacher innovators. It serves as a framework within which the reader can place the other papers. In the present context, especially, this paper should be regarded as one team's attempt to develop a systematic conceptualization of a teacher who would function in the classroom as an innovator, that is, as an effective teacher who studies educational forms and tries to create and implement new ones. Many of the components of that program were developed from ideas provided in the source papers which form the bulk of this volume.

The second paper was written by Elizabeth C. Wilson, Curriculum Director of the Montgomery County Public Schools, and addresses itself to the problem of creating schools which can serve as centers of innovative activity, such as the "school as the center of inquiry" conceptualization developed by Robert Schaefer, Dean of Teachers College, Columbia University. Dr. Wilson addresses herself to the development of the political and technical procedures which need to be undertaken in order to bring into existence schools which can serve as "centers of inquiry" and as centers for a teacher education program.

The third paper, by David E. Hunt, Professor of Psychology at the Ontario Institute for Studies in Education, provides a conceptual framework for matching teacher training procedures to the personality characteristics of the students in order to accomplish two purposes. One is to increase the creative potential of the teacher candidate and the second is to enable him to live in an environment in which he is comfortable.

The fourth paper, by Carl Weinburg, Professor of Educational Sociology at the University of California in Los Angeles, deals with the question of helping students who are training to be teacher-innovators to develop innovative values and to maintain those values within the bureaucracy of the school while attempting to debureaucratize education and create a more humanistic model.

The fifth paper, by George I. Brown of the University of California at Santa Barbara, suggests procedures for helping teachers become self-actualizing and to treat teaching as a creative act in which their own self-actualization and that of their students become one.

The sixth paper was written by Louis Smith, Professor of Education and Psychology in the Graduate Institute of Education at Washington University, St. Louis. His studies of the classroom suggest that we can take our clues for teacher education from the structures that experienced teachers use to develop and manage their groups and to institute educational activities. Smith also suggests ways that techniques used by anthropologists, psychologists, and sociologists can be used to help young teachers comprehend the classrooms they observe and also to understand their own behavior as teachers.

The seventh paper, by Ed Sullivan of the Ontario Institute for Studies in Education, suggests ways of identifying the developmental psychology content that should be taught to teachers—content to help them apprehend the individual differences of students and to identify the means for providing educational environments which are matched to the characteristics of the students they would teach. In essence, Sullivan's paper is a platform on which content from developmental psychology can be selected for inclusion in a teacher education program.

The seventh and eighth papers, by Bruce Joyce of Teachers College, Columbia University, and Michael Apple of the University of Wisconsin at Madison, are analyses of the types of performance models or conceptualizations of teaching which were developed by all ten projects funded by the United States Office of Education. Joyce investigates the range of conceptions of teaching and schooling which were developed by the ten teams and suggests ways that teacher educators can draw on those models for ideas about the creation of teacher education programs. Apple analyzes the problem of applying behavioristic techniques to describe teaching and organize the training of the teacher.

The reason for publishing this series of papers is to provide the teacher education community a set of conceptualizations which they can use to approach the design of the various aspects of the teacher education program or even its totality. Most of these papers are addressed to the twin problems of helping teacher education become a humanizing experience for the teacher and helping him to learn how to make education of his own students a humanizing experience also. The great challenge to the American culture is to knit itself together again, to find ways of humanizing itself so that its citizenry can counter the alienating forces which affect them in their daily lives and can learn to create a society in which all individuals are treated in such a way that they can develop themselves as fully as possible. Potentially both pre-and in-service teacher education can contribute to this much needed and massive societal effort. The most serious challenge which requires that there be a renaissance in teacher education is the creation of a more humane United States and world culture. There is no more important task at hand. These humble ideas are presented in the hope that they may stimulate others to the creation of a more humanistic world through education and, specifically, through the education of the teacher.

1

The Teacher Innovator: A Program for Preparing Educators

BRUCE JOYCE

The papers appearing in this volume were part of an effort to build a rationale and program for preparing teachers who would be teacher innovators. As alluded to in its title, the *teacher innovator* makes certain assumptions about the nature of the schools and the roles of the people who operate in them. The program is geared to the notion that the schools we see before us today will not long be with us. Instead, new educational forms and methods that more adequately serve our nations and the young people will be created. Part of the rebirth will be by graduates of these very teacher education programs we now seek to reform, for teacher education is, in a real sense, the midwife of educational change. As a result, this program places heavy emphasis on the teacher as a person who participates in the creation of new educational forms even while he executes the old. He is seen as both an innovator in his own right and as a faculty member of a school which is continuously recreating itself. However, the present context of teacher education is paradoxical. For despite the fact that teacher education must now be future oriented and prepare people who can help create the educational institutions of the future, its graduates must be able to perform within the existing institutions and to help define presently practical as well as new roles for teachers. Exactly how to do this is one of the riddles of teacher education. What kinds of preparation will enable the new professional to operate both as an innovator and at the same time relate coherently to the profession as it is when he enters it? It is to the various aspects of this problem that the papers in this volume address themselves and to its solution that this program, which draws heavily upon their analysis, is dedicated.

The Teacher Innovator:
Considerations for a Program Rationale

A HISTORICAL CONTEXT

The need for and dimensions of a teacher innovator role are, perhaps, best illustrated within a historical context. In 1900, a teacher was able to graduate from a normal school, take a job and spend forty-five or fifty years of her career in classrooms that were identically equipped, and teach in one manner that did not change. The motion picture came in, but she did not use it much nor was she required to do so. Television appeared, but there were no televised courses that required her attention. She worked in a social institution that did not change in any essential way during that entire time. *Because that institution did not change it slowly became irrelevant to its society and its young people.* By the time the teacher retired, the prestige of the school and the prestige of the teacher were gone in large measures. And as we turned around, we found that the institution was being blamed, rightly or wrongly, for many of our societal problems.

In response to these charges, new educational possibilities have been and are emerging at a rapid rate bringing with them new institutional forms, new roles for teachers, and new technologies. In contrast to most of our present educational forms, which were developed at a time when the text-book and the fixed course of study were the preferred way of preparing young people, instruction is beginning to take place in many ways and settings. For example, Philadelphia has developed a "school" whose walls are the boundaries of the city. The art museum is the "classroom" for art, the library for reading and independent study, the natural history museum and parks for the study of nature, the industries for the state of industry, and social institutions for the social institutions. The literary figures of the city assist in the study of creative writing and literature, government officials and private political groups assist in the education of the young. New technologies mediate independent instruction. Self-instructional courses consisting of taped lectures are made available to the student. For the diagnosis of their basic skill needs, students go to skill centers where they are also taught how to teach themselves, using self-instructional materials or person-alized methods created for their own particular sets of needs and person-alities.

Aspects of this proposal are already in effect, and these ideas for the creation of new institutions are precursors of what will come. The implica-tions for a teacher education program are clear. The product of this teacher education program must be equipped to work out the details of such new institutional forms as well as their accompanying new teacher roles and technologies. For instance, with the introduction of teacher aids into the classroom the teacher becomes the manager, helping groups of professionals carry out a wide variety of functions. Self-instructional materials are freeing teachers to use themselves in creative and personalized ways and help children in areas heretofore neglected. As subject matter becomes more rigorous, elementary school teachers are becoming more specialized in terms of disciplines.

Thus, the graduate of today who teachers forty-five years will see his role transformed innumerable times in that span. At some point in his career he may teach entirely over television. At another time he may work entirely as a creator of written materials for children. At yet another point he may be a director of a computer-based instructional center. Because of this, the teacher innovator program gives as much attention to the teacher as an institution builder, as a scholar, and as an innovator as it does in preparing him to work directly with children. If the teacher innovator program is successful, the teacher will be able to help shape the institution in which he will work, to teach himself those new roles, and to test out new educational ideas.

The actual development of the program for the preparation of teacher innovators requires new patterns of teacher education which find their roots in a rationale purporting new definitions of professional competence, new methods for the creation of effective teachers, and a fundamental support for educational change. Let us examine more closely some of the considera-tions involved in constructing such a rationale.

CHANGE

Teacher education must be rooted in a commitment to educational change. The young teacher needs to be prepared, not by socializing him to the existing structure and form of the school, but by preparing him to par-ticipate in the re-creation of educational forms and substance. Unquestion-ably, the young teacher needs the cooperation of the existing school if he is to try out new educational procedures. He cannot have in a kit by his side the computer terminals that he might need to institute computerized instruction. Nor is he able to carry game-type simulations with him wherever he goes, or to become a new type of specialist in a school that does not recognize that specialty. He needs to know, therefore, not only about the kinds of alternative educational forms that are developing, but what it takes to bring them into existence in the institution or the school. Beyond this, he needs to have the opportunity to work where innovation is the byword.

A teacher education program has to be integrated with schools and clinics where educational experimentation is the norm, and where the teacher receives training and support services long after his preservice education has been completed. In fact, the world of education is changing so rapidly that the distinction between "preservice" preparation as a period of intensive training followed by an "inservice" period in which training is less intensive or even haphazard, is not valid. An increasingly high proportion of the "service" will be consumed by reeducation and experimentation.

A teacher education which would prepare teachers not simply to carry out present educational practices but to create new ones or assist in their implementation must satisfy the following conditions: In the first place, it must bring teacher candidates and inservice teachers together in educational experimentation. The program will not succeed if it simply pits "the new ideas" of the new teachers against the "old ideas" of the inservice teacher. Most educational innovations cannot be accomplished by teachers working alone. They require institutional change and institutional commitment. Therefore, the school and the school district are really the units of cooperation with the teacher education program. Within schools devoted to scholarship and innovation, experienced teachers and teacher candidates can work together in joint inquiry.

The second condition is that the creation of an innovative teacher education program requires the simultaneous creation of innovative schools. In the inner city, for example, one cannot simply prepare young innovators and then send them into the existing ghetto schools to let *them* do the changing of those schools. The city, the college, the young teacher and the inservice teacher, the community, the student body of the school, the teachers union, and the administration of the city public schools have to join together to sanction the creation of a new type of social institution within the ghetto. Anything short of this is simply to prepare the new teacher for disillusionment. In her paper (Chapter 2) Elizabeth Wilson describes the creation and workings of such a cooperative, inquiry oriented educational system.

UNCERTAINTY

The new teacher enters a world in which we are very uncertain about the ends and means of education. Although it will no doubt make him uncomfortable to find this out, the only honest teacher education will confess to the young teacher from the beginning that he will need to be a participant in the study of education as well as in the process of teaching. He is entering a world in which alternative models for curriculum and instruction are being created and tested at a very rapid rate. The young teacher might wish that he could be taught the "right" methods or even the "best" methods for accomplishing any purpose, but no such certainties exist. New ways of doing things are being created at an accelerating rate and if the young teacher is to be effective he needs to know how to participate in the selection of these things and their incorporation into school life. Consequently, to prepare him to work in a "self-contained" classroom or on a teaching "team" or in any other single model would be a mistake. He needs to be prepared at a more generic level so he can help create new goals and help assemble the means for carrying them out. Perhaps most critical, he needs to learn to train himself for new educational roles.

These demands may seem obvious, but they are surprisingly difficult ones to act on. Nearly all teacher education programs in the past have been centered around a powerful apprenticeship component whose purpose was to socialize the young teacher to one of several prevailing or new educational patterns. Early childhood teachers, for example, have generally been trained to the "Montessori" system, or to the "play-school" theories, or to "academic" approaches. In both student teaching and internship programs the young teacher frequently has learned only to accommodate himself to the existing school, rather than to make independent curricular and instructional decisions that reflect an advanced knowledge of curriculum materials and learning. Hence, it is frequently discovered at the end of a conventional teacher education program that the young teacher has not been prepared to make decisions concerning objectives or appropriate learning activities. It is necessary therefore to build a program which takes advantage of the virtues of the existing school and which prepares its students to work in them, but which avoids the overstabilizing effects of student teaching and internship which result from most present practice.

SCHOLARSHIP

The present state of knowledge about teaching and learning is such that the teacher who would live rationally must be a competent scholar of teaching and learning. He must be prepared to create and test out original solutions to educational problems; to create and study, and to research if necessary, curriculum materials that are prepared by other people; and to create with his colleague what Robert Schaefer calls a school that is a center of inquiry.[1] This is the kind of goal that arises from the dilemma of

[1] Robert Schaefer, *The School as the Center of Inquiry* (New York: Harper and Row, 1967).

the universities' commitment to the development of rational man. Although it will be extremely difficult to prepare large numbers of teachers who will have the capacity to inquire into teaching and learning, it is essential that the attempt be made. Otherwise, we turn away from the possibility of a reasoned life and a reasoned approach to education. We simply cannot support the conception of a teacher as an applier of formulas.

As roles in education become more differentiated, it will become more possible to prepare teachers for a high level of scholarship. The specialist in computer simulation, for example, will be in a far more manageable role than is the multipurpose nursery school teacher of today, whose role is too diffuse to permit mastery in performance, let alone scholarship. Teachers with specialties and support systems such as those defined recently by Joyce[2] will be in a position to create new procedures and new knowledge about their effectiveness.

COMPLEXITY

Another consideration is the exceeding complexity of teaching. Teaching is not a single process. Some of the processes of teaching are scholarly in character (for example, analyzing the modes of inquiry of scholarly discipline). Others require great interpersonal capacity (as working with others to change the character of a school). Yet others are primarily technical abilities (for example, diagnosing learning difficulties). Consequently, the components of a teacher education program will not all look the same. Single methods in teacher education are unlikely to produce the complexity of competencies that are necessary to the teacher. Some components need the kinds of methods that are characterized by training in psychology. Other components require feedback techniques that enable the learner to monitor his own performance. Yet other components should be characterized by scholarly inquiry, and still others may involve an almost therapy. The strategies of a sound program will be as multiple as are its components.

Building the Rationale for Teacher Education: Four Roles of the Teacher Innovator

After taking these kinds of issues into consideration, the next step was to formulate a rationable which, in effect, would furnish the design specifications for a program. In doing so, we needed to develop a performance model of a teacher—a conception of teaching that would include the competencies necessary to help create new educational institutions and to study teaching

---

2 Bruce R. Joyce, *The Teacher and His Staff: Man, Media and Machines* (Washington, D.C.: National Commission on Teacher Education and Professional Standards and Center for Study of Instruction, National Education Association, 1967).

and learning as well as to work in the existing institution. To create a model of a professional is to identify the areas of reality that he needs to control in order to define and solve educational problems.

Our rationale, then, identifies the areas of reality which the teacher should control if he is to function effectively with children, create new educational forms and bring them into existence, and participate in the quest for knowledge about teaching. We identified four roles (areas of realities) and within each role the kinds of control that appear necessary to carry out our conception of teaching. From these conceptualizations, we would then be able to move to the second stage in the creation of a program for teacher education—the development of curricular systems which could bring these about.

THE INSTITUTION BUILDER (SHAPER OF THE SCHOOL)

We found that some of the jobs of teaching seem to relate to the school or to the wider educational institution rather than to encounters that occur in the classroom or in other places where teachers work directly with children. In other words, some of the processes of teaching seem to be institution related. We came to call these the institution-building processes. They are the processes of creating educational institutions, and working with colleagues, members of the community, and students; a teacher has to identify the objectives of the school and the methods and procedures which will be used to achieve these objectives. Curricula have to be developed or adapted for the local school. Staff deployment patterns have to be made. Provisions for meeting individual needs of students have to be developed. Learning materials, including books, motion pictures and other devices need to be put together and made available to the students.

The social system of the school has to be planned for. As we identified the institution-shaping processes, it became evident that teacher education has in the past paid much less attention to institutional functions of the teacher than it has to the functions that take place within classrooms. For example, teacher education pays much less attention to curriculum, than it does to instructional methods. Also the young teacher frequently does not envision himself as a future institutional decision-maker. He generally feels that his goal is to prepare himself to work with particular groups of children within classrooms. As we realized the neglect of the institution-shaping processes of teaching by both teacher education programs and by their students, it became obvious that the components to achieve control over these processes would have to be entirely new ones for teacher education. It also became apparent that institution building is a very complex set of processes. Hence, these were divided into three general categories which overlap somewhat but make it possible to divide the teacher education task into more manageable components. The first is creating curricular patterns for a school (developing the missions of the school and determining the particular means that will be used to accomplish those objectives). Second is the process of developing the social system of the school (the organization of faculty, organization of students, and the blending of these into a coherent social system). The third is the development of the technical support systems within the school (assembling the media components, library, and self-instructional systems).

THE INTERACTIVE TEACHER

To most familiar teaching role occurs during *contact with children.* At that point the teacher needs strategies for making instructional decisions which are tailored to the characteristics and needs of the students. He can work with groups of children to build effective democratic structures through which they can conduct their education. He controls a wide variety of teaching strategies and wide range of technological assists to education. He is a student of individual differences and he has the interpersonal sensitivity to touch closely the minds and emotions of the students and to modify his own behavior as a teacher in response. He is able to bring structure to chaotic situations without being punitive. The teacher does this in company with his colleagues. He rarely works alone, partly because he is more effective when teamed with others but also because he needs the shared analysis of teaching and learning that is a continuous part of their professional life. With them he controls techniques for designing continual small experiments of teaching and learning.

THE INNOVATOR

The teacher innovator needs the capacity to resist the slide into routine that tempts everyone. He has to approach problems with zest and flexibility, and see himself as a creator of new things. He has to cope with the bureaucratic structure of the school and work with his colleagues to develop professional climates where innovation is the norm. To be an innovator rather than a bureaucratic functionary, the teacher has to combine personal creativity with the ability to work with others.

The Interpersonal Processes of Innovating

Teaching is not a solitary business. Teachers have colleagues who know a great deal about them and who influence them. Students, parents, and administrators all have a candid view of the teacher in action. Teaching is done inside a very well-defined social institution. It has been traditional that the institution has been a bureaucracy whose functionaries play out the ascribed roles that are common within the schools in the western world. Innovative activity clashes with bureaucracy by definition.

Being an innovator involves dealing with colleagues, students, parents,

administrator, and the character of the bureaucracy. All of these are difficult to cope with. Especially, the enormous weight of bureaucratic behavior
saps the energy of the innovator. Even students become accustomed to
reacting to certain patterns of teaching and they resist when "the language
game of the classroom,"[3] is changed. They, too, perpetuate routine. Hence,
creative teaching includes interacting with colleagues, students, parents, and
administrators in productive ways; learning to analyze the ways interpersonal
relations are stabilized; and to master the strategies of inducing change
without creating chaos or undue discomfort. Working with others to create
interpersonal climates which are interdependent, and where the arrangements of living and teaching are negotiated, subject to scrutiny, and continuously improved, are as essential a part of teaching as the selection of
educational objectives and the creation of the appropriate means of carrying them out.

The Personal Aspects of Innovating

The development of a creative personality is another critical element.
Generating unique solutions to problems, creating new educational forms
and testing them out, finding new ways to reach students, and adapting to
a wide range of student and faculty personalities, require a creative self. The
teacher must handle information and theories flexibly and accurately. He
must strive for minimal personal bias but act with resolve. He must be able
to control himself when children challenge established authority and standards; he must provide a mountain of support for the frightened and insecure
child. The teacher must become able to assess his own behavior objectively
and then to work deliberately to improve it—he cannot afford to be defensive about his personality or practices.

A strong component then of a teacher education program has to be
devoted to helping the teacher learn a creative personality. He has to
master the processes of flexible and continuous re-creation of his personal
and professional life. George Brown, in his paper (Chapter 5), presents
one perspective on the development of a creative and flexible personality.

THE SCHOLAR

As Robert Schaefer puts it, we cannot "wind the teacher up like an
old victrola and hope that he will play sweet cerebral music forever." Continuous scholarship renews him and adds to knowledge about education.
He controls techniques for studying the processes of interactive teaching
and theories of learning. He specializes in one discipline until he knows the

---

[3] See Arno Bellack, et. al. *The Language of the Classroom* (New York:
Teachers College Press, 1966).

nature and the modes of inquiry of that discipline. Equally important, he knows how to engage in research that relates that discipline to the lives of young children. He controls structures for studying the school and for studying teaching and learning so he can design and carry out educational experiments. He masters a range of teaching strategies derived from different views of learning, and more importantly, controls techniques for developing and testing new ones.

Outline of a Program for
Preparing a Teacher Innovator

The roles of the *interactive teacher,* the *institution builder,* the *innovator,* and the *scholar* become the sources of the methodology and structure of a teacher innovator program. We can think of the program as having an outer covering or framework which shapes and supports these four parts. The outer covering is the general procedures or structures which unify and serve the activities of all of the four components. The components themselves have been developed around each of the roles of the teacher innovator and are specifically designed to yield control over the areas necessary to the role. The four major components are interrelated and overlapping but each has its distinct rationale and organization.

In this program the development of the teacher innovator is achieved in three ways:

The technology for change prepares him to shape the school to make and carry out instructional decisions, and to employ and test out contemporary technological assists to human behavior.

Commitment to the role as an innovator enables him to work with groups of his peers and faculty members, making and testing out new educational forms and methods. The entire mode of operation of the program is designed to envelop him with a community in which he will be part of an innovation team from the time of his admittance to the program.

Emotional preparation for innovation tries to teach the young teacher to understand the problems of changing the social institution, and the emotional hazards of doing so; it helps him cope with his own feelings of anxiety and alienation. Without preparing him emotionally we should not be fair to him, for to commit a person to change is to expose him to uncertainty and anxiety. To do that without preparing him to cope with it would be a cruel thing. As a result, we give as much attention to the teacher as a person as to the teacher as a technologist.

Let's look first at the general methodology and structure of the program and then at the kinds of activities within each of the four components.

GENERAL METHODOLOGY AND STRUCTURE

Cooperative Inquiry

Cooperative inquiry is the basic teaching strategy in the program and carries with it certain structural requirements. The essence of the strategy is the creation of democratic "inquiry groups," each group consisting of about twelve teacher candidates and functioning as a miniature democracy. That is, the students assisted by faculty counselors educate themselves as they work their virtually self-administering substantive components. En route they will react to many situations. As this happens, they will discover basic conflicts among their ideas, attitudes, and perceptions. Out of this conflict, problems for study can be identified and the group can organize itself to carry out the investigation. In no activity is a faculty member more than a seminar leader. The structure of each component is explained to the inquiry group which then, with the help of the faculty, negotiates the activities.

The cooperative inquiry method, combined with the democratic organization of the program, accomplishes three purposes:

1. It teaches the teacher candidates how to organize an educational program that operates as a democracy with the hope that there will be reasonable transfer to their teaching situation.
2. It involves the teacher candidates in continuous experimental activity which is supported by a group of their peers. This group eventually can function as a reference group, anchoring the experimental norms for each member.
3. It involves the teacher candidates in the shaping of their own educational activities—a highly motivating activity. The students will probably form a tight community, an experience which should be of personal value and provide increased effectiveness of professional education.

Contact Environment

This element provides for the teacher candidates to be in contact with schools and children. After an initial period of student teaching in a public school situation, new contact is provided to give the teacher candidates the opportunity to study schools, teachers, and children. This is so that they can master a wide repertoire of teaching strategies, practice making curricular and instructional decisions, and engage in educational experimentation.

These contact experiences can occur in several types of environments. At Teachers College we have found it possible to provide much of the contact by organizing educational programs for neighborhood children. There is a great demand for remedial programs in all school subjects, and for enrichment programs as well. Both after-school programs and summer programs are possible. By offering such programs the candidates serve the neighborhood and create a contact laboratory for themselves in which frankly experimental teaching can be the norm. In addition, teacher candidates can engage in experimental activities in the Inquiry School as described by Robert Schaefer.[4]

Contact with schools and children begins in the first weeks of the program and continues, ideally, into the first year of paid teaching. Only the initial phase includes apprentice teaching of the type most familiar in traditional student teaching programs. The remainder of the experience is in experimental teaching in which candidates are mastering a variety of strategies and carrying out teaching units which they develop with research designs.

The Differential Training Model

The third element is a model for individualizing instruction which is based on the work of David E. Hunt of the Ontario Institute for Studies in Education (Chapter 3). Hunt has taken the position that an optimal educational environment can be prescribed for individual teacher candidates. This environment would function in two ways: it would increase the learning of ideas and skills, and it would increase the personal flexibility of the teacher candidate. Hunt's model provides for modification of educational procedures to take into account the competency level, feedback preference, value orientation, and cognitive orientation of the teacher candidate. All of these characteristics are related to achievement personal flexibility.

The components of the teacher innovator program are organized so that *pacing by competency level* is accomplished in the skill areas through procedures that the candidates administer directly to themselves. For example, a candidate needs to practice a teaching strategy only until he has mastered it; the means for determining mastery are built into the component in which teaching strategies are the central concern.

The other aspects of the differential model are carried out by the action of the faculty member as he works with the inquiry group. Basically, he modifies his role in order to change the educational environment that is presented to the candidates. For example, the faculty member may modify his behavior so that candidates who prefer feedback from authority figures receive much from him or other faculty, whereas candidates who prefer peer feedback receive less authority feedback and greater measures of peer judgment. Or, the faculty member may modify the amount of structure and task complexity that is presented to the teacher candidate. For example, candidates of low cognitive complexity operate best in environments which

4 Robert Schaefer, *Inquiry.*

are fairly well structured and in which task complexity is not too great. Highly complex individuals, on the other hand, operate best under low structure and high task complexity. Hunt's theory suggests (and he presents much research to bear him out) that when there is a substantial mismatch between cognitive complexity and the environment, the individual not only does not achieve as well but he also is unlikely to grow in flexibility. An optimal environment for growth in flexibility is one in which the amount of structure is somewhat less and the amount of task complexity is somewhat greater than what is optimal for achievement. In other words, a slight, controlled mismatch has the effect of pulling the individual toward increasing cognitive complexity and flexibility.

The General Methodology Summarized

The program, then, is operated as a democracy with small self-regulating units of students monitoring their own progress and administering the program to themselves with the assistance of faculty counselors. The faculty counselor modifies his role to provide an optimal educational environment for each individual according to the differential training model. Contact with schools and children is organized to provide the teacher candidates with opportunities for study, micro-teaching, and experimentation rather than to socialize them to the school as it presently exists. The contact stretches over a long period of time in order to insure the development of realistic skills, but it is carefully designed to discourage teacher candidates from believing that "realism" means accepting and maintaining the school as it is today.

THE FOUR COMPONENTS

The activities comprising the four components take place within the context of the cooperative inquiry strategy, the provisions for individualizing instruction (the differential training model), and the environment for contact with schools and children. In this section we describe briefly the thesis and activities of the various components. Most of them are built upon ideas suggested by the source papers appearing in this volume and the reader is referred to these papers for more complete explanations of the rationale and training techniques for a particular component.

The Innovator Component

This component is developed in a thesis by Carl Weinberg and presented in a source paper in Chapter 4. Weinberg maintains that the school as we presently know it is a bureaucracy, and that the roles of a teacher, like all bureaucratic roles, represent stabilizing forces in the institution rather than forces which encourage change and adaptation to the individual. The average teacher engages in much routine activity and teaches with some methods simply because they have "always been done." Moreover, deviation from these routine patterns of behavior is quickly questioned and sanctioned. As the novice teacher learns the bureaucratic roles within the school, he becomes alienated because he recognizes that many of the things that he is going to do as a teacher are not educative for youngsters so much as they serve to maintain the bureaucracy. He can resolve his conflict by leaving the school (which many young teachers do) or by accepting the bureaucratic roles, thus alienating himself from teaching (which many apparently do); or he can learn to understand the bureaucratic forces and develop his capacity to create *authentic teaching roles* and even engage in *innovative activities* through the school.

To achieve this, the student, is exposed to the school as an apprentice and permitted to learn whatever roles are given to him by the teachers to whom he is apprenticed. As he learns the bureaucratic roles, he will experience alienation, and is helped to analyze both the bureaucratic process and the feelings of alienation which he is having. He studies the social system of the school and the ways in which it stabilizes itself and prevents change and innovative activity from coming about.

From that point, he works in a group carrying out exploratory and experimental teaching strategies. It is hoped that this group (the inquiry group) will become a reference group for its members—a group whose norms are experimentation and innovation. In the common cause, they will support each other and help each other anchor the commitment to change and experimentation. When the inquiry creates its section of the remedial and enrichment school, they study how to teach in nonbureaucratic ways and how to build a community of teachers and students devoted to authentic and personal learning experiences. Throughout the intern period every effort is made to keep this inquiring group in contact with one another so that when they experience resistance to scholarly teaching and innovative activity, their solidarity will bolster them.

The Interactive Teaching Component

It is in the area of interactive face-to-face teaching that the most precise level of competence must be reached. To begin with, the professional self-concept of the teacher depends on his belief in his capacity as an interactive teacher. No matter how well he is able to build institutions and study education, he will not feel authentic or adequate unless he knows he can teach well. Then also, performance in today's schools depends largely on competence in face-to-face teaching. The teacher must be able to unite groups of children into communities of learners and needs to command a range of teaching strategies which induce many kinds of learning. In addition, only a very high level of technical competence enables innovative activity and an awkward or inept teacher would have serious limitations as an innovator.

Hence, this component is the most precise and requires the most definite standards of performance. Four subcomponents focus on different aspects of teaching.

INSTRUCTIONAL DECISION-MAKING. This subcomponent is designed to teach the teacher candidates a range of strategies for making instructional decisions. The activities stress decision-making in terms of testable hypotheses—that certain procedures will affect particular learners in such and such a way. Teacher candidates experience decision-making activities in a variety of ways.

Initially they may begin with simulated situations. For instance, "The Teaching Game" is a lively game-type simulation which confronts the candidates with several general principles, e.g., that teaching strategies have differential effects, that several aspects of the environment affect the learner, and that there are several defensible theories of learning which relate to different kinds of educational objectives. Another phase of the component may take place in a simulated school which consists of three elements: a set of data banks on many aspects of fourteen children (including tests and observational data, samples of written work, expressions of attitudes, family experiences, etc.), data on three communities (Spanish Harlem, a New England town, an English town), and a set of decision-making tasks. The tasks bring the candidates into contact with common teaching decisions and lead them to the study of decision-making strategies. They examine strategies based on their psychological theories and strategies within the area of their specialty.

After decision-making in simulated situations, teacher candidates may practice making decisions and carrying them out in their contact environment. In addition, the inquiry group may make plans to teach a four- to eight-week unit in their specialty to build and test teaching strategies and instructional materials.

MODELS OF TEACHING. The goals of the "models of teaching" subcomponent are the mastery of a range of teaching strategies which have been derived from theoretical positions on teaching and learning, and the ability to create and test strategies tailored to individual students.

Before mastering teaching strategies, the teacher candidate practices basic "moves" in small group teaching situations. These moves or maneuvers underlie a number of teaching strategies and function to induce academic and value inquiry, as well as to structure (or induce the structure of) procedures.

The students then set about to master several basic teaching strategies, each developed from a theoretical position on learning. A teaching strategy or model of teaching describes guidelines, specifies a broad pattern of behavior, and attempts to make the various learning theories operational for the classroom teacher. The model alerts the teacher to the key moves and provides him with a map for organizing and viewing his instruction.[5] Some of these are inductive strategy, group inquiry approach, nondirective teaching, inquiry training, operant conditioning, concept attainment, jurisprudential approach to the analysis of values, approach to creativity, advance organizer strategy for expository teaching, and group dynamics approach. Together these strategies constitute a fundamental repertoire and later, candidates develop, adapt, or test a variety of strategies.

FLEXIBILITY TRAINING: REACHING THE WORLD OF THE LEARNER. Although a teaching strategy is a theoretically based guide for teaching and curriculum-making, it should not operate as a juggernaut, rolling over the students, regardless of how they respond to it. Strategies should be reshaped as the child reacts (or fails to react) to them. Sometimes a strategy should be discarded entirely, and a completely different approach begun. Often, teaching should begin, not with a strategy, but with an encounter between the world of the student and the world of the teacher. Flexibility is required to adjust teaching to the competence of the learner and to his preferred modes of working. It also insures that the procedures enhance the learner's feelings about himself, builds concepts between the learner and what is to be learned, and accommodates an emotional reaction to the material. Flexibility includes the processes of entering the world of the learner and of modulating the teaching activity to "fit" or capitalize on the learner's world. *Flexibility training* refers to the attempt to help the teacher become more sensitive to the world of the child and modify his behavior appropriately.

In the opening stages of the flexibility training component, the teacher candidates study the children in their small group classes using procedures developed by Ruth Formanek.[6] These procedures are designed to sensitize the teachers to "coping" behavior of children and to point out that all student behavior is significant.

Then they engage in teaching situations called "communication tasks" in which they teach children or adults who play a particular role relating to the objectives of the lesson. The roles are contrived so that the "learner" gradually reveals to the teacher a competency level, affective state, or cognitive orientation. Success in the task requires that the teacher figure out the characteristics of the learner and modify his strategy to take the learner

5 Bruce R. Joyce and Marsha Weil, *Models of Teaching* (Englewood Cliffs, N.J.: Prentice-Hall, 1972).
6 Ruth Formanek, *Course Outline and Workbook for Elementary Education 105* (Hempstead: Hofstra University, Department of Elementary Education, 1966).

into account. The teacher candidates practice in communication tasks until they are able to diagnose learner characteristics easily and modify their teaching accordingly.

THE SOCIAL SYSTEM OF THE CLASSROOM.   One of the most important aspects of interactive teaching is helping the children develop a social system and a sense of community. Even a group of youngsters who work together on a short project need to develop a rapport and a *modus operandi* that enable them to work and grow together. A classroom group which works together for a year or more has an overpowering need for community.

Many teachers have great difficulty establishing an effective social system, especially in inner city classrooms. This dimension of interactive teaching is so complex and difficult that a special subcomponent has been devised to ensure that significant effort is made to help the teacher candidate develop the understanding and skill which is necessary if he is to build strong and effective communities of children.

The purpose of the subcomponent is to provide the teacher candidate with techniques for analyzing the social system[7] of the classroom and to provide him with techniques for developing a stable, cooperative, person-oriented social system in a classroom, even when starting from chaotic conditions.

The component begins with the analysis of classrooms using techniques developed by Louis Smith[8] (Chapter 6) to analyze activity structure and social dynamics and to identify tasks involved in establishing a cooperative social order.

In the next stage the candidates analyze the social aspects of teaching strategies (amount of structure and training for roles as learners) and experiment with varieties of strategies, studying the effects on the social behavior of the children. They proceed to experiment, diagnosing the needs of the children, selecting a strategy, and analyzing the effects. (In an unruly group, for example, they might decide to institute a structured social situation, select a highly structured strategy, and observe the effects on disruptive behavior.)

In the candidate-operated school, the next stage involves the planning of the social system by the inquiry group, the development of a strategy for achieving it, and testing of the strategy.

The Institution-Building Component

Teaching is a large scale social enterprise. The school as an institution is an effective educational force in its own right. Moreover, the character

[7] See Louis Smith, Chapter 6 of this volume.
[8] See Louis M. Smith, *Complexities of an Urban Classroom.* (New York: Holt, Rinehart and Winston, 1968).

of the school greatly affects what the individual teacher can do. When it comes to innovation and scholarship, the institution is all-important. Hence, an extensive component is devoted to the process of creating institutions.

Throughout their educational experience, teacher candidates study and test strategies for developing the curricular, technological, and social systems of the schools. Then, as they formulate the candidate-operated school, they practice institution building—planning and testing out curricula, interpersonal climates, and support systems. They can also study the institution-building techniques used in the Inquiry School, especially the arrangements that permit scholarship and experimental teaching.

The Teacher Scholar

We make the assumption that all teachers should be specialists both academically and pedagogically. Toward this goal, provision is made to teach them theories for studying the school, teaching and learning.

With respect to the study of teaching, teacher candidates are asked to work together analyzing their teaching behavior using the Bellack, Flanders, Gallagher-Aschner, and Joyce systems, each of which analyzes teaching from a stance that illuminates teacher and learner in a distinctive way. They are also asked to construct small studies of teacher-learner interaction, generalizing the studies to help themselves study particular techniques of teaching, to study their own progress toward mastery of strategies, and to develop experiments on the response of children to teaching behavior.

The other subcomponent focuses on the study of cognitive and affective development in children. Teacher-candidates are asked to become familiar with the work of various developmental theorists. The chapters by David E. Hunt (Chapter 3) and Edmund Sullivan (Chapter 7) are particularly helpful here. In addition, small-group activities and studies are designed so that the teacher is equipped to study the child and assay the effects teaching has on him.

Summary

The activities of the teacher innovator program involve the teacher candidate in continuous experimentation. He studies institution building and subsequently experiments with strategies he learns. He masters teaching strategies and experiments with them and others he creates. He studies his own teaching and tests its effects on children. He works in a school as a center of inquiry where teaching-scholarship is the norm, and he develops and offers his own educational programs to children.

If the program succeeds, it will be because the inquiry groups become reference groups which urge innovation and scholarship and which continue to have significance in the teacher's life long after he graduates. If the democratic organization of the program is implemented vigorously, then the program will change rapidly, will be different for each inquiry group, and will require the faculty to reeducate themselves continuously. If enough inquiry-centered schools are established, the entire program can take place in *them.*

2

Can the School Become a Center of Inquiry? A Design for Institution Building

ELIZABETH C. WILSON

Many people believe that Elizabeth Wilson is one of the leading public school educators in the nation—certainly she is one of the most sophisticated curriculum directors.

In the following essay she brings her experienced eye to bear on the problem of engineering schools modelled after Robert Schaefer's vision of schools in which colleagial groups of teachers study learning and teaching because they recognize that our fundamental ignorances about education forbid us from teaching *without* studying what we are doing.

She reviews the astonishingly small impact that the reform movements of the last fifty years have had on schools and analyzes the reasons for their limited effect. She then asserts that the reform of education requires the systematic changing of the entire institution: "It is the monolithic and homeostatic quality of the school system and the school as a part of that system which must be attacked." Further, although we have great ignorance about techniques of change, our problems are not so much ones of technology as they are problems of politics—the social matrix which does not support change, and even makes it desperately difficult.

To provide a base for technical development, social support, and political leverage, Dr. Wilson suggests the formation of an interagency institution-building complex which would function "to create a series of different models of 'center of inquiry' schools and simultaneously to redesign the two parent institutions so that they generate rather than prevent growth of these inquiry schools."

The development of a series of models is necessary because of our ignorance. By trying a number of conceptualizations of inquiry schools and ways of building them, the agency would gradually develop valid conceptions for further work—conceptions which would constitute the strategies for bringing into existence schools which would function as centers of inquiry.

Dr. Wilson provides us with the specifications for the personnel, support systems, management systems, and political organization necessary to operate the interagency institution-building institution. Her model should be useful to persons in a variety of professional roles. Teacher educators have long been stymied by their inability to create adequate settings for clinical practice. School and curriculum planners need a strategy for institution building. Systems planners need models to help them analyze the institution-building process. Teachers who wish to initiate and maintain change will find much to reflect on in Dr. Wilson's essay.

We have no more urgent task at present than to redevelop and rejuvenate our social institutions. In many fields, including education, progress has been virtually halted because the institutional setting inhibits progressive human activity.

Elizabeth Wilson's essay provides a solid base on which we can begin the practical task of creating humanistic, inquiry-oriented schools —a task absolutely necessary to progress in educational practice.

Introduction: The Case of the Punjab

The Washington Post for Thursday, July 11, 1968 carried the following story:

> The farm revolution in the Ludhaina district of Punjab State—and revolution is a just word for a wheat output that has more than tripled and a harvest of all food grains that has more than doubled in seven years—can be traced to a remarkable conjunction of people, technology, and wise policy.
> The people are the Punjab's Sikh farmers, an extraordinary breed of aggressive, hard-working Indians, eager to seize on new techniques to better their lot. . . . The most important [scientific breakthrough] has been the high-yielding strains of wheat developed by the Rockefeller Foundation in Mexico. . . .

Moreover, agronomists at Ludhaina's Punjab Agricultural University have themselves developed improved strains of Mexican wheat that raised the average yield [from 2,000] to 4,000 pounds.[1]

The design and execution of basic technological and cultural change in underdeveloped countries have long been problems of enormous difficulty.[2] The case of the Punjab is a near miracle for the student of planned institutional change, whether the desired change be focused upon agriculture or upon education.

Questions tumble over one another. Why did this break through occur in the *Punjab?* What were the components? Who was responsible? How long did it take? What can we learn from an agricultural revolution in the far off Punjab which has relevance for the problem of creating a new kind of school? *What does it take to rebuild an ancient and honorable institution like farming or like the school?*

The Punjab miracle, it seems, depends upon the existence of many interlocking factors and events. We note that the Punjab had already done a big job on the irrigation of land—seventy percent is now irrigated. The farmers suddenly found themselves relatively free from their traditional dependence upon the monsoon. Similarly the Punjabi have what one dealer there called "tractor-mania." Ludhaina, at this point, has 3,000 tractors working for it—an enormous number of machines for an underdeveloped nation. We observe that the Ford Foundation, after an intensive study by experts, published a report in 1958 which "urged India to focus its resources on some promising farm districts that would serve as models for the nation."[3] We add the fact that an existing agricultural college transformed itself into a university and extended its functions to include research, and the training and staffing of village specialists who in turn instructed new generations of experts.

Another ingredient included the cooperation of the Punjab State which put fifty extension workers into the villages of Ludhaina to work with the specialists and supported prices so that farmers got handsome and stable rewards for their hard work and acceptance of change. Financial support has also been supplied by U.S. aid dollars, which provided farmers with the credit necessary to buy the required new seed and fertilizer.

Finally we return to the people of the Punjab themselves—their aggressiveness, physical capacity, general ethos, and particularly self-pride. How quickly the revolution, well started in the Punjab, will spread across all of India remains to be seen. The author of the article, however, concludes

[1] *The Washington Post,* July 11, 1968.
[2] Cf. Margaret Mead, ed., *Cultural Patterns and Technical Change* (New York: The New American Library, 1955).
[3] *The Washington Post,* July 11, 1968.

by saying that "...the new techniques and the new seeds appear to be irresistible. It now takes a very reckless prophet indeed to forecast the inevitability of famine in India."[4]

Perhaps the author is too hopeful, but may be optimism built upon some successes is an important frame of mind for would-be institution builders. And if analysis of the Punjab's experience has transferability for the school world, we must take note of other vital elements. A history of successful experimentation, familiarity with and enthusiasm for technology, and an aggressive tough-mindedness seem to characterize the local setting. A collection of cooperating institutions with varieties of expertise appears necessary as does the ability to find, use, and adapt existing scientific knowledge and technology. We should not overlook the funding from a variety of sources—monies which make possible continued support of the total complex as well as stable rewards for the innovators. Nor should we forget time and space factors. It was ten years *after* the Ford report before the task for *one* district in *one* province really broke the institutional change barrier.

Thus, institutional change, even when the ends and means of the institution are concrete, easily observable, and relatively simple, requires an extraordinarily complex series of reinforcing agents upon a small target. Our goal of creating a new kind of school, one which is a center of inquiry,[5] calls for an even larger order of magnitude—a concentration of many resources. Maybe we do not yet have the knowledge or the material or the fortitude to design and create the "critical mass" essential for the conception, gestation, birth, and growth process of Robert Schaefer's dream school. We are, however, reminded of Alfred North Whitehead's remark recently featured by Westinghouse Broadcasting Company: "Ideas won't keep. Something must be done about them."[6]

The School as a Center of Inquiry[7]

But what is the idea that won't keep? Why is Schaefer's inquiry school so unusual? The building of laboratory and demonstration schools is hardly a new concept. Schaefer's ideal school is, however, not a laboratory school in the conventional sense. Rather,

> ...a school organized as a center of inquiry...[is]...an institution characterized by a pervasive search for meaning and rationality. Fundamentally such

4 *Ibid.*

5 Robert J. Schaefer, *The School As A Center of Inquiry* (New York: Harper and Row, 1967).

6 *Time,* 92, 4, July 26, 1968, 12–13.

7 Robert J. Schaefer, *Inquiry.*

a school requires that teachers be freed to inquire into the nature of what and how they are teaching. . .[8]

Schaefer's school quite properly demands drastic modifications of teaching loads so teachers can read, reflect, and design research. This modification of present practice is predicated on other important interlocking components such as self-directed learning on the part of students; the nourishment of "colleague authority" with peers, administrators, and college professors; major change in the role of administration and supervision within the school; a commitment toward sustained study of the behavioral sciences, structure and processes of the disciplines, and foundations of educational thought; and the development of creative productive school-university collaboration.[9]

Such dimension are far more complex than those required of a demonstration school. The school as a center of inquiry becomes a *producer* as well as a *dispenser* of knowledge about teaching and learning. Schaefer is profoundly depressed by our ignorance of the nature of teaching and learning and by the stultifying quality of the everyday working world of the teacher.

Creating the Schaefer school implies institutional changes of startling proportions. Such changes are, moreover, far from simple as a brief analysis of recent history can attest.

Recent Attempts to Change the Schools

Well over ten years have elapsed since Sputnik and the frantic outcry of the public about the inadequacy of our schools. That event and its immediate aftermath climaxed a series of increasingly strident criticisms of the public schools and paved the way for the so-called curriculum reform movement. That movement, now no longer a baby, was to put some backbone into the curriculum and shape up the schools by sponsoring creative marriages between great scholars and great teachers. These marriages, well endowed with material resources, did in fact produce offspring which are provocative and several light years away from the everyday curriculum in practice in the majority of public schools across the nation. Yet despite these curricular innovations—some ideas about organizational change within the school and some minor flirting with architectural design and TV—the basic contour lines of the public schools have remained remarkably untouched. The same statements hold true for the majority of teacher training establishments which were successfully bypassed by the university curriculum builders. Oddly enough, it seems as if the more polished the new curriculum

---

[8] *Ibid.,* p. 3.
[9] *Ibid.,* pp. 60–76.

and the better organized the packages, the farther off stage these ideas and materials get pushed. The innovators of the sixties, it seems, were naive about the realities of the institution known as the public school.

Another strategy which has been less than successful was to train and import cadres of young people from liberal arts colleges to supplant the old line teachers' college teachers and thus circumvent the school establishment. But even the most elite colleges and universities working with bright imaginative young people untainted by schools of education have not had much impact in wealthy suburban districts, much less made a dent on ghetto school problems. The lack of effect upon the basic structure of the schools by the MAT programs across the nation illustrates the situation in suburban districts. A beautiful case study of the impact upon inner city schools may be found in the *Harvard Educational Review*.[10] Paul Lauter, author of that article, is to be commended for his willingness to make a thorough autopsy of the project. (Such dissections are *real* innovations in the educational world.) The project was undertaken in the hopes that a series of major social and educational issues could be solved by bringing to bear on the problem an experimental set of liberal arts colleges, some new unorthodox staff, and a community and school interested in changing its face. A brave hope it was, but *the issues were much more complex* than had been anticipated by the liberal groups working on the project. At the end of the first year, the director and most of the new white staff left in frustration; the curriculum at the request of the parents returned to the traditional three R's; and "establishment" professionals moved back to promote a "black is beautiful" attitude in the children. The erstwhile director ends his article as follows:

> . . . The issues of community participation, teachers' attitude and preparation, classroom organization and curriculum, and the roles of outside agencies must be worked out together or the educational fabric will unravel almost as quickly as it is stitched.[11]

The innovators of the sixties were not only unacquainted with the complex structure of the public school system, they also did not predict the potency of the power struggles which have torn at the vitals of all schools— the universities as well as the grammar and high schools. The last several years have been characterized by an increasing cry for autonomy by a revolt of the underdog both socially and academically. It takes the form of black power, of parents demanding control of local schools, of teacher militancy, of student militancy, starting at the university and seeping into

[10] Paul Lauter, "The Short, Happy Life of the Adams-Morgan Community School Project," *Harvard Educational Review*, 38, Nov. 2, 1968, 235–62.
[11] *Ibid.*, p. 262.

the high schools. Indeed, it is at our best academic and scholarly universities where the strikes are most strident.

No longer is it possible to look to the university as a model and savior of the flagging public schools. It too has feet of clay. In fact, as an aside, it could be that the kind of cooperative relationship between schools and colleges fostered and required by the National Science Foundation has aspects of the blind leading the blind. It could be that the university professor knows no more about relevant curriculum than the public school teacher —maybe less.

Conventional wisdom concerning what to do about the schools has had several rude shocks. Time-honored ideas like redoing the curriculum, getting some new good teachers educated outside the establishment, and giving the power to liberal university elements divorced from the existing bureaucracies, have been tried and found wanting. Ten years ago the idea of a complete redesign of both schools and colleges would have fallen on deaf ears. Today if either institution is to stay alive, the whole complex must be reexamined from head to toe. At the least, some well-defined exploratory probes on a small scale could ascertain whether the disease can be treated or whether the condition is so far advanced as to be inoperable.

Some Operating Assumptions and Obstacles

What is the state of the art? What assumptions or ideas exist which may be used? What obstacles will be encountered? Such an engineering endeavor is surely more of an art than a science, but that fact does not mean that the foundations of an operational plan need to be irrational. The discussion which follows is an attempt to pinpoint the ideas which are relevant and the roadblocks which must be considered.

Creating the school as a center of inquiry means changing the whole institution. This assumption is implicit in the title of this essay, and in all that has preceded this section of the article. Changing the whole institution is a task that demands a *systems approach.* In its generic sense, a systems approach means simultaneously considering all components of a situation or problem. In terms of the school, a systems approach includes the school for children and the school system to which it belongs, together with the school for teachers (the teacher training institution) and the academic community of which it is a part.

Tinkering with one piece of the whole or another has, as we have learned the hard way, not produced the revolutionary results which are needed. Further, when one section of the whole "gets ahead" of another in complex institutions or social phenomena, there is inherent difficulty. The introduction of modern medicine into underdeveloped countries with resultant huge population growth is a case in point. Similarly, within the life of a given institution, while one department or office or school or individual may periodically take great leaps forward, that phenomenon has no lasting impact upon the institution unless the movement is accompanied by some pulling of the whole with it.

Actually it is not the system *qua* system which needs changing since it is probable that the schools of tomorrow will require the kind of support and differentiation of function which necessitates complex organization. In other words, there seems to be no way in the modern world to get away from systems as such. Rather the problem is to *redo* the educational system so that it focuses upon its primary task of facilitating learning and producing knowledge rather than upon simply maintaining itself. It is the monolithic and homeostatic quality of the school system and the school as a part of that system which must be attacked.

In a very real sense a good performance by one part of a large social institution or organization often disrupts the whole. *All organizations, even the best of them, behave in an irrational fashion much of the time.* That is to say, they are busy taking care of the needs of the group rather than focusing group energy upon the primary task. These covert processes get in the way of the work of the organization. Such hidden agenda becomes more and more the order of business as groups become more and more threatened.

Notice that the task of creating a school which is "systematically reflective about its work"[12] requires an upheaval of existing attitudes and beliefs. So does the development of a colleague relation between scholar-teachers and college professors as envisioned by Dean Schaefer. The world to be created is an unfamiliar and thus a frightening one. Both types of teachers will feel less competent than they do now. This fact, plus the intrinsic difficulty of changing beliefs and attitudes, must be considered as the model for institution building is planned.

Related to the security needs noted above is the familiar sociopolitical phenomenon of the assassination of the leader. When a leader really pushes a group and/or an institution toward change, particularly if he is successful in keeping the organization focused upon its central mission, his tenure as a leader is often short-lived. In other words, the forces of conservatism and security-seeking within the group often catch up with him and make his sacrifice upon the altar of change almost inevitable. Perhaps the most dramatic phenomenon of this kind may be found in the short administrative lives of the cabinet members ruling over large governmental bureaucracies in Washington. Those cabinet members who actually move programs forward

12 Schaefer, *Inquiry*, p. 1.

or succeed in changing the power structures within a bureaucracy, almost always are committing political suicide.

The political dimension of educational institution-changing has never been given the credit it deserves. Somehow students of the schools and of the educational process have wished to sweep that component under the rug or, if it is recognized, to consider it a dirty part of the job.

We are reminded of the remarks made by M. Jean-Jacques Servan-Schreiber concerning European reluctance to examine its industrial weaknesses. The French publisher and political analyst says:

> ...we have to realize that politics is more than the short-term adjustment of power and of interest groups.
>
> .   .   .
>
> *There is no doubt that the problem is political.* ... Political rigidity and self-defensive reflexes act as a brake on change, often dramatically so. Technological aptitude is not what is missing, but the will to change the rules of the social game....[13]

The conventional wisdom in educational research and evaluation has often hindered progress on the part of a school or school system. The education profession has become so nervous about itself and its place in the world that it has been unwilling to move away from the narrowly objective and descriptive instrumentation believed to be "scientific." As a result we have too often focused only on that which can be accurately measured or quantified, and have lost track of bigger issues. These require all the rational faculties we can muster but because they are outside of the data processing orbit they are downgraded by educational leaders. Robert B. Davis, Director of the Madison Project in Mathematics, suggests that we have been:

> ...clinging to scientific generalizations, which provide a safe buffer between educational research and the problems of practical reality. What is needed is something more like an Arthur Schlesinger, a Walter Lippman, a James Reston, or a Harrison Salisbury. We are here more in the domain of the historian, the journalist, or what Allan Dulles has called the "craft of intelligence." ... If we cannot begin to cope with such data, then education (which probably ranks second only to defense among major industries in the United States) seems destined forever to elude systematic study.[14]

Davis notes the candor with which certain hospitals have managed to study

[13] Jean-Jacques Servan-Schreiber, "The American Challenge," *Harper's Magazine,* July, 1968, p. 41.

[14] Robert B. Davis, *Mathematics Teaching—With Special Reference to Epistemological Problems,* Monograph Number 1, Fall, 1967, *Journal of Research and Development in Education,* Athens, Georgia, p. 50.

themselves and wishes that schools could engage in the same kinds of reality testing. He angrily asks, "Are we too polite (or too lacking in courage) to tell the truth when, in fact, we know it?"[15]

Davis perhaps forgets that the medical profession has arrived as a profession and has the kind of professional and social status which permits it to be less defensive than the educational profession. Teaching is indeed an underdeveloped profession and needs face-saving devices just as do our less fortunate colleagues in the proud but poor nations of the world.

Building a new institution out of an old one is an extraordinarily difficult task. In fact, it may be impossible. As we have seen, the obstacles are many in number and multifaceted in nature—economic, social, political and psychological. In addition to a systems approach to change, the creation of an inquiry school probably has no chance of succeeding unless leverage is applied from outside of the institution being recreated and unless some catalytic agents exist both within and without the institutions in question.

Requirements for Change:
A New Catalyst Institution

The process of educational change may be considered in terms of the targets of change, the innovators or change agents, and the mechanism for change—in this case a new catalyst institution. Schaefer's idea envisions the re-creation of the school so that it may serve not only as a major agent in the education and reeducation of teachers, but also in the advancement of knowledge about the teaching/learning process and the change process in school. The creation of this heuristic school will, according to Schaefer, grow out of a "sustained school-university collaboration."[16] This joint school and university collaboration will affect the nature of the teacher training institution or university as well as the school proper. If we use the terms as they are defined by David Clark and Egon Guba,[17] experts in the study of educational change, there will in effect be two target systems for change: (1) the school or school system and (2) the college or university which has heretofore assumed the major responsibility for the education of teachers.

Schaefer also is promoting the development of scholar-teachers who will take the leadership in creating the school as a center of inquiry. These scholar-teachers or change agents and innovators would be supplied by both the schools and the collaborating university.

In addition, we are talking about the invention and development of a

---

15 *Ibid.,* pp. 52–53.
16 Schaefer, *Inquiry,* p. 75.
17 See David L. Clark and Egon G. Guba, "An Examination of Potential Change Roles in Education," Essay Six in *Rational Planning in Curriculum and Instruction* (Washington, D.C.: NEA, CSI, 1967), p. 115.

change mechanism. It is very likely that the scholar-teachers or change agents who are part of the change mechanism will need to be reasonably at home in both camps. Indeed, if Clark and Guba are correct, the task of recreating a new institution "may call into play a complex interaction of intra-and extrasystem individual and institutional changes."[18] Change strategies in these instances must be supported by as much power as can be organized.

This paper posits the hypothesis that *the complexity of the task, the need for support* to both target systems during the process of change, *and the provision of retreat from the psychological heat generated by the change* within either institution *requires a new base of operations. Such a base of operations we see as a semi-autonomous interagency complex,* created and sustained by both of the target institutions, but having enough power and autonomy to serve as an escape valve and as a catalyst and support system for both institutions.

We return to Clark and Guba for advice about the way in which such an agency might be organized. They state:

> Colleges and universities must come to recognize development activities in education as a legitimate function of the institution similar to their development programs in engineering and agriculture. They must accept a role as one agency in an inter-agency complex attacking these problems and should probably be prepared to organize some type of functional unit to carry out this responsibility.... Local school districts...should initiate and participate actively in inter-agency development compacts, and provide substantial released time for the best of their own personnel...to perform as development team members.[19]

The primary function of this new interagency complex is institution building, not of itself, but of others. Its main task is to create a series of different models of center of inquiry schools and simultaneously to redesign the two parent institutions so that they generate rather than prevent growth of these inquiry schools.

The primary goal of the new interagency complex and the schools it creates is the development and use of conceptual schemes or intellectual orderings of complex sets of phenomena. From the writer's point of view they are like James' ideas—ideas which:

> ...help us to get into satisfactory relation with other parts of our experience, to summarize them and get about among them by conceptual short-cuts instead of following the interminable succession of particular phenomena.[20]

18 *Ibid.,* p. 114.
19 *Ibid.,* pp. 127–28.
20 William James, *Essays in Pragmatism* (New York: Hafner, 1955), pp. 147–48.

Bruce Joyce calls the building and use of such conceptualizations the ability to "de-center" from the concrete phenomena which fill every waking moment of the practitioner's life. Robert B. Davis speaks of paradigms. He feels that paradigms

> ...come in all sizes, from something as small as a self-consistent philosophy of one man to something as large as a system of orthodox belief and orthodox practice shared by an entire generation of scholars. Probably, for our present purposes in education, we can make do with more-or-less "medium-sized" paradigms.[21]

It is no accident that most of the analogies used in this essay come from architecture and engineering, or medicine. They are applied arts and sciences which have accumulated enough workable concepts, paradigms, and theories to make up a respectable body of professional knowledge. Education desperately needs the same kind of knowledge to save the practitioner from the mindless empiricism which characterizes the present state of the art.

The present state of the art, however, is nowhere near an "umbrella conceptualization of education which embraces all of the present approaches and important ideas..."[22] *Diversities of models and programs are essential,* as are the *practical,* the *quasi-practical,* and the *eclectic* modes of thought so well described recently by Joseph Schwab.[23] For as Schwab points out:

> The problem slowly emerges...as we search for data, and conversely, the search for data is only gradually given direction by the slow formation of the problem.[24]

The diversities have to do not only with the lack of a coherent theory about teaching and learning, but also with the "organic connections among the diverse organs of the school, the school community, and the educational establishment."[25] It is well known that the public school is highly dependent upon the support of a relevant community. Such communities are diverse in basic values and assumptions and want different educations for their children. We repeat: *A series of school models is imperative.*

---

[21] Robert B. Davis, "Can We Organize The Content, The Children, The Adults, and The Resources?" A position paper prepared for a conference on the Teaching of Mathematics and Science in Elementary Schools, Belmont, Maryland, June, 1968, pp. 15–16. (mimeographed)

[22] *Ibid.,* p. 48.

[23] Joseph J. Schwab, *The Practical: A Language for Curriculum* (Washington, D.C.: NEA, CSI, 1970), p. 2.

[24] *Ibid.,* p. 4.

[25] *Ibid.,* p. 9.

Creating the Interagency Complex

If a new catalyst institution is to be built, what are its dimensions? How can it avoid the pitfalls experienced by the curriculum reform movement of the sixties, and the obstacles inherent in institutional change? What kind of a blueprint can be designed which helps to make Schaefer's school a reality and thus serve education in the United States as the Punjab farms have served agriculture in India? How can a systems approach be applied to the problem?

The remainder of this chapter outlines some plans for action. It assumes some form of interagency coalition consisting of three interlocking components—a small headquarters unit, a teacher support center, and well stocked learning centers for children. The hope is that out of such a complex could emerge the energy and know-how to develop and to sustain a school as a center of inquiry.

SELECTION OF SITE

Let us return now to the case of the Punjab. That "miracle," we note, occurred in a place already favored by the aggressiveness of its people, by the existence of considerable technological know-how on the part of the farming community, and by the bringing together of already progressively oriented governmental and university groups. We propose to follow the Punjabi example and to choose a university and a school system already known for their readiness to move, for their collective brains, and for a history of successful innovation. In other words, we hope the institutions represent strength and not weakness in both mental and material ways. The task will be difficult enough at best. It is therefore very important that initial moves take place where there is some possibility of success—not necessarily where the need is the greatest. If a first experience proves successful, the project may wish to take on larger adversaries.

ORGANIZATION OF THE CATALYST INSTITUTION

There are no precise examples or models of the new institutional arrangements we are here promoting, but there are institutes and teaching and learning centers which bear careful study and examination. For example, it would be interesting to study the genesis and present organizational structure of the Ontario Institute for Studies in Education. That independent organization grew out of the activities of a curriculum group allied with a large teacher organization and later incorporated into itself the Departments of Educational Research and Graduate Studies of the Ontario

College of Education. Undoubtedly the Ontario Institute is a much more formal and formidable kind of an institution than is needed or wanted at the beginning of this enterprise. It does, however, represent an unusual alliance between scholar-teachers and a graduate center. Of interest also is the fact that the Ontario Institute grew in Canada's wealthiest and most progressive province.

A plan which combines some of the components of this proposed institution-building agency may be found in the Center for the Study of Instruction's *Rational Planning in Curriculum and Instruction.*[26] The consortium there outlined had the task of developing "settings in which the rational planning of curriculum and instruction can be studied in operation and through which a nucleus of catalytic agents may be identified and nurtured."[27] That proposal (not funded) also envisioned a new kind of educational cooperative consisting of

> ...a small headquarters unit with ready access to scholar-consultants in the fields of curriculum and instruction and to an established dissemination network, four school systems whose discrete problems and programs represent those most often encountered throughout the country, and a group of observers from schools in settings similar to the testing sites.[28]

This conceptual scheme also took note of a variety of curriculum and teaching paradigms, which were to be screened for local relevance, suitability, and feasibility by a moving group of scholar-consultants and school site personnel. Pilot sites, in turn, were to be serviced by a small headquarters unit which acted as a link between the scholars and the schools as well as a coordinating and communication center for the whole.

Other similar interagency complexes include the League of Cooperating Schools allied with the University of California at Los Angeles and the IDEA complex of the Sloan Kettering Foundation, the Center for Coordinated Education in Santa Barbara, and possibly some of the new regional laboratories.

The second important component in this organization is the kind of teacher support center described by Bruce Joyce in his *Man, Media, and Machines.* These instructional support centers include "specialists who create or organize instructional materials and programs for direct-instruction teams and provide consultant help."[29] The specialists are both professionals and paraprofessionals and possibly work out of what might be called a

[26] Elizabeth C. Wilson, "A Model for Action," *Rational Planning in Curriculum and Instruction* (Washington, D.C.: NEA, CSI, 1967).

[27] *Ibid.,* p. 173.

[28] *Ibid.,* p. 161.

[29] Bruce R. Joyce, *The Teacher and His Staff: Man, Media, and Machines* (Washington, D.C.: NEA, NCTEPS, and CSI, 1967), p. 12.

"souped-up" instructional materials center. That center contains a computer support center, a self-instruction center, an inquiry center, a materials creation center, a human relations center, and a guidance and evaluation center.

Other teacher center models also provide support for teachers and time for them to plan and organize their living. Larry Cuban, in an article in the *Washington Post* dated Sunday, May 5, 1968, recommends for Washington, D.C.:

> ...eight to ten Staff Development Centers, each with a contractual university affiliation located in or near the schools. The staff for each center would include supervisors and curriculum specialists (heretofore assigned to central offices); experienced teachers (assignment to an SDC would mean promotion yet continuation of classroom teaching, thereby creating a career slot above that of teacher); university staff; clinical psychologist; a social worker; and a community organizer. The staff would teach, observe, confer, and provide assistance to the principals and teachers of the immediate area, being always accessible and visible to school and community.

Cuban's description is reminiscent of teacher centers established in England which have been very successful in moving innovative practices into some of the schools in the United Kingdom. Those centers, run by teachers, sponsor local teacher study groups and provide both material assistance and the opportunity for Schaefer's "productive colleagueship."

In addition to teacher support centers in the Joyce sense, the better schools are increasingly developing learning centers for children, the third component of our intra-agency complex. Such centers are supported again from a sophisticated instructional materials center and probably would contain some of the same materials Joyce describes in his pamphlet. In Montgomery County, Maryland, for example, art and music centers for children are growing in number—places where children go not only for formal lessons, but, more importantly, for individual experimentation of various kinds. The city of Philadelphia is finding this device useful in breaking up old teaching patterns.

We professionals have tended to be fuzzy in our conceptualizations of the types of support needed by schools, teachers, and children—often confusing one for the other. The Goodlad idea of differentiating by distance away from the learner is helpful, as is the recent paper by Joyce and others on the "Dimensions of a Curriculum Bank: Support Systems for Schools, Teachers, and Children."[30] That article, generated at the request of the Sloan Kettering Foundation, describes three kinds of curricular data banks:

---

[30] Bruce R. Joyce, *et. al.,* "Dimensions of a Curriculum Bank: Support Systems for Schools, Teachers, and Children," June 7, 1968, p. 5. (mimeographed)

One would serve as a support system for making curricular decisions at the institutional level (that is, by schools and school systems). A second would function as support system for the making of instructional decisions by teachers. The third bank would provide materials for use by children. *The materials for the children should not be all of the same kind.* The materials for children need to flow from different views of self-instruction as those conceptions fit different curricular and instructional purposes.[31]

Joyce's book *Alternative Models of Elementary Education*[32] and his (unpublished) article called "The Principal and His Staff: The Multiple Systems Approach to Curriculum" (May, 1968), also help by describing varieties of curricular modes and teaching strategies. All these, in turn, add to the tool kit of the scholar-teachers destined to assume "colleague authority" in the new schools to be created by our institution builder.

But such professional tools as exist must be readily available at all levels of inquiry, and the organization must have the capacity for inventing and producing more supports. They are to the teacher and the learner what the pharmaceutical companies, the medical suppliers, the dispensary, and the clinic are to the physician and his patients. They are also to the teacher and learner what the research physiologists, the nurse, medical technician, the orderly, and the nurse's aide are to the medical profession. Thus, the support system idea includes ideas, people, material, and services. Indeed, the institution-building agency we envisage might well grow into a "teaching-hospital-with-allied-dispensaries-and-clinics" model.

This model is an extension of Conant's idea of calling the supervisor of practice teaching a "clinical professor" and Schaefer's hope for his school. Says Conant:

> . . . I remind the reader that a clinical professor of surgery is an outstanding surgeon who continues his practice and gives only part of his time to students. His status is equal to that of a professor of surgery or a professor of medicine, both of whom nowadays are expected to be primarily research men. The clinical professor, on the other hand. . .[has]. . .status. . .assured by his accomplishment as a practitioner. . . .[33]

Conant goes on to note that while educational sciences are not as "well developed as their counterparts in a school of medicine,"[34] they have the same relationship to the training of teachers as the medical sciences have to

31 *Ibid.,* p. 5.

32 Bruce R. Joyce, *Alternative Models of Elementary Education* (Waltham, Mass.: Blaisdell, 1969).

33 James B. Conant, *The Education of American Teachers* (New York: McGraw-Hill, 1963), p. 142.

34 *Ibid.,* p. 144–45.

the training of doctors. Conant also feels that those assuming basic responsibility for the induction of teachers should have professorial rank.

Schaefer mentions Conant's clinical professor of education and moves the analogy a step further as he expresses the hope that "schools organized as centers of inquiry would become comparable to teaching hospitals in the medical profession and like teaching hospitals could "serve as a unifying force in welding together...practitioners and...professors."[35]

In any event, this institution-building model has three integral parts: (1) a small think tank operation with a movable and moving "faculty;" (2) a teacher support center stocked with the material, the technology, and the services needed by teachers to study themselves, the teaching-learning act, and the environment and school organization required to create schools as centers of inquiry; and (3) learning centers for children, also well stocked with organized instructional materials. These three parts may or may not be physically housed under the same roof. Such perhaps would be desirable. More important than physical propinquity is the establishment and maintenance of an open two-way communication system between the differentiated parts. The whole internal system, moreover, needs to be loosely, but powerfully tied to the parent organizations so that the whole operation functions in a synergistic fashion. A synergistic structure means that the total organization has more effect than the sum of the parts would indicate —the effect of "killing two birds with one stone."

STAFFING AND ACTIVITIES OF THE INSTITUTION-BUILDING CENTER

This interagency coalition would be staffed jointly by members of the collaborating university and the school or school system entering into contract with that university. In addition to a group of professors and scholar-teachers, the institution-building center will need to have access to a series of consultants not necessarily allied with the university in question. Particularly, we are thinking of the disciplines from which education draws, such as philosophy, sociology, social psychology, psychology of learning, and so on. It is most necessary to create a great deal of ferment and inquiry within this small institution since it is charged with the task not only of designing, producing, and maintaining schools which inquire, but also with the task of recreating that particular phenomenon in its parent institutions, the university and school system. The dimensions of the task it will set for itself are not known at this time. Therefore, the possibility of easy access to a series of scholar-consultants is paramount. For example, such a small institution might well want to establish periodic contact with the National Institute

[35] Schaefer, *Inquiry*, pp. 74–75.

for the Study of Educational Change at Indiana University, of which Egon Guba is now director, or with the Maxwell School at Syracuse University, a school dedicated to the study of institution building particularly in the under developed areas of the world.

Aside from a small think tank group of individuals who are moving and fluid in nature—that is to say, not part of the permanent staff of the interagency center—there would need to be a relatively large rotating staff recruited from the parent institutions for varying periods of time. These joint task forces have the central task of inventing, designing, demonstrating out, installing, and institutionalizing a series of models of new schools.

A corps of teacher-leaders who would be the shapers and movers of the new school will spend at least a year together inventing and designing the school they wish to put into effect. During this creative process the teachers would be backed up by the think tank people and by the entire teacher and learner support system. Indeed, all the services of the institution builder would follow them as they move from the design and invention of the school into its actual institutionalization. At that point, the services of the interagency complex would probably need to become more mobile than was necessary earlier.

Examples of projects allied to the central task are further investigations of the nature and use of support systems; careful documentation of the failures which are bound to occur; and studies of "teacher belief" systems or "cognitive schema," as Robert Davis calls them.

In this connection, Davis remarks:

> The teacher in the classroom swims in an ocean of sensory information and must respond by a rapid fire sequence of hastily made decisions. The perception and interpretation of all of this data, as well as this stream of decision making, will be shaped in very pronounced ways by the teachers' "belief system" or "cognitive schema."[36]

Teacher-scholars need time to become aware of their own belief systems in order that they may examine them, modify them, categorize them both in process and content. They thus acquire another tool to help other teachers gain access to the same insight and control over their teaching techniques.

There is no question but that these teacher tasks call for a quality of leadership in the profession which does not exist in great numbers. Thus, we are not talking about all teachers. Rather, we need the scholar-teacher, the artist-teacher, who can assume the colleague authority Schaefer describes,

[36] Robert B. Davis, *Mathematics Teaching,* p. 12.

and who has the brains, guts, and power to focus the school upon its primary task of inquiry into the learning process, into teaching as a function of the learning process, and into the nature of the institution *which promotes both.*

Actually, it is as important that the center study the parent institutions as it is to create and maintain alternaive models of schools which inquire. All of us, from time to time, have had experience with schools which approach this goal. The problem is not that some samples have never existed as a result of happy accidents or fortuitous concatenations of events and people. Rather the profession needs to learn how to control the ingredients so that happy accidents have a higher probability of turning up and replication is a conscious possibility.

One of the hypotheses to be field tested by this institution-building center is that the present organizational setup of school systems and teachers' colleges hinders rather than helps the creation of inquiring teachers and inquiring schools. Should this hypothesis prove to have any validity, paradigms for the redesigning of *those* institutions may also be a necessary product of this oddly constructed consortium.

In essence, the consortium will be promoting and resurrecting "the much-abused concept of action research."[37] Other terms for this kind of systematic and rational study are "program" and "operations" research. These remarks bring us back again to Robert Schaefer who elaborates so beautifully the habits of mind to be acquired by the teacher-scholar and promoted by colleague authority:

> The commonality among all these approaches is their dependence upon rational thought and analysis. They emphasize the systematic study of what teaching is and scrupulously avoid the familiar hazards of defensiveness and tender-mindedness. Schools serving as centers of inquiry must foster all such disciplined efforts to achieve understanding.... What is crucial is not that a particular mode be adopted but that the art of teaching (and we would add all the institutions which surround it) be subjected to vigorous continuing inquiry.[38]

But why, asks the old time progressive, does this center for institution building not mention a vigorous continuing inquiry into the learning of children? Is it not important? Yes, we reply, it is the central concern of education, *but has not been the central concern of the school.* The problem addressed by this essay is how to realign the institution and the teaching act as a support rather than as a hindrance to learning. Previous studies

[37] David Clark and Egon Guba. "Roles in Education," p. 131.
[38] Robert Schaefer, *Inquiry,* pp. 72–73.

of learning have had little effect upon the school as an institution. Perhaps if the school changed, existing learning studies could really be used.

PROBLEMS OF POWER AND AUTHORITY

In any interinstitutional liaison, the extent to which a partner gives up power and authority to an outside agency is of prime importance. The failure of many such enterprises can be traced again and again to the difficulties which occur over the issue of power. In this connection, recognizing teacher militancy as a new power on the horizon, we recommend including leaders from the local teacher organization in the early stages of the planning for and the setting up of an "institution builder." Authorities should welcome such teacher interest and extend a warm invitation as a possible partner.

Whatever the outcome of these explorations and invitations, negotiations must proceed with great care and great clarity. Eventualities need to be explored openly in a series of discussions between the authorities of all institutions and agreed upon in writing. A good deal of attention needs to be paid to the set up of the governing body. There are various alternative arrangements. There are boards of trustees and/or governing boards which have the power to hire and fire directors and have control over the budget. There are directorates, assisted by advisory committees which sit regularly, and are powerful in that they are selected out of the power structure of the institutions they represent.

Other managerial questions include the kinds of funding which are possible, arrangements for personnel selection, and the amount of autonomy to be exercised by the institutional coalition. Again, there are various degrees of autonomy. These must be identified in whatever contractual arrangement is built by the parent groups. It is central that the agency have some funding of its own which it does not borrow from its parent institutions. In like manner, it needs the power to select its own "faculty" and consultant groups, and should have a decided voice in setting up the criteria for the selection of the individuals who will move through the centers toward the building of a school as a center for inquiry.

Let us be sure that the new institute does not get so bound up in entangling relationships and obligations to its parent organizations that it loses mobility and freedom. It must have these two qualities since, it will be remembered, the reason for its existence is that the homeostatic qualities of school systems and teacher education institutions have prevented the collection and organization of a sufficiently critical mass to break through the inquiry barrier. Both institutions tend to be bound by their own institutional habits and protocols. They are overly concerned with "keeping school," with business as usual, and with the maintenance of the institution. These are their real tasks. As a consequence there is little energy to pursue further inquiry into themselves, much less create a series of new schools. Further, as we have seen, such innovations as they do invent or adopt seem to flare up briefly, enjoy a short period of public acclaim, and then return to normal mediocrity. The "system" somehow manages to take its toll either by making it impossible for the creation to happen, or by draining off the energy required to institutionalize the creations which do occur. Thus, the new coalition must at all costs avoid falling into the trap of overinstitutionalization itself. Perhaps the best analogy that we can think of is that of the scaffolding set up to assist in the process of building a new building. It is there while the building itself is getting under way, but is not functional after the building can stand by itself. Note, however, that heavy support needs to be built into the building if it is to stand alone.

This analogy suggests a small continuing staff as the directorate of such an institution. The main work would be done by task forces organized upon an ad hoc basis, recruited from both the schools and the university. It also suggests that the support system for teachers and children be not only available at the center during the invention and design phases of the creation of a new school, but that much of the same kind of support be built into the new school as it establishes and institutionalizes itself.

Obviously, the new agency will need funds. It will need money to buy brains in the form of outside consultants, and to buy time for the artist-teachers and university professors who will be selected to move in and out of the institution. It will need money to set up a model support center for teachers and children and to conduct such evaluation as it deems important. It may well be that the institutions forming this coalition will wish to underwrite many of the costs listed above. Well and good. The more they contribute the more likely their active support of the consortium. But the consortium must not be dependent upon this kind of largesse. Without some independent funding, or at least monies earmarked for this agency, the new institution could lose its leverage in relation to the "establishments" and get swallowed up just as have other innovative arrangements.

At the same time that the interinstitutional agency needs freedom and independence, it also needs sanction from the power structure within each of the organizations it serves. Thus, some mechanism must be devised so that the building agency has direct access to the power structures within the establishments. There may also be need to ally this institute with given segments of the larger establishments. For example, we note that the Ontario Institute grew out of a curriculum arm built by the Ontario Teachers Federation, and that a research office here or a curriculum office there may already be serving a university or a school system as an unofficial planning and development office. These are the kinds of ties which need to be built into contractual arrangements. They will vary from school to school and from institution to institution. Suffice it to say that as contractual arrangements are developed, it is important to locate the places within existing institutions which bear the closest resemblance to centers of inquiry already, and to use that strength in a well defined systematic relationship.

The End Products:
Recapitulations and Conclusions

In summary, this essay underlines the Schaefer leit-motif that the artist-teacher and the scholar-teacher must work hand-in-glove if the system itself is to change. It adds to this idea the hypothesis that no inquiring schools can be created which will sustain themselves and be replicable unless the system itself, the total system, is changed from the bottom up. Thus, the small agency with allied support system centers here described contracts with its parent institutions not only to invent, design, field test, and establish alternative models of schools which are themselves centers of inquiry, but also to recommend those changes in the parent institutions which will reward and foster this kind of institution building.

The new agency will need to look into all levels of institutional decision making. For example, in big school systems it is important to examine the budget-making process, the personnel selection process, the amount of decentralization, the role of middle management, the organizational communication system and so on. Similarly in teachers' colleges and universities such matters as rank, the place of research, and the reward system of the institution should be areas for study. All systems must be willing to engage in serious self-examination. Since that kind of study hits at the power structure of any institution, only relatively secure organizations (or organizations with their backs to the wall) will be tempted by this possibility or attempt to take part in it. In other words, only mature institutions willingly fight about their primary tasks. The first order of business, then, is to find the institutions which are consciously ready to cooperate in such an alliance.

The second order of business consists in organizing, staffing, and funding the interagency consortium. Essential at the beginning are the directorate, the "shadow faculty" to serve as the yeast for the new institution, a teacher support system as described by Joyce and Cuban, and a highly selected small group of artist-teachers destined to be the first faculty of the first model school.

Out of the first year of this organizational structure will grow the first school. Its precise dimensions cannot be clearly foreseen at this point since the task of the first year of the "institution builder" is to build these plans in detail. It seems likely, however, that the school will:

1. build around a learning center for children well stocked with a wide variety of multimedia instructional materials within easy access of teachers and children.
2. use a variety of organizational patterns as means to different educational ends.
3. have considerable control over its own budget and personnel.
4. organize a faculty dominated internal governmental system which concentrates efforts on instruction.
5. spend considerable time and energy in articulating its goals, and in studying its successes and failures in achieving these goals.
6. require a variety of differentiated responsibilities and specialists in its staffing arrangements.
7. adapt its curricular modes and teaching methods to local needs and tastes.
8. attend to the system of interlocking components which must work together, i.e., curriculum, diagnostic and evaluative procedures and instruments, organizational patterns, teaching methods, and staff education.

As the first model school becomes operational, the institution builder begins to take on the dimensions of a teaching hospital. Indeed, this combination of shadow faculty, teacher support center, and first school model should help identify and nourish the "clinical professors" needed by the teaching hospital. They might be active school practitioners; they might be educational engineers from the teachers colleges and universities. In any event it is expected that they would assume the kind of leadership for the new institute and for the model schools that the medical profession now exerts in hospitals, buying the kind of managerial and administrative assistance that is needed but holding the reins of policy and planning for the school in professional hands whose first concerns are instruction, not administration.

If all goes well, the center for institution building will soon have the capacity (1) to create other models of inquiring schools, (2) to serve as training grounds for other scholar-teachers, (3) to investigate the nature of the institutions which help and which hinder the creation of a "new tough-minded progressivism."

Obviously, the quality and catalytic capacity of the leaders of this consortium is of primary importance to its successful operation. They need both the intellect to conceptualize and create, and the ability to build the environment where inquiry is rewarded and supported. The directorate should probably combine the talents of several people, who are at home in both the schools and university world and who together can be equally forceful in thought and action.

A major component in the creation and operation of the center for institution building is provision for the basic emotional needs of the staff as well as the push toward the primary tasks of inquiry and institution building. The kinds of changes here envisioned are bound to upset the habitual order of the day as well as run head on into political power struggles. We have already noted the psychological phenomenon of assassination of the leader and the need for providing a periodic haven for those who in fact do lead well.

The idea of mobile groups moving through the teacher support center makes for some possibility to take care of these needs. Another is to make a major business of the institutions a series of well-defined projects which have a beginning and end and which do not require individuals to abandon entirely their need for touching home base from time to time. The point is that whatever the particular strategy, the organization must recognize the need for recharging emotional batteries and provide regular escape hatches for even the most mature staff members.

But the center need not always be a place for Puritan hard work, nor for agonizing wrenches from old and familiar habits and patterns. The norm created can also be exciting, fun, stimulating, and intellectually and emotionally rewarding. Such a mood can be created by careful selection of continuing leaders and by changing and enjoying an inquiring and irreverent mix of real professionals. In summary, we see the moving staff which works through the "teacher support center" as staying long enough to invent and design new models or pieces of models of schools which will inquire in the Schaefer sense. They may periodically return to redesign, retool, or escape from the heat of the kitchen. They will come singly or in teams. Teams will surely be the order of the day as new school models are designed and become operational.

This support system, moreover, will continue to be operative as the groups leave the institute to try out, to demonstrate, and to institutionalize their inventions. These supports may well be a small version of the teaching hospital—a clinic or dispensary—designed as a support system for the local children and teachers and/or a mobile support team which would move from the teaching center out to the places where invention and design were being tried out. Thus, while the institution builder per se might move on to erect more scaffolding around more new schools, sustained support for the old would be built into the system, support which would continue to engender inquiry and which could, in turn, make a real profession out of teaching. As Martin Mayer remarks and Robert Schaefer notes in his prologue:

Given almost unimaginable good luck, American education could develop into a predominantly scholarly enterprise, in which the masters of a study would feel an obligation to communicate, and the teachers of children would feel an obligation to communicate, and the teachers of children would feel an obligation to discipline their common sense and seek out the uncongenial idea. . . . Teachers could participate in the invention and propagation of teaching ideas, in the elimination of what is inconsequential, stupid, misleading, or unnecessarily difficult and in the adaptation of pedagogic models for differing groups of students.[39]

This essay outlines one way of creating a situation where unimaginable good luck will be the order of the day.

[39] Martin Mayer, "Changes in American Education in the Next Decade: Some Predictions," in Matthew B. Miles, *Innovation in Education* (New York: Bureau of Publications, Teachers College, Columbia University, 1964), pp. 626–27.

3

Matching Models
for Teacher Training

DAVID E. HUNT

David Hunt is a psychologist who has developed two closely related lines of inquiry that apply to education. With his associates, Harold Schroder and O. J. Harvey, he has developed a personality theory which has special interest because it does not create a dichotomy between cognitive and affective behavior. Rather, it describes human development as an integrated process of personality growth which can be observed in terms of intellectual, social, and personal growth.

Hunt and Joyce,[1] with a variety of collaborators, have conducted a series of studies which indicate that both the cognitive and affective aspects of teaching styles are related to personality as described by conceptual systems theory. Several independent replications have been made of this work, including an extensive recent one by Murphy and Brown,[2] which found that many aspects of the behavior of student teachers were related to conceptual (personality) level.

Hunt's second line of inquiry has been oriented to the relationship between environmental differences and the behavior and growth of individuals. If we conceive of personality development as a progression

---

[1] See, for example, D. E. Hunt and B. R. Joyce, Teacher Trainee Personality and Initial Teaching Style, *American Educational Research Journal*, 4, 1967, 253–59.

[2] P. D. Murphy and M. M. Brown, Conceptual Systems and Teaching Styles, *American Educational Research Journal*, 4, 1970, 540–99.

toward increasing complexity and integration of behavior (which Hunt does), then we may ask the questions (as Hunt does) : In what environments do individuals of particular complexity function best, and which environments are likely to increase the complexity and flexibility of the individual's response to his tasks and surroundings? Since personality and teaching style are related, the personality of the teacher may be the key, if teaching behavior is to change.

The importance of these orientations for teacher education is twofold. In the first case, we want to organize teacher education so that the individual differences of the teacher candidates are optimally matched to training methods and interpersonal climates so that learning will be comfortable and effective. Ideally, the climate of teacher education should modulate to the teacher candidates, so that a variety of conditions can meet the needs of the individuals.

Second, conceptual (personality) development is itself a significant goal of teacher education as we conceive of it. For Hunt's conception of personality is directly linked to the creativity, flexibility, and complexity which are essential to the innovator. His hypotheses about how we can increase conceptual development thus provide us with strategies for shaping teacher education to increase personal capacity in areas which are critical to our conception of the teacher.

The training of teachers, like the education of children, requires adaptation to individual differences. Teacher trainees vary enormously in skill level and in personality, yet most programs for training teachers are designed for an "average trainee" with few options to accommodate trainee variation. A teacher training program which provides alternative experiences modulated to trainee differences is not only more likely to produce an efficient direct effect, but it will also be indirectly beneficial in providing the teacher trainee an experimental example of what is meant by individualizing instruction and "meeting the needs of the student."

In teacher training, adaptation to individual differences requires a system for coordinating differences in educational environments (or training intervention) with trainee characteristics. We will use the concept of "matching" to describe the appropriateness of a particular training intervention for an individual trainee to accomplish a specific training objective.

Matching has been used in earlier work (Hunt, 1966a; Hunt, 1970a, b) to describe situations in which the training agent himself radiates an environment toward a person, e.g. a teacher presents a didactic lesson which is either "matched" or "mis-matched" to a student, given certain objectives. However, analysis in terms of matching should be equally useful here, and requires only that we use the term *training intervention* to make clear that the environment in differential teacher training refers to intervention procedures directed toward the teacher trainee, as distinct from those environments which he will learn to radiate later toward students.

Matching models for teacher training should provide the basis for coordinating trainee characteristics such as skill level and aptitudes with variations in training intervention. Trainee skill level will determine the specific *content* of the training intervention while the trainee's aptitudes or "accessibility characteristics" will determine the *form* of the training intervention (Hunt, 1970b). A matching model states two knowns—the immediate training objective and the relevant trainee characteristics—and prescribes the third: a specific training intervention. Matching models are based on the assumption that different people learn different things in different ways; thus, the planning and design of any educational program, including the training of teachers, should provide differential alternatives toward the same or different goals. The notion that there is no single best program for training teachers is fundamental to this view. The reader is likely to nod in agreement with this belief as he might agree with the importance of meeting the needs of each child. However, if one intends only to give lip service to the idea of adapting training to individual differences of trainees, then the specific prescriptions outlined here will serve little purpose.

Several assumptions underlie this differential training approach. First, the design and planning of a training program must begin with a thorough understanding of the variation in trainees who will attend, i.e. it is not developed according to general specifications ignoring trainee characteristics. Second, there will be sufficient variation among trainees to warrant adapting training intervention to such trainee differences. Third, regardless of the amount of variation among the trainees, a careful analysis of the "match" between trainee and intervention is likely to force a more explicit analysis of the process involved in how trainees change during training.

In what follows, this analysis consists of: (1) stating certain training objectives; (2) considering certain trainee characteristics relevant to intervention; (3) specifying related aspects of training intervention; and finally, (4) deriving those trainee-intervention combinations most likely to produce the desired objectives.

The Machining Model

TRAINING OBJECTIVES

The training of teachers is considered one example of the training of training agents. The term *training agent* (Hunt, 1966b) describes a person who provides an interpersonal environment (E) for the person or group (P) with whom he interacts to produce a particular behavioral effect or change (B). Therefore, although the model will be described specifically for the training of teachers, it should also apply to the training of other training agents: psychotherapists, counselors, social workers, industrial trainees, and even parents.

One of the most useful forms for specifying objectives is to state them in terms of components characterizing the effective training agent. Component analysis permits initial characterization of a trainee in terms of a component profile, and subsequent evaluation of various forms of intervention by noting the degree of component change produced. For example, we have used three components—adaptability, motivational orientation, and interpersonal competence—to assess Peace Corps trainees (Hunt, 1965), and to suggest how different component profiles might be required for different Peace Corps assignments, e.g. teaching, community development. Harrison and Oshry (1967) have developed an Organizational Behavior Describer Survey for use in industry which consists of four components: rational and technical competence, verbal dominance, emotional expressiveness, and consideration. In the area of psychotherapist and counselor effectiveness, Truax and Carkhuff (1967) have suggested three essential components: empathy, nonexpressive warmth, and genuineness.

More specifically relevant to the training of teachers are the components suggested by Joyce (1967): (1) making and using knowledge, (2) shaping the school, (3) teaching with strategy, (4) creating interpersonal climates, and (5) controlling the self. Teacher sensitivity (the capacity to react appropriately to the learner's frame of reference) and teacher strength (the capacity to structure and organize the classroom) have also been used as two components useful in assessing and planning for differential treatment of teacher trainees (Hunt, 1970c).

Another system of component analysis (Hunt, 1966b) which we will use here as a major illustrative approach, consists of: (1) skill in discrimination, (2) skill in radiating environments, and (3) skill in flexible modulation from one environment to another.

When training objectives are expressed in terms of components, they can be operationally defined, permitting an assessment of each trainee's present position on a component profile. An inspection of the trainee's component profile indicates those areas in which further training is required. In order for a component system to serve as the basis for planning a training program, some understanding of the relations between the components is required. If a trainee is deficient in several components, then the first practical issue is to decide on which component he should first receive training, a decision which requires considering the order and sequence of components. In the "model for analyzing the training of training agents" (Hunt, 1966b, summarized in Table 3-1), it was assumed that the three subcomponents in discriminative skill—discriminating between environments, discriminating between behaviors, and discriminating between persons—were prerequisites for skill in radiating an environment to produce a specific behavior, some recent research, conducted in a different conceptual context (Brooks, 1967), supports this assumption.

Order of intervention may also be determined by the potential ease or difficulty in inducing change in a component since it may be advisable to begin with a component on which change is more likely to occur. Also, there is the question of how many of the components can realistically be expected to change in the training time available. If planners are willing to settle for a circumscribed set of component skills, then, of course, this will affect strategy in specifying objectives. For example, it is unrealistic to expect every trainee to acquire skill in radiating all possible environments.

The components in Table 3-1 are based on the following ideal definition of training agent effectiveness:

> the capacity to radiate a wide variety of environments, to select from this variety a specific environment to be radiated toward a particular person or group with the aim of producing a particular behavioral outcome, and to shift from one environment to another under appropriate circumstances. In education, for example, the teacher's capacity to present the same lesson in a variety of educational environments, to select and use that specific educational environment most appropriate to produce a specific learner outcome with a particular group of students, and to shift to a new form of educational environment when appropriate would constitute the operations for teacher effectiveness. (Hunt, 1966b, pp. 138–39.)

This definition, and the components associated with it, are admittedly ideal for reasons which should not require explication; in many instances, only a few of these objectives can be aimed for, or realized. Nonetheless, Table 3-1 provides a model for matching and coordinating the trainee's present skill level with the content of the training intervention. For example, if a trainee is lacking in discriminative skill, this component would be the initial focus

TABLE 3-1 Training Objectives

Objective	Definition of Objective		
Skill in discrimination	To discriminate between environments $E_x/E_y/E_z$	To discriminate between behaviors $B_1/B_2/B_3$	To discriminate between persons $P_I/P_{II}/P_{III}$
Skill in radiating environments	To radiate a variety of environments $E_x:$ $E_y:$ $E_2^2:$	To radiate that environment which will produce a specific behavior $E_x:\ \to B_1$ $E_y:\ \to B_2$	To radiate that environment which will produce a specific behavior from a particular person $E_x:\ P_I \to B_1$ $E_y:\ P_{II} \to B_1$
Skill in flexible modulation from one environment to another	To shift from one environment to another under appropriate circumstances (Time 1) $E_x:$ $P_1 \to B_1$ (Time 2) $E_y:$ $P_1 \to B_3$		

Code: E = Environment
  B = Behavior
  P = Person

After Hunt, 1966b.

of the intervention before attempting to induce change in skill in radiating environments.

TRAINEE CHARACTERISTICS

Before describing specific trainee characteristics thought to be most important for guiding intervention in a differential training program, it will be useful to review some underlying assumptions. A matchng model framework for training teachers requires that one begin with the trainee—where he is now and his change-relevant characteristics—in order to intervene to produce change. The rationale here is identical to the belief that, in planning education intervention for the classroom, the single most important aspect is the child and "where he is now." Although it is fairly obvious and reasonably well accepted to assume that one must "begin with the child", it is less frequently assumed in the training of teachers that one must begin with the trainee. In this sense, the present model may be seen as a "trainee-centered" training program.

The major problem with almost every attempt to individualize instruction or to devise a "person-centered" educational program is the inordinately large number of individual differences which might be considered. The educational planner is overwhelmed by the myriad differences among persons, and further confused by the fact that very few of these differences are coordinated with specifically appropriate educational interventions. Faced by this double dilemma—"Every student (or trainee) is unique" and "Because of his uniqueness, every student must be treated differently"—the educational decision-maker is likely to abandon all efforts toward individualization or differential treatment because of its apparent impossibility.

We are not concerned with cataloguing all of the ways in which trainees vary. We are concerned only with those characteristics which are systematically related to selecting the most appropriate training intervention. Two classes of trainee characteristics will be considered: (1) trainee skill level, which will be coordinated with the *content* of the training intervention (Hunt, 1966b), and (2) trainee accessibility characteristics which will be coordinated with the *form* of the intervention (Hunt, 1970b). Put simply, if we know what the trainee knows and can do, this prescribes *what* he needs to learn; if we know his modes of accessibility, this prescribes *how* the content should be presented. There are, no doubt, many other important trainee characteristics, but we will be concerned only with those which are related to differential training procedures, either theoretically or empirically. Since no program can treat every person as completely unique, the practical issue becomes what are the most important adaptations to make.

Skill Level

The trainee should be characterized in terms of his present position on skill components: skill in discrimination, skill in radiating environments, and skill in flexible modulation from one environment to another. These skills, and means for assessing them, are discussed in detail elsewhere (Hunt, 1966b). Other components such as those described in other chapters might serve as well. It is important to assess the trainee's present skill level so that this diagnostic information can be used to make the most effective differential placement.

Accessibility Characteristics

Using Lewinian terminology, the change process is described as one of first "unfreezing", producing change, and then "refreezing". Viewed in such a way, the immediate problem is to specify the procedure for "unfreezing" or "reaching" the trainee. We consider this issue by characterizing trainees in terms of accessibility characteristics. It is not sufficient to describe the trainee only as he is now on a skill component profile, and to indicate that component on which change is desired. We must also characterize the trainee in terms which will be directly translatable to that mode or form of training intervention to which he will be most open or accessible. When we deal with a physically handicapped student we are aware of the importance of accessibility channels; though less dramatic, the concept of "tuning in" to the most appropriate channel for all trainees is equally important.

Four accessibility characteristics are described: cognitive orientation, motivational orientation, value orientation, and sensory orientation.

1. *Cognitive orientation.* Cognitive orientation is an important accessibility characteristic because it indicates how a trainee will organize and interpret his experience (i.e., training intervention). Specific measures of cognitive orientation are conceptual level (Hunt, 1966a; Hunt, 1970b) and integrative complexity (Schroder, Driver, and Streufert, 1967). Conceptual level (CL) and integrative complexity are sufficiently similar that a description of CL will convey the flavor of the dimension of variation in cognitive orientation. CL was originally based on a theory of conceptual development (Harvey, Hunt, and Schroder, 1961) which hypothesized that, under ideal training conditions, a person develops from a low level of conceptual development (low CL) in which he is cognitively simple, dependent, and not capable of generating his own concepts, to a higher CL in which he is more cognitively complex, independent, and capable of generating his own concepts. CL has been used in several investigations of trainee characteristics (Bundy, 1968; Heck, 1968; Hunt, 1970c).

2. *Motivational orientation.* Motivational orientation affects preference for and reaction to different forms of feedback and reward. Praise is more effective than criticism for "introverts" and "failure avoiders", while criticism is more effective than praise for "extroverts" and "underachievers" (Schroder and Hunt, 1957; Thompson and Hunnicutt, 1944; Van de Riet, 1964). French (1958) demonstrated that persons high in affiliation motivation solved problems more effectively under conditions of feeling-oriented feedback, while persons high in achievement orientation solved problems more effectively under conditions of task-oriented feedback. Similarly, Wells (1957) found that persons who were other-directed worked harder under conditions of experimenter-defined feedback while inner-directed persons worked better under conditions of self-defined feedback. Other studies have demonstrated the differential effects of peer approval vs. authority approval.

3. *Value orientation.* Whether trainees will be likely to learn skills designed as intervention procedures which will achieve objectives they do not believe in, or that they disagree with, is a question about which there is little evidence. However, on the basis of available information plus intuition, it seems important to include the trainee's value orientation as a classification characteristic for differential training. Teacher trainee attitude toward the best way to teach, i.e., inductive-deductive, has been related to the teacher trainee's preferred style of communication (Hunt, 1970c).

In an educational context, it is probably inadvisable to use a single dimension to measure a trainee's value orientation. What is most important for the trainee is whether he can accept a variety of procedures as being useful at different times. Unless the trainee who favors inquiry and inductive lessons can also accept the necessity for structured lessons and didactic presentation, he will be much like the "rigid liberal", and as difficult to change as a trainee with exactly the opposite values. This point was especially clear in observing some trainees in an urban teacher preparation program who valued giving students freedom, and refused to establish order in the classroom or learn procedures for doing so.

Measures of value orientation (e.g., Minnesota Teacher Attitude Inventory, Attitudes to Teaching, Hunt, 1970c) will require revision and extension so that they do not simply classify the trainee on a single dimension. It seems necessary that they also include what Sherif has called the person's "latitude of acceptance," or that area on the dimension to which the person is "open" to information.

Much of the lack of knowledge about the relation between value orientation and the acquisition of skill comes from lack of information about the role of awareness—how does explicit knowledge of one's instrumental quality affect the learning of teaching skills? As we learn about this role, we will better understand how values are likely to inhibit or facilitate skill acquisition. Bereiter's suggestion is appropriate in this regard:

> What we should try to do is give students the increment in IQ without all the agony of belief and disbelief that hampers its coming. This is not easy, but there is a time-honored principle that is applicable to the effort. The principle is, "Should follows Can". Try in every way to get students to where they have the capability of applying a new way of thinking before putting them in a position to pass judgment upon it. (1969, p. 75.)

How much it is possible to postpone the "should" question without affecting trainee's acquisition of skills and understanding is an area which deserves much more investigation. Perhaps then we will learn the answer to the question, "How does the awareness of what you are doing affect your learning to do it?"

Another factor linking value orientation and skill acquisition is the trainee's feeling of adequacy. One reason for a trainee's disinclination to acquire a skill which is at odds with his present value orientation may be the threat that learning this skill would pose to his feelings of adequacy.

4. *Sensory orientation.* Most forms of presentation in training intervention involve both visual and auditory spheres. However, in some instances, there may be an option, and it seems useful to consider the trainee's preferred sensory modality.

Summary of Trainee Characteristics

First, the trainee should be characterized in relation to his position on the skill level in question, e.g. if the objective is skill in discriminating between environments, then his level on this component should be assessed. If he is weak on the component, then consideration must be given to his accessibility to intervention aimed toward increasing his skill level. To do this, he should be characterized according to an accessibility profile: (1) cognitive orientation, i.e., conceptual level or the complexity with which he processes information; (2) motivational orientation, i.e. importance of certain interpersonal needs; (3) value orientation, i.e. his position and "latitude of acceptance" on relevant dimensions; and (4) sensory orientation, i.e. preference for visual or auditory presentation.

TRAINING INTERVENTION CHARACTERISTICS

A trainee-centered program requires procedures appropriate for the trainee. Taken literally, the training program would be developed on the basis of trainee characteristics *after* the trainees had been selected. Although such literal adaption is clearly impossible, the training program must be kept flexible with numerous options available.

Planning a training program with flexible options for intervention sounds like a reasonable idea; however, the implications of such flexible planning should be briefly considered. Frequently, new training programs are built around the most popular new form of training as their central single feature, e.g. T group sensitivity training, video feedback; but a differential training program cannot be fixed to a single procedure in an across-the-board fashion. This is not to say that equipment for video feedback training should not be available in a differential training program, but rather that such equipment should be regarded as one of the many resources available for accomplishing certain training objectives with certain trainees.

Perhaps the most difficult feature in adopting a flexible program is that program planners have to forego the security of a fixed four-year or one-year curriculum outline. Also the staff in such a program will never be quite sure what forms of training they will have to provide in the future. Cronbach has made an interesting suggestion in this regard:

> I suggest that we set out to invent interactions. Specifically, *we ought to take a differential variable* we think promising and design alternative treatments *to interact with that variable.* (Cronbach, 1967, p. 32.)

The logic for selecting the following intervention characteristics follows Cronbach's rationale in that only those program features directly related to variation among trainees are discussed. Variations in training procedures, therefore, are considered in two general categories—content and form—which are related to the two trainee categories, skill level and accessibility characteristics.

Content of Intervention

Training procedures designed to produce the objectives in Table 3-1 have been described elsewhere (Hunt, 1966a, pp. 144–45, 150–52, 154), and will only be briefly summarized here. Procedures for training discriminative skill may consist of (1) variations of psychophysical techniques that give the trainee direct instruction in making discriminations between various environments, behaviors, or persons, or (2) some form of sensitivity training (e.g. Heck, 1968) which deals directly with the enhancement of interpersonal discrimination. Procedures for training skill in radiating environments have been described extensively in other chapters of this volume. Such procedures include: learning by modeling, learning by instruction, and learning by trial and error. A major value of the skill-content matching model summarized in Table 3-1 is to define that specific content which a trainee needs to learn; thus, if he is deficient in the capacity to discriminate between environments, he should be trained in this area.

Form of Intervention

Among the countless variations in intervention procedures, only those dimensions will be considered which are related to trainee accessibility characteristics, and these are summarized in Table 3-2.

TABLE 3-2 Relation Between Trainee Accessibility Characteristics and Form of Training Intervention

Accessibility Characteristic	*Form of Intervention*
Cognitive orientation	Structure of presentation
Motivational orientation	Form of feedback and reward
Value orientation	Value context of presentation
Sensory orientation	Modality of presentation

1. *Structure of presentation.* Structural variation includes both the structured-flexible dimension, or the degree to which the trainee can interact responsively with the material, and the degree of organizational complexity of the material. Short-term structural variation is exemplified by variations in rule-example sequencing in which the example-only form represents low structure while the rule-example form represents high structure. Structural variation over a longer time period is represented by variation from the low structure of a discovery approach to the high structure of a lecture approach; from independent study to highly organized study; and from student-centered approaches to teacher-centered approaches.

Several examples of measuring the intervention procedures in terms of their degree of structure are available: environmental complexity (Schroder, Driver, and Streufert, 1967); structured-flexible programs (Hunt and Hardt, 1967), and reflective environments (Hunt and Joyce, 1967).

2. *Form of feedback and reward.* A trainee may receive information about his performance in many different forms. For example, he may receive feedback directly through self-viewing on video, or he may simply be told about his performance. The source of feedback may vary: he can be informed by his supervisor or he can be informed by his fellow trainees (authority-peer variation).

Reward may vary not only in its nature (positive-negative), and its source (authority-peer), but also in its informational quality (informational-approval). Informational reward, e.g. "that's right", is essentially identical to feedback while reward in the form of approval ("I like the way you're doing that") carries information only about the source's evaluation, not about trainee performance.

3. *Value context of presentation.* A matching model should specify the optimal disparity between the trainee's orientation and the presentation (Hunt, 1970a, pp. 16–18) Ordinarily, the most effective training presentation is neither identical to the trainee's present position, nor too disparate from it. Rather, it should be close to his present position, within his "latitude of acceptance".

In some cases it may be possible to maintain a "value-neutral" context. If skill acquisition requires some involvement and affective arousal, however, the positioning of the presentation on a value dimension becomes important. Although forms of training intervention have not typically been considered on specific attitudinal dimensions, it should be helpful to view various interventions as either "absolute", i.e. presentation differs in a predetermined amount from the trainee's position, or "gradual", i.e. presentation begins at a point very close to that of trainee's position, and gradually deviates from it (Harvey and Rutherford, 1958).

4. *Modality of presentation.* Variation in modality has become more apparent with the increased use of video feedback and films which usually provide both self-viewing and self-listening. Little is known about the general or differential effects of multimodality (self-viewing and -listening) versus single modality (only self-listening); the distinction should be made in intervention procedures when possible so that such information can be accrued.

RELATION BETWEEN TRAINEE ACCESSIBILITY CHARACTERISTICS AND FORM OF INTERVENTION

Having described the variations in trainee characteristics and intervention procedures, we now consider how specific trainee characteristics can be used to determine the most specifically appropriate training intervention. Table 3-3 contains the relations which were described in Table 3-2, but in Table 3-3 specific examples have been added. Only the form in which the content is presented is dealt with so that in using Table 3-3 to prescribe the most effective form of intervention, it is assumed that the content has already been matched to trainee skill level according to Table 3-1.

In what follows, the principles for prescribing the best intervention for an individual trainee are derived. Issues such as grouping and how many trainees to put together, will not be considered since these issues frequently depend upon available resources, urgency of producing change, etc. Many of the examples of differential effects are from areas other than the training

TABLE 3-3 Trainee Accessibility Characteristics as a Basis for Prescribing the Most Appropriate Form of Training Intervention

Trainee Accessibility Characteristic	*Prescribed Form of Training Intervention*
Cognitive orientation:	*Degree of structure*
Low Conceptual level	High structure
High Conceptual level	Low or intermediate structure
Motivational orientation	*From of feedback and reward*
High social approval	Extrinsic reward and/or normative feedback
High intrinsic motivation	Intrinsic reward and/or self-defined feedback
Value orientation	*Value context of presentation*
	Within "latitude of acceptance"
Sensory orientation	*Modality of presentation*
	Adapted to primary sensory "channel" i.e. visual auditory.

of training agents because the differential approach has not been used frequently for training; however, the same principles should apply.

RELATION BETWEEN TRAINEE COGNITIVE ORIENTATION AND STRUCTURE OF PRESENTATION. The structure of the presentation should be modulated to the trainee's conceptual complexity, or CL (Hunt, 1970b): the higher the trainee's CL, the more likely he is to be accessible through a more complex presentation or one which is interdependent; conversely, low CL trainees are likely to be more accessible through a more structured, less complex presentation. Bundy (1968) found in training educational administrators to make more effective decisions, that high CL administrators were adversely affected by a structured guide while those lower in CL tended to profit from the structured guide. Heck (1968) found in training to increase communication skill, that high CL trainees profited more from the unstructured form of sensitivity training while low CL trainees profited more from a more structured human relations training program.

Relation between trainee motivational orientation and form of feedback and reward. Self-viewing, or video feedback, has recently become a frequently employed device in teacher training programs, and its effectiveness also depends upon trainee characteristics, as Salomon and McDonald (1970) stated:

> ...reactions to self-viewing of one's teaching performance on video tape are determined largely by the viewer's predispositions. That is, his satisfaction with how own performance determines what will be noticed on the screen, how it will be evaluated, and to what attitudinal change it will lead. (Salomon and McDonald, 1970, p. 285.)

These authors reported more specifically that teacher trainees who were dissatisfied with their teaching performance and low in self-esteem, when compared with more satisfied, high self-esteem trainees, were less favorable in their attitudes toward teaching after self-viewing. The low self-esteem trainees were also more likely to attend more to physical cues of their appearance. In contrast, trainees who were more satisfied and had a higher self-esteem, improved their self-evaluation, and were more likely to attend to cues related to their teaching performance.

Several examples of the motivational orientation-feedback relation were described earlier, e.g. persons high in affiliation functioning more effectively with feeling-oriented feedback, and persons high in achievement orientation functioning better with task-oriented feedback (French, 1958). Whether the feedback or evaluation comes from an authority figure, e.g. supervising teacher, or from a peer is especially relevant in teacher training; Harvey's finding (1964) that persons high in affiliation were more accessible through peer-based statements while authoritarian persons were more accessible through authority-based statements illustrates such a differential effect.

RELATION BETWEEN TRAINEE VALUE ORIENTATION AND THE VALUE CONTEXT OF PRESENTATION. Specifying the precise optimal distance between the training presentation and the trainee's present position on the value dimension is complicated by factors such as the trainee's latitude of acceptance and his intensity of belief. However, Harvey and Rutherford (1958) found that the absolute approach was more effective with authoritarian persons while the gradual approach was more effective with nonauthoritarian persons.

In another attitude change study, McClintock (1958) found that persons high in other-directedness were more susceptible to an informational approach than to an approach aimed to give them insight into their attitudes. The insight approach, however, was found to be effective with persons moderate or low in ego defense. These investigations need to be extended to the training domain so that we can learn more about the limiting or facilitating effects of various training procedures upon trainees with varying value orientations.

RELATION BETWEEN TRAINEE SENSORY ORIENTATION AND MODALITY OF PRESENTATION. This form of differential training effectiveness is nicely illustrated by studies investigating the effect of filmed intervention versus other forms of instruction. Snow, Tiffin, Seibert (1965) summarized their findings as follows:

> Thus, ascendant, assertive individuals and individuals who are relatively irresponsible apparently do not learn as well from film as they do from live presentations. When shown in darkened rooms without provision for active

student participation, films may foster a spectator attitude which, while having a deleterious effect on the learning of active, assertive students, may be comfortable for their more submissive peers. Possibly, film provides an atmosphere in which the more interpersonal attitudes of responsibility and conscientiousness are required while self-assertiveness is frustrated. (Snow, Tiffin and Seibert 1965, p. 320.)

Also relevant is an investigation by Koran, McDonald, and Snow (1969) investigating the differential effects of film-mediated modeling versus written modeling. They reported that, while video modeling was more effective for trainees who were relatively low in analytic ability and high in visual memory, the written modeling intervention was more effective for trainees who were highly analytic but low in visual memory.

ILLUSTRATIVE APPLICATION OF THE MODEL : INCREASING FLEXIBILITY IN TEACHING

To give an example of how the matching models might be used, consider how they might be applied in a specific case: increasing teaching flexibility. Flexibility in teaching is, in many ways, like creativity in the learner: both are value-laden, generally desirable states which are usually poorly specified and given inadequate operational definitions.

In defining teaching flexibility, we follow Joyce and Hodges (1966) who stated in their discussion of instructional flexibility training that "a teacher who can purposefully exhibit a wide range of teaching styles is potentially able to accomplish more than a teacher whose repertoire is relatively limited (Joyce and Hodges, 1966, p. 409). Their definition of flexibility includes only the capacity to radiate a wide variety of environments, and does not explicitly include their use under differentially appropriate circumstances, as described in Table 3-1. However, we take this simpler definition of flexibility because it is clearly a prerequisite to a more comprehensive form of flexibility.

This definition does not refer to the stimulus situation (variation in learners) in which the variation in response (radiating an environment) occurs. Scott's (1966) critical analysis of the terms flexibility, rigidity and adaptation from a stimulus-response view can be applied to flexibility in teaching behavior. Scott criticized the unqualified endorsement of flexibility as always desirable. He classified forms of response variation by noting their relation to stimulus variation, or in teaching terms, variation in teaching behavior as a function of variation in student behavior. "Stimulus tracking" refers to response variation which is completely determined by stimulus variation (teacher changes procedure whenever students change), while "spontaneous alternation" refers to response variation which is unrelated to stimulus variation (teacher changes procedure for no apparent reason).

He pointed out that neither adaptation nor flexibility, can be adequately defined simply in terms of spontaneous variation or stimulus tracking. Scott concludes by noting:

> It is possible that adaptation may best be facilitated if the person conceives of his various requirements in a hierarchy of importance, treating some of them as "goals" or "ultimate values" and others as "means". The constancy or "rigidity" may be adopted with respect to the goals, and flexibility with respect to the means. In terms of our behavior categories, this is to say that modification of the environment to meet the person's requirements is best accomplished if behavior patterns expressing ultimate goals are maintained relatively fixed in the face of changing circumstances, while means-relevant behavior patterns display spontaneous variability and stimulus tracking. (Scott, 1966, p. 397.)

A related issue in defining flexibility in teaching is to consider teacher behavior in what Bell (1968) called a "direction of effects" model. Using the parent-child paradigm, Bell pointed out that this dyadic interchange is almost always viewed in one direction, namely the effect of the parent upon the child without acknowledging that the child "pulls" differential responses from the parent. In the classroom, direction of effects simply emphasizes the common-sense notion that the students affect the teacher's behavior (Turner, 1967). A comprehensive formulation of teacher flexibility must eventually take account of Scott's notions and of direction of effects.

While teaching flexibility requires skill in using a variety of teaching environments, we consider only two in the present example—ability to present material in a structured fashion and in a reflective, or interdependent fashion (Hunt and Joyce, 1967). The first step in applying the model to this objective, therefore, is to assess the trainee's present skill level to determine whether he can radiate the same material in both a reflective and structured context. Assuming that the trainee cannot radiate one or both these environments, (but is capable of making the prerequisite discriminations in Table 3-1), we consider how to apply the models to planning such trainee-specific intervention.

Planning Content of Intervention

One example of the content for inducing two kinds of teaching is found in a study by Shaver (1964) who attempted to induce the teacher's adoption of Socratic and recitation styles, which are generally similar to reflective and structured environments. Shaver defined the intervention as follows:

> The orientation of the teachers involved several steps: (1) General discussion of the two teaching styles as an integral part of the total research project; (2) the reading of a theoretical description of the two styles; (3) a session

of approximately two hours spent in discussing points which needed clarification and problems which might arise in applying the theoretical models in
the classroom situations; and (4) impromptu conferences after teaching periods
to discuss specific problems which occurred in attempting to conform to the
teaching styles. (Shaver, 1964, p. 260.)

Planning Form of Presentation

1. *Structure of presentation.* If the trainee's cognitive orientation is
relatively simple (low CL), then the material should be presented in simple, concrete form, e.g. providing typescripts or clear demonstrations from
which the trainee can model. If the trainee's cognitive orientation is more
complex, then the material should be organized in more conceptual, theoretical form, e.g. theoretical rationale for procedure.

2. *Form of feedback and reward.* If the trainee is more susceptible to
peer influence than authority influence, the procedure should be adapted
accordingly. For the trainee who is rigidly adherent only to reflective
teaching, he might be given student feedback indicating its lack of effectiveness. For example, an intervention procedure might be designed in which
the trainee's task was to teach a student a particular skill which could be
taught only through a structured procedure. The intervention procedure
might then be programmed so that the student would not learn unless the
trainee employed a structured procedure.

3. *Value context of presentation.* Since there is a relation between
value orientation and preferred teaching style (Hunt, 1970c), a trainee
capable of radiating only one environment, e.g. using only a reflective approach, is likely to have a negative attitude toward the other environment.
This negative attitude toward structured teaching is especially likely to
occur in trainees classified as "weak-sensitive" (Hunt, 1970c), or those who
believe the *only* teaching approach is a reflective, open environment. Such
trainees are unlikely to acquire skill in structured teaching through a "value
neutral" approach in which it is a skill to be acquired with no questions
asked. However, if a "gradual" approach is used so that the trainee gradually
becomes aware of the possible usefulness of structured teaching, this is
more likely to produce the desired results.

4. *Modality of presentation.* Studies such as those by Snow, Tiffin, and
Seibert (1965) and Koran, McDonald, and Snow (1969) will be helpful
in guiding these decisions. Special attention should be focussed on trainee
characteristics associated with susceptibility to multimodal approaches as
distinct from single modality or presentation.

LIMITING FACTORS IN THE USE OF MATCHING MODELS

Matching is useful only when certain trainee characteristics interact
with modes of intervention in producing the objective. As Cronbach puts it:

> Aptitude information is not useful in adapting instruction unless the aptitude and treatment interact—more specifically, unless the regression line relating aptitude to payoff under one treatment crosses the regression line for the competing treatment. (Cronbach, 1967, p. 30.)

For example, Schroder and Talbot (1966), in attempting to increase teaching flexibility through two forms of intervention, concluded that their results

> . . .indicated that the ability to sense and utilize another person's perspective in communication is a relatively stable personality characteristic which persists despite short-term lecture and video feedback training methods. (Schroder & Talbot, 1966, p. 12.)

Experimental studies investigating the validity of the present matching models will therefore not only need to control for initial trainee skill level in investigating the relation between *change* in skill level and trainee accessibility, but will also need to partial out the initial relation between the trainee accessibility characteristic and skill level. In other words, more investigations are required into correlates of what Lewin called plasticity, "the ease with which a relatively lasting and stable change can be made in the structure of a region" (Lewin, 1946, pp. 161–62).

Matching models are only general guides for planning intervention at a particular time, and must be continually updated to index any changes in the trainee. Different approaches may be required for the same trainee at different times, e.g. the trainee's motivational orientation may change over time.

It is frequently observed that the introduction of an educational innovation is relatively easy, but providing conditions under which the innovation will be maintained is very difficult. Probably the most under-emphasized reason for this difficulty lies in the training agent's motivational orientation, especially his need for novelty. These factors of the teacher's motivational orientation are especially important in planning inservice training programs.

The prescriptions in the models for deriving trainee-specific intervention vary in their empirical support so that the models should be regarded only as provisional statements which will permit empirical exploration into the problem of developing more effective differential training programs for the training of teachers.

References

BELL, R. Q., A reinterpretation of the direction of effects in studies of socialization. *Psychological review*, 73, 1968, 81–95.

BEREITER, C., Commentary. In J. Herbert and D. P. Ausubel, eds., *Psychology in*

Teacher Preparation (Toronto: Ontario Institute for Studies in Education, 1969), pp. 73–76.

BROOKS, H., The effect of alternative techniques for modifying teacher behavior. Unpublished doctoral dissertation, Stanford University, 1967.

BUNDY, R., An investigation into the use of a programmed guide on the effectiveness of problem analysis behavior. Unpublished doctoral dissertation, Syracuse University, 1968.

CRONBACH, L. J., How can instruction be adapted to individual differences. In R. M. Gagne, ed., *Learning and Individual Differences* (New York: Macmillan, 1967), pp. 23–44.

FRENCH, E. G., Effects of the interaction of motivation and feedback on task performance. In J. W. Atkinson, ed. *Motives in Fantasy, Action, and Society.* (Princeton: Van Nostrand Rheinhold, 1958), pp. 400–408.

HARRISON, R., and B. I. OSHRY, The impact of laboratory training on organizational behavior: methodology and results. Mimeographed technical report, National Training Laboratories, Washington, D.C., 1967.

HARVEY, O. J., Some cognitive determinants of influenceability. *Sociometry,* 27, 1964, 208–21.

HARVEY, O. J., D. E. HUNT, and H. M. SCHRODER, *Conceptual Systems and Personality Organization.* New York: Wiley, 1961.

HARVEY, O. J., and J. RUTHERFORD, Gradual and absolute approaches to attitude change. *Sociometry,* 21, 1958, 61–68.

HECK, E., A study concerning the differential effectiveness of two approaches to human relationship training in facilitating change in interpersonal communication skill and style of interpersonal perception. Unpublished doctoral dissertation, Syracuse University, 1968.

HUNT, D. E., A component pre-training assessment program for Peace Corps trainees in Tanzania X. Report to Peace Corps, Washington, D.C., 1965.

HUNT, D. E., A conceptual systems change model and its application to education. In O. J. Harvey, ed., *Experience, Structure, and Adaptability* (New York: Springer, 1966), pp. 277–302 (a).

HUNT, D. E., A model for analyzing the training of training agents. *Merrill-Palmer Quarterly,* 12, 1966, 138–56 (b).

HUNT, D. E., Matching models and moral training. In C. Beck, B. Crittenden, and E. V. Sullivan, eds., *Moral Education* (Toronto: University of Toronto Press, 1970).

HUNT, D. E., A conceptual level matching model for coordinating learner characteristics with educational approaches. *Interchange,* 1, 1970 (b).

HUNT, D. E., Adaptability in interpersonal communication among training agents. *Merrill-Palmer Quarterly,* 16, 1970 (c).

HUNT, D. E., and R. H. HARDT, The role of Conceptual Level and program structure in summer Upward Bound Programs. Paper presented at Eastern Psychological Association, April 1967.

HUNT, D. E., and B. R. JOYCE, Teacher trainee personality and initial teaching style. *American Educational Research Journal,* 4, 1967, 255–59.

JOYCE, B. R., Method and methods in teacher education: *Geist,* form, and substance. Paper presented to the University of Alberta Conference on teacher education. Alberta, October 1967.

Joyce, B. R., and R. E. Hodges, Instructional flexibility training. *Journal of Teacher Education*, 17, 1966, 409–16.

Koran, M. L., F. J. McDonald, and R. E. Snow, The effects of individual differences on observational learning in the acquisition of a teaching skill. Paper presented at American Educational Research Association, 1969.

Lewin, K., *Principles of Topological Psychology* (New York: McGraw-Hill, 1936).

Lippitt, R., J. Watson, and B. Westley, *The Dynamics of Planned Change* (New York: Harcourt Brace Jovanovich, 1958).

McClintock, C. G., Personality syndromes and attitude change. *Journal of Personality*, 26, 1958, 479–93.

Salomon, G., and F. J. McDonald, Pretest and posttest reactions to self-viewing one's teaching performance on video tape. *Journal of Educational Psychology*, 61, 1970, 280–86.

Schroder, H. M., M. Driver, and S. Streufert, *Human information processing* (New York: Holt, Rinehart and Winston, 1967).

Schroder, H. M., and D. E. Hunt, Failure-avoidance in situational interpretation and problem solving. *Psychological Monographs*, 71, 1957, No. 3 (Whole No. 432).

Schroder, H. M., and G. T. Talbot, The effectiveness of video feedback in sensitivity training. Peace Corps Report, Princeton University, 1966.

Scott, W. A., Flexibility, rigidity, and adaptation: toward clarification of concepts. In O. J. Harvey, ed., *Experience, Structure, and Adaptability*, 1966, pp. 369–400.

Shaver, J. P., The ability of teachers to conform to two styles of teaching. *Journal of Experimental Education*, 32, 1964, 259–67.

Snow, R. E., J. Tiffin, and W. F. Siebert, Individual differences and instructional film effects. *Journal of Educational Psychology*, 56, 1965, 315–26.

Thompson, G. G., and C. W. Hunnicutt, The effect of repeated praise or blame on the work achievement of "introverts" and "extroverts". *Journal of Educational Psychology*, 30, 1944, 75–85.

Truax, C. B., and R. R. Carkhuff, *Toward Effective Counseling and Psychotherapy* (Chicago: Aldine, 1967).

Turner, R., Pupil influence on teacher behavior. *Classroom Interaction Newsletter*, 3, 1967, 5–8.

Van de Riet, H., Effects of praise and reproof on paired-associate learning in educationally retarded children. *Journal of Educational Psychology*, 55, 1964, 139–43.

Wells, H. H., The role of two processes in determining reactions to two forms of failure stimulation. Unpublished Masters Thesis, Yale University, 1958.

4

Problems in the Presentation of the "Real" Self

CARL WEINBERG

Carl Weinburg, an educational sociologist from the University of California in Los Angeles, was asked to reflect on the problem: How can we help young teachers to internalize a strong commitment towards innovation? To live a life as an innovator is a very difficult thing. It seems almost too much to ask a young teacher not only to learn how to teach and how to cope with a wide variety of individual differences and the very complex institution of the school, but also to take on the life of the innovator, a person who reaches out continuously into the unknown, who risks the safe world of the present for the risky world of the future, and who exposes himself continuously to the kind of criticism and difficulty that seems to beset every innovator in our culture. Yet, the task must be attempted.

Weinburg addressed himself to the problem of creating a strong tightly knit group of students who could work together as a reference group. He dipped into the social psychology of reference groups for clues to how a group could be developed which would be tightly knit and which would have norms built around a commitment to innovation. He suggests that if the students in a program can be welded into a tight group centered around innovative norms that the power of that group will influence the anchoring of the values for the student. Consequently, as a student works in his teaching, he will be conscious of his allegiance to that group and of the responsibility of living up to the innovative values. The group will provide a home for those values and can serve as a conscience for the individual. As a result of his recommendations, we shaped the Columbia University Model Teacher Education Program so that each of the inquiry groups (the small groups of students who administer the program to themselves), would be brought together early in the program and would be given an opportunity from the onset to engage in innovative activities. In this way, innovation could become a characteristic of their group activity and they could develop norms which would support that kind of activity as they later worked alone or in teams in the classroom.

Weinburg had another suggestion which influenced us heavily. He described the process of learning to teach as a potentially alienating one. According to his conception the young teacher enters teaching with hopes that teaching will be a very personal business in which he will minister to the needs of individual students. As he is exposed to the school, however, the young teacher very often finds that it functions as an exceedingly impersonal institution and that it has become bureaucratized in many ways. Consequently, he finds himself teaching things which have become traditional in the school rather than things which had been created as an authentic response to the needs of the children. He finds himself giving grades which increase competition rather than meeting the needs of each individual to be respected and appreciated on his own terms. When these things begin to happen to the young teacher, they tend to alienate him from himself and from education. He becomes left with two choices unless we help him in some way. One of those choices is to withdraw from education and to avoid it in order to avoid being alienated from oneself and from one's conceptions of teaching as a personal function. Weinburg suggests that many of our finest young people take that course and refuse to go through the establishment and become part of it. The other choice is to learn to function in the bureaucracy and to supress or put aside one's feelings of alienation.

Neither of these choices is very pleasant. In order to avoid them, Weinburg suggests that we expose young teachers to the schools early, not to apprentice them but rather to have them study the bureaucratic behavior—how it functions and how it may alienate them. If they do not understand the bureaucratic phenomenon and the social problems they are to face, they cannot innovate within the institution and create an authentic education based on the needs of the children. From that point on, he suggests, we should make certain that during their program the young teachers are never subjected to an experience which requires them to take on the characteristics of the bureaucracy. They should work in innovative reference groups where, as the bureaucracy attempt to impede their innovation, they can take comfort in the group, return to it to anchor their values and to continue their attempts at humanizing the educational institution of our time. Weinburg's paper is provocative and interesting; he sees many sides of the situation and offers new and relevant ideas.

Introduction

Each person contains two selves. One self is linked to the regularities of social interaction and is founded upon the expectations of a particular society with respect to appropriate kinds of behavior in social situations. Thus, as a person relates to others he assumes postures or selves that correspond to his definition of his role in a particular social situation. The other self (which may or may not be referred to as the "real" self, depending upon the definition of "real") contains the elements of uniqueness, the invariant personality characteristics which are only slightly modified by varying social conditions. Often the unique self is subordinated or submerged beneath an ideal standard of behavior as defined by society. In other words, individuals often become estranged from their unique selves and pattern their behavior according to social expectations. When this happens, the necessary energies and support for change and innovation are destroyed.

This paper addresses itself to the problem of developing the capacity to transcend the confinements of traditional social expectations and definitions in such a manner that self-estrangement can be avoided and commitments to innovations in the social world can be made.

The notion of self-estrangement, as it has been utilized in sociological literature, refers to a circumstance in which people devalue their self in terms of ideal standards.[1] This phenomenon arises from a negative comparison of the part of the self-image related to actual behavior to the ideal standards incorporated through socialization or represented in the behavior of others. Members of professional occupational groups, such as teachers, have undergone a long period of socialization to a professional role. Out of the socialization may develop certain idealized behavioral standards. Teachers evolve a definition of a "real professional self" against which they compare their actual performance. The demands of the professional world, with its bureaucratic bogs, administrative restraints, and requirements for success in a status system, often force persons to abandon their real goals,

---

[1] Melvin Seeman, On the meaning of alienation, *American Sociological Review*, December, 1959, pp. 783–91.

to cease performing in terms of their real motivations, and to accede to the limitations of the ongoing system in which they occupy a role.

We need to ask: How do persons in standard social situations develop the capacity as well as the commitment to deviate from the institutional restraints inherent in the social systems to bring about changes in those systems? A fruitful place to begin is to explore those restraining elements in the social system and the processes by which they operate to impede the individual's real self and hence, his capacity and commitment to change. Once this is done we will have a better understanding of the various levers of change and can design teacher education programs to take account of them. The first part of the paper discusses three aspects of the social system —the institutional structure, social typing, and social roles—and their influence on an individual's real self. The second part suggests possibilities for orchestrating these levers in new ways so that the individual's capacity and commitment to change is enhanced.

The Social System

THE STRUCTURE OF INSTITUTIONS AND GROUPS

The structure of institutions and groups is composed of its values, beliefs, roles, and role relationships. These components interact to restrain change in the following manner. Families, churches, schools, peer groups, etc., contain a system of beliefs and values about what constitutes desirable behavior. These values, as a collective tradition, mold the direction of the group and set the criteria for the evaluation of the performance of the members. In order to attain the cultural goals of the unit, persons are arranged in coordinated and hierarchical role relationships such that effective communication and control over the behavior of members is possible. These role relationships become patterned through a system of rewards and punishments. When these expectations become internalized, the system is assured its equilibrium.

If role occupants consider the expectations associated with their roles legitimate ones, the institution may achieve long-standing stability. Legitimacy of expectation is determined by the relative effectiveness, in terms of control and communication, that networks of role relationships have. Interpersonal relations, taking this structural view, are analytically interpreted as functional relationships associated with one of the major functions of social systems.[2]

---

[2] Talcott Parsons postulates four dominant functions of social systems: (1) Adaptation—moving the group efficiently towards its goal, (2) Pattern Maintenance —committing the group to the cultural values of the system, (3) Goal Attainment—

Max Weber delineated five characteristics of bureaucratic structures which are relevant to any study of professional alienation.[3] We may think of these as the formal structural elements, the means by which bureaucratic beliefs, values, norms, and roles are officially incorporated in the institution. As we consider the cumulative characteristics of bureaucratic systems, we find a portrait of a system that would appear to discourage any attempts to help persons relate to others in ways not completely prescribed by those systems.

The characteristics, as outlined by Weber, are as follows:

1. Bureaucracy has fixed jurisdictional areas governed by administrative regulations. Each job has a description which contains the duties of that position.
2. A bureaucracy contains a hierarchy of authority. Most authority is invested at the top, and persons in those positions have the responsibility, as one component of their authority, to control the behavior of those below them.
3. Management of the bureaucracy is based upon written documents, minutes of meetings where decisions are reached, extensive filing systems and personnel records.
4. Recruitment to bureaucratic roles occurs in terms of specific criteria and training. These criteria help to control the stability of role enactment, stable in the sense of being congruent with the expectations for behavior held by others in the system.
5. Bureaucratic roles are prescribed by an exhaustive set of regulations, manifest rules, which control the behavior of members.

From the vantage point of social systems, the notion of a real self, or even of a person who can become self-estranged or alienated, becomes irrelevant. Innovations or changes within the system can only be viewed as structural accommodations to new system functions. Where new demand are placed upon the system or group from the general culture or even from within, a rearrangement of these structural components occurs, and new roles become integrated into the *ongoing* network.

SOCIAL TYPING

Social typing, that is, identifying someone else or oneself as a general "type" skews the authenticity of interpersonal relations. Social typing func-

---

defining specific goals of the system and committing members to the attainment of these goals, also legitimating these, and (4) Integration—the function of developing solidarity of members so as to ensure the coordination of roles towards the end of accomplishing the purpose of the system. See: Talcott Parsons, *The Social System* (New York: Free Press, 1951).

3 From Max Weber, *Essays in Sociology,* H. H. Gerth and C. W. Mills, eds. (New York: Oxford University Press, 1958).

tions in two ways. First, it artificially molds our perception of ourselves and the construction of our social personality. Second, and conversely, it orders or affixes our responses toward others. In the first instance, persons choose roles within social situations and continue to perform consistently as long as their choice continues to be rewarded. Very often roles chosen in childhood (e.g., the scholar, the leader, the athlete, the good friend) persist into maturity. In this sense the real self is submerged in the interest of assuming a comfortable and available role. In the school setting, the classroom clown may be the most intelligent student who has, because of circumstances and selection, chosen an alien role. The simple fact that he is good at it forces others to relate to him in such a way as to inspire greater acts of clowning. Thus, the forces of social approval and disapproval, in informal as well as formal interaction, conspire to shape a relatively permanent social personality. These forces, then, in the broadest social psychological sense, are the microstructures which influence adaptations to the social world. The professional or the occupational self simply adds functional components to the basic and socially determined self. Interpersonal relations thus evolve into a process of presenting all of these components to others and responding to a like presentation.

Secondly, social typing controls the predictability of behavior of persons in social roles. It orders relationships in organizations and provides the basis for maintaining stability of the stratification order. Typing persons, for example, as destined to achieve certain occupational goals, provides the kind of definition of self that enables persons to achieve these goals. Sociopsychological typing is also an obvious aid to the individual in ordering his social relationships. The complex worlds, particularly the urban world, are most efficiently organized when persons can be categorized. Such typing insures that few interactions require a total interrelational exploration before communication begins. Typing also appears to be the most efficient way of managing social growth without anxiety.

As we have seen, most interpersonal relationships, particularly within bureaucratic structures, occur as a process of relating to types. Klapp's classification of dominant types as heroes, villains and fools may not be a complete classification system, but it is a useful illustration of the *kinds* of definitions persons use to organize their interpersonal interaction.[4] These categories of types are defined in terms of some attitudinal position or ideology in most bureaucratic interactions. And in most cases the classification occurs as a result of a person's assessment of *that position* in relation to his own. A teacher, for example, may be defined by some females as a hero to whom they relate with affection. He becomes a hero because he per-

[4] Orin Klapp, *Heroes, Villains and Fools* (Englewood Cliffs: Prentice-Hall, 1962).

sonifies the qualities that many middle class girls aspire to attain and represent, such as wisdom, morality, and decorum. Many lower class males, however, may define a teacher as a fool because he has spent so much time getting an education and then makes so little money. Any attempts this teacher may make to present himself in some basic and honest way will be defined by these boys as a simple extension of the fool model. Consequently, the influence of the teacher is not only negated, but may have a negative effect.

We can assume, then, that the dynamics of social typing complicate any attempt to help persons relate to others on some basic or even correct grounds. Even if we could socialize persons to forget about the kind of "front stage" and "back stage" behavior Goffman talks about[5] (that is, role playing shifts in terms of varying situations), we still would need to solve the problem of how to avoid the dysfunctional consequences occurring as a result of the social typing or stereotyping employed by others.

SOCIAL ROLES AND SELF

We have considered social roles as a structural component, as a shaper of interpersonal relations and now as an influence on the development of self. Psychology has several ways to describe a person. Personality theory, for instance, defines a person as holding a position on a scale of psychological traits. Our concern, however, is with the phenomenological self, that is, the way in which a person perceives himself in relation to his social world. The phenomenological self is defined not according to a scale of traits, but according to the way in which persons want to be seen by others, and according to the relative importance the person places upon the evaluation of specific characteristics which he possesses. As Sherif suggests, the human person actively sets levels of attainment and goals of achievement in matters of significance to him.[6] These are components of his self image, and as such, motivate him to maintain consistency in pursuing his objectives. But the self system is not a unitary structure, as Sherif has noted; it contains components (attitudes, identifications, commitments) which contradict one another. These, then, become the source of internal conflicts.[7] Thus, the self is internally committed to maintain consistency within the person, but often finds a conflict between it and the role, the expectations of others in the ongoing system.[8]

[5] Erving Goffman, *The Presentation of Self in Everyday Life* (Garden City, N.Y.: Doubleday, 1959).

[6] Muzafer and Caroline Sherif, *Reference Groups (Exploration into Conformity and Deviation of Adolescents)* (New York: Harper and Row, 1964).

[7] *Ibid.*

[8] Theodore Sarbin and Vernon L. Allen, Role Theory, in *Handbook of Social Psychology*, Gardner Lindzey and Elliot Aronson, eds. (Reading, Mass.: Addison-Wesley, 1960).

Components of the self system are usually objectified by the person into his social situation, for they help maintain the consistency of the self. Social psychological literature sees these objectified components as reference groups. These are groups with whom persons affiliate, to whom they confer loyalty, and in terms of which they define themselves. Often these may be groups with which persons only aspire to affiliate, but the mechanics of identification remain the same. The significant others for the actor who wishes to stabilize his self system are representative members of these reference groups. From these persons the actor gets cues for his self-presentation. Often, however, even these constructs are anxiety producing, for actors may find themselves ensconced in roles with contradictory expectations. Even though persons in each group may be defined, at least situationally at one point in time, as part of a significant reference group, any contradictions, defined as real by the actor, become real in their consequences. That is, they cause him to reduce the dissonance he perceives in the impinging expectations at the same time maintaining loyalty to both groups. Such role conflict will be seen to be relevant to building a system in which we can advance a case for the development of an institutionalized pattern for relating to others in terms of a real self.

The presence or absence of role conflict often relates to the way in which the role is assumed. A useful distinction posited by Turner is that between "role taking" and "role playing."[9] Role taking can be viewed as a commitment or internalization of the expectations such that the cues for behavior come from the self. Role playing involves assessing what is appropriate from the situation and acting accordingly, regardless of one's own predisposition in a given situation. Mobility, or even survival, in an occupational system such as teaching, is related to the degree to which one has internalized the norms for interaction, and the extent to which teachers can perceive the appropriateness of behavior in different contexts. Sociologically, the process of role taking or playing is not affected by the accuracy of the perception of expectations.

Teachers are often caught in a role conflict produced by the discrepancy between what is espoused as the professional role of the teacher and what is, in fact, practiced by their prime reference group of colleagues. Consequently, a young teacher internalizes one set of role expectations (role takes) and later defers to role playing, looking only for cues of appropriateness rather than basing his interactions on internal cues or standards.

In classroom social systems these cues emanate from three sources (1) from the external environment which would represent the expectations of the community; from school administration and teachers as role types

---

9 Ralph Turner, Role Taking, Role Standpoint, and Reference Group Behavior, *American Journal of Sociology,* 61, 4, January, 1956, 316–28.

rather than persons; (2) from the internal environment, which is made up of daily interaction with role occupants such as administrators, teachers and pupils; and (3) from the professional reference group which reflects the wisdom of professionalism, often traced to graduate and undergraduate studies and professional literature.[10] The person is a member of each system and receives cues from each. As cue systems, the three may be highly congruent. But such congruence is generally only an ideal. Normally, (1) the traditions require strict adherence to a set of rules which permit limited flexibility; (2) interactions present the actor with the definition of acceptable behavior at one point in the social history of the group and this is frequently a compromise between demands for control and expectations for creative leadership; and (3) the professional ethos expects a dynamic involvement in the institution and the application of up-to-date knowledge, plus a positive attitude towards experimentation and innovation. The teacher as actor is typically forced to accommodate all three systems. This, in actuality, cannot be accomplished by the real professional, since a commitment to one or the other set of cues usually produces strains around the other. Accommodation to all three cue systems can be accomplished only if there is no commitment, but rather a desire to survive in the institution.

In a study of 535 school teachers, Weinberg, McHugh and Lamb discovered that alienation among these teachers was very low.[11] The researchers inferred that these teachers generally had abandoned their real self to achieve security in a system which was not, and is not, significant in their lives. Such teachers either identify with the new reference group whose commitment is primarily to stability, or they are simply role playing in the sense of doing what is expected. Their jobs are secured, and mobility, if they wish it, is not endangered. Another possible interpretation of the findings is that self-role conflicts are obviated by the disappearance of the self. As long as the person's expectations for his own behavior are incongruent with the expectations of others within the system, and as long as these expectations of others prevail (which they invariably do in schools), there will be alienating effects. The fact that the teacher alienation study was unable to discover many of these effects suggests that the self component was so rationalized, or that the dissonance was so reduced, that the incongruence did not confront these persons. Since Stauffer[12], and subsequently others, have demonstrated that role conflicts are reduced situationally, it is useful to look at the kinds of reduction mechanisms which apply to our specific situation.

10 Carl Weinberg, *Social Foundations of Educational Guidance* (New York: Free Press, 1970).
11 Contexts of Teacher Alienation, USOE Report number 5-10-170.
12 Stauffer, Samuel, "An Analysis of Conflicting Social Norms," *American Sociological Review*, 14, 1946, 707-17.

One way in which female teachers reduce dissonance is by deferring to their primary role of wife and mother; another is to convince themselves that one individual does not make much difference since students are exposed to so many other forces; a third is to believe that the stability of the school is the major goal. The latter becomes easy to accept, since disruptions in the school milieu are consistently defined as undesirable. It is the opinion of the authors of the Teacher Alienation Study that the teachers have been co-opted by the system, have been integrated in roles which require an abandonment of awareness of their own needs related to position in the structure, and have submerged their selves to system interests which they were made to feel were personally important.

Role playing (or appropriateness) as a critical definition of the basis for interaction obviously maintains systems in equilibrium and precludes change, particularly when appropriateness simply means what has been expected in the past. If we can somehow shift the meaning of appropriateness of social action substantively to refer to innovation, which could very well be an integral part of the real self of the trained teacher, then presentation of that self in social and professional relationships could become institutionalized.

Enhancing the Real Self and Promoting Educational Change: Some Possibilities

Educational change and innovation is possible only if a "real self" can emerge and transcend the existing social expectations or if the existing social expectations are redefined to create a new social ideal which stresses innovation. Applying these two strategies let us examine the three social influences we discussed earlier, this time taking into account these two strategies.

CHANGING THE CHARACTER OF THE BUREAUCRACY

Alienation is a common characteristic of contemporary bureaucratic life, and it would seem most obvious that one way to reduce alienation would be to change the character of the bureaucracy. Although the mechanical structures of bureaucracy may remain the same, the substance that has been institutionalized would be quite different. For instance, teacher educators need to present ways in which job descriptions, recruitment criteria, and manifest regulations can be changed or circumnavigated. We could also require that all teachers undergo a period of basic encounters or that authority be decentralized (moved to the classroom). With our students we might explore such needs as earning a steady living and gaining status within a bureaucratic system in terms of control mechanisms that are used to regulate behavior rather than need systems. In other words, in addition to changing the character of the structure directly we need to equip our students with an understanding of the formal elements of a bureaucracy and the ways these operate to maintain the system and shape individual behavior.

THE CONTROL OF SOCIAL TYPING

We took the position earlier that social typing sets in motion a mechanism often referred to as the "self-fulfilling prophecy" which drives persons to achieve or abandon goals which they believe they should or should not attain. We have also argued that typing sets the tone of interpersonal relationships such that persons respond to others in ways related to these often rigid definitions. The students' social typing can easily subvert the teacher's best intentions simply because the students ascribe qualities to the teacher which they reject in themselves. The presentation of the self, and the maintenance of consistency in that self, *cannot* be managed in environments where rigid typing controls the ways in which persons are perceived.

As most of us know, stereotypes diminish with frequency of interactions. *The American Soldier* demonstrated that integration of army units reduced prejudice amongst the white soldiers involved.[13] The solution for teachers attempting to avoid the invidious consequences of typing would appear to lie in the kind of interpersonal relationships they develop with students. However, this is only a partial answer. The other tack would require a neutralization of the structural possibilities for typing. The ecological arrangement of the classroom is important. Teachers' desks and the physical position of the students can communicate a specific kind of structure for interaction. The fact that the interaction of teachers and students involves an evaluative procedure is another component of that structure. Another most obvious factor is the flow and direction of communication, and the authority intrinsic in it; students use these structures to define the situation and the persons in them. Even though we are aware of these situations in which a fresh approach brings about a reevaluation of stereotypes, we cannot yet talk so much about a long-range overhaul of the traditional structures. We must face the immediate problem of a reduction of tendencies on the part of students to define the situation prematurely and rigidly, and consequently type personnel in the old way.

Despite attempts to disrupt persons through the mechanics of controlled disorganization, they will always attempt to normalize the situation and account for unpredictable behavior in normal ways. Garfinkel has

13 Samuel Stouffer, *The American Soldier: Combat and Its Aftermath* (Princeton, N.J.: Princeton University Press, 1949).

empirically demonstrated that persons react to unexpected behaviors on the part of persons they know or have typed by attempting to bring the behavior into some kind of normal perspective, e.g.: "he is only acting that way because he is sick."[14] Suppose a teacher walked into the classroom for the first time and told the students, "You can call me Buck instead of Mr. Smith; you can say anything you want in this room; you can even curse if you feel the need to. Nothing will happen to you. You can leave your seat when you want, go to sleep if you want, and cry or scream if you are unhappy. You can shout with joy if you're happy." Students in a normal school situation know that this person is a teacher. What will be their response to this declaration? They will probably immediately assume either that he is crazy or that he is inexperienced and hasn't learned how to act as a teacher. Or they simply may not believe him.

The point is that the standard definition of the role of teacher includes a large number of expectations, which, if violated, will be treated as deviant. Persons will either disregard deviation from the stereotype, or attempt to bring it into focus in terms of the earlier standards. Obviously, the teacher who wishes to redefine his role to avoid typing or stereotyping, must somehow manage others in such a way as to be accepted in his presentation of self.

There are at least three ways of effecting the types of change this paper has seen as desirable. Only one of these possibilities is feasible within the confines of the present project, yet each should be clarified. The first option is that we start from scratch, redefining all traditional role characteristics which interfere with personalized interaction. This requires an experimental model, and the financial sponsorship to effect a new institutional context.

The second constitutes taking the present context and systematically eroding all the traditional definitions, rewarding behavior that was not earlier rewarded and punishing behavior previously proscribed. There can be several variations on this theme. One might be to choose selected behavior (such as volunteering, or unsolicited talking), and reverse the traditional sanctions associated with these. Another variation might be to randomize techniques of sanctioning and the behaviors to be sanctioned up to the point where students can no longer rely upon traditional expectations; after unsettling the expected patterns we then begin to seed in a new stability by consistently rewarding or punishing specific behaviors.

The third alternative, which seems most appropriate for this project, is to prepare students to undergo a resocialization experience. That is, teachers will need to be trained to manage a group of students in the reorganization

[14] Harold Garfinkel, "Studies of the Routine Grounds of Everyday Activities," *Social Problems* II, Winter, 1964, 225–50.

of their routines and expectations. The student teachers must rediscover ways of knowing what the expectations of each context are. As teachers, they must leave off their own stereotypes of how middle or lower class, black or white students expect to be related to. They may use these typings to structure their initial action in reverse fashion so as to observe the reaction of the student group. For example, a teacher may wish to talk about norms rather than "our neighbors" in a second grade class, and he may want to do it in such a way as to avoid providing the specific factual information he thinks the children expect. If they do expect this, he will know it from the way they respond to his approach, from the positive demoralization that occurs when the children become confused. At this point in the new method, the teacher should make possible a discussion of symptoms of confusion or disorganization. This discussion should be institutionalized within the routine of the discussion and students must be forced to explain the basis of their expectations so that they can be mutually examined. They must be forced to remark that teachers X or Y did things this way or that, that they always got detentions for calling out, that such and such has never been permitted and such and such always expects it. A discussion of this sort only has meaning as students strive to achieve some consistency in their own behavior, which they see as being retarded by the teacher.

Resocialization is a difficult task in a bureaucratic setting, and the realities of the situation are such that only small approximation of what we need to do can be done.[15] But if we are to avoid the pitfalls of the certain kind of typing which retard the tendencies toward the presentation of the "real" self we must begin to make some motions in that direction.

INTEGRATION BETWEEN SELF AND ROLE

The opposite of alienation is integration in the sense of a *congruency between the self and the role*. While role expectations may conflict with the self, the person may still be integrated within the system in several ways. If the structure provides the means for effecting changes and for bringing the role in harmony with the self, the person is thus integrated and has power. An integrated self perceives a meaningful relationship between the goals of the institution and the self; it ascribes legitimacy to the ways and means of accomplishing these goals; it perceives a congruence with other persons in the institution in terms of agreement about means and ends; and it uses the institution as a vehicle of self-fulfillment.

An integrated self interacts in a desirable manner with others in social relationships. That is, the role components which are alien to that self do

---

[15] Peter McHugh, "Social Disintegration as a Requisite of Resocialization," *Social Forces,* 44, March, 1966, 355.

not intervene in such relationships. To see such an integrated person as a reality should be one of the goals of our teacher training program. At this point in our study we must find components of action which might achieve that end, and we must rationalize such components of integrated action in the light of our discussion of alienation and bureaucracy.

To begin, teachers need to see and understand the school as a social system. They must attack the problem of authority structures, and learn about expectations and value systems. More important, as a basic gesture toward achieving an integrated self, they must attack the question of the legitimacy of authority structures. They must solve the problem of how various role participants decide the parameters of authority and the basis on which legitimacy is assumed. Students, for example, either reject or accept the authority of teachers to the extent that teachers meet certain criteria (e.g., fairness, consistency) and perform in certain ways (e.g., how they relate to student leaders or administrators).

To answer problem of authority in the schools, future teachers should learn to conceptionalize the interaction components which characterize bureaucratic positions, and in terms of these interactional routines, assign legitimacy to authority. It is not enough, for example, for a student teacher to return from an experience in a classroom and report that her best intentions to be her real self have been frustrated. She must begin to conceptualize the basis of frustration. Such discovery and analysis takes us beyond the sheer awareness of being alienated to a conceptualization of the *structure* of alienation, a subtle and refined distinction, which is based not so much in the formal rules of the organization as it is in the informal definitions of expectations and of the routines which legitimize constraints. Very simply, the teacher educator's first task should be to familiarize future teachers with actual behaviors, in the form of patterns, which restrain the development of an integrated self. It is not, for example, that administrators refuse to permit participation by teachers in deciding objectives and strategies. It is a whole system of patterned interactions which makes such participation difficult.

Once the student teachers have begun to clearly see the social system in which they must function as integrated selves, the next important experience should be one in which they are forced to experience characteristic restraints, frustrations, and inhibitions. We might think of this as enforced organizational impotence, or as education for alienation. This can be effected in two ways: (1) by placing these persons in a real school setting where institutionalized restraints are highly visible, and (2) by simulating the processes of alienation. The simulation process should make students feel powerless—that the meaning of what they are doing is unclear, that they must deviate from the norms to survive, that they are isolated in terms of what they think should happen, and that their best capacities are being misused or not used at all. After the students have experienced the process, extensive and intense discussions should be organized so that the students may analyze the way they feel and determine what actual behaviors, on the part of others as well as themselves, made it occur. Finally, the discussion should center around strategies for changing the alienating structures in schools. If, for example, the isolation component can be seen as relevant to certain patterns of disaffiliation on the part of the staff (either teachers or preteachers), then strategies for organizing persons with common concerns and similar feelings of isolation can be formulated.

An excellent follow-up experience might be a simulation of an integrated system where all the components of integration could be guaranteed. It would be a simple matter to insure influence, clarity or meaningfulness, togetherness, success through institutionalized means, and the utilization of the best (the way he wants to be seen and evaluated) in persons in an experimental situation. Although highly problematic in the real situation, at least the student teachers will become able to recognize what is missing and focus upon the behavioral patterns which inhibit the establishment of an integrative system.

Another focus for solving the problem of the integrated self would be to attack the problem of the role rather than, or perhaps concomitantly with, the problem of self. At this point, let us consider the problems associated with an analysis of role. Most institutions expect that socializing agencies, particularly those related to preparing persons to follow professional vocations, are required to make individuals into types compatible with the roles they are about to assume. In contrast, we should not only concern ourselves with problems of enabling persons to relate interpersonally in a way that is both difficult and unclear in the institution, but also we should focus upon ways of shifting the informal structural components to insure a reduction of self-role conflict extrinsic to the self. As Cicourel and Kitsuse note in their discussion of the selection of school counselors, the kinds of people who were chosen to make important educational decisions for hundreds of students were those who were compatible with the way in which the particular institution defined the counselor's role.[16] In the upper middle class community studied by Cicourel and Kitsuse, expectations for counselors centered around a definition of a role occupant as one who possessed a lot of psychological knowledge and a commitment to worry

---

[16] Aaron Cicourel and John Kitsuse, *The Educational Decision Makers* (Indianapolis, Ind.: Bobbs-Merrill, 1963).

about maladjustive behavior in psychotherapeutic ways. In the same way, the traditional, normative expectation for teachers in Harlem would be for behavior that could absorb conflict, routinize frustration, and teach basic communication skills without resorting to conceptual thinking.

At every level, student teachers and teachers must articulate and inspect educational roles. Students must somehow be socialized to believe that innovations are not only desirable but possible. Certainly, educational in-novation is an illusive phenomena, yet some basic ideas about change can be communicated which indirectly sensitize persons to a belief in its feasi-bility. Thus, the realization of an integrated self depends upon the re-organization of educational roles and a redefinition of the rights, obligations, and expectations surrounding them. The Teacher Alienation Study has demonstrated that alienation is structural, is implicit in the routines of educational systems, and operates independently of the configuration of personality types which enter the system. As such, role structures need to be reorganized, and students who hope to survive as an integrated self within school systems should begin thinking about the problem from this structural perspective.

Earlier we discussed the role playing or cue-guided behavior that teachers often adopt in order to reduce discomfort and to aid them in responding appropriately to their social situations. We can think of these cue systems as multiple reference groups. Individuals who take these cue systems into account often find themselves filled with conflict because of the conflicting natures of the cue systems to which they respond. Thus, the development of a professional self through the kind of model proposed by the project must anticipate that strains in reacting to the other two systems will be inherent in the experience of the teacher as a member of an ongoing cultural and social system. If we assume that building a professional self involves a commitment to a set of ideas about education on the one hand, and a similar commitment to maintaining an integrated self in interpersonal relations on the other, then we can begin to assume that we have made the future teacher ready to maintain consistency in her future role enactments. The remaining problem is how we can reduce the strains incumbent in the other cue systems. The answer would seem to lie in two directions, only one of which is relevant to our specific problem of teacher. The first direc-tion is to work towards redefining the culture of the school from a restric-tive, institutionalized formality with structured relationships (which may no longer be functional to contemporary educational goals) to a system which values change and experimentation. This would involve the kind of attack on role structures discussed earlier in this paper. The second direction, based also upon some of the propositions already mentioned, would involve the development, in the program, of a cohesive professional reference group.

Teachers, as a *professional* collectivity, exist only in the abstract, and as such do not control the behavior of members due to a lack of opportunity for frequent interaction. Teachers, upon graduation from college, are dispersed throughout the broader system and frequently become isolated in a new culture, simultaneously losing their identity. What is required is a way of developing this reference group such that mutual support for presentation of the integrated and professional self is possible. This should be initiated as part of the training experience, and maintained throughout the careers of persons. Such a reference group *is* possible, and in the final pages of this paper we will present a description of the form of this reference group and a rationale for its incorporation.

The popularity today of basic encounter groups is obviously a function of the depersonalization of interpersonal relations. People run to a legion of such sessions to discover who they are and to be educated about how to be themselves. T groups and the like are beginning to be used in educational programs. The function of the reference group is not so much intended to help persons find out who they are so they can present the real self, but to reinforce a standard of behavior desirable for innovative, creative functioning in a bureaucratic setting. Since it is professional definition of self we wish to support, the consistency within the self we are seeking can only be maintained with the help of an ongoing reference group. An abstract set of standards which can be violated without fear of sanctions does not serve this function. Socialization to a profession is a process of building an internalized set of beliefs about what one is in relation to clients, consumers, patients, or students and teachers. It appears that it is necessary, given the lack of control that colleges of education have over their students after they assume professional roles, to personalize the standards through controlled, continuing interaction. This will guarantee a viable reference group from whom cues for action and interpersonal relations can be taken.

The success of organizations like Alcoholics Anonymous and Synanon can be directly attributed to the same mechanism, providing members with a reference group to whom they must account (this becomes internalized) if they violate the standards. Of course, teachers or future teachers do not need to be "rehabilitated" in the same sense, but we can take instruction from the structure of such groups, if such a reference group is desirable. In such groups, persons will develop habits of expressing and supporting such standards as honesty and integrity in the presentation of self which should carry over into the organizations in which they work. The viability and the strength of the reference group may depend on a specific activity such as the Reference Group Game (or the Integrated Self Game) and can be usefully prolonged after graduation.

THE INTEGRATED SELF GAME[17]

Student teachers should be exposed to an integrated self game (Reference Group Game) in which a group of preteachers undertake to castigate the professional performance of one of their members. The game itself develops a core attitude through attacking persons in terms of a set of ideal standards to which all ideally subscribe. Unlike T groups, sensitivity training, and therapy, a reference group game would have the effect of always posing the total group against each individual. In this way each person who is being attacked does not personalize individual hostilities but rather, since all members of the group attack the same behavior in the same way using the same standards, he will begin to perceive the generalized standards as they apply to each individual posture, attitude, or behavior. All preteachers should be sent out into situations in small groups such that someone will be able to pick up data which can be used in the game— something that might come out as an *indictment* such as:

> I noticed you assigning those stupid grammar drills last week. Is that the best you can do after all you got here? You're a Neanderthal man.

or:

> One of your students told me that you want them to memorize a bunch of names and dates. What the hell does that accomplish?

It may well be that the indictments are exaggerations of real behavior, but in the process of reducing the exaggerated indictment to the level of reality, the person may still reveal a violation of the cues for behavior that he should have taken from the reference group. We might imagine the following exchange taking place in such a game.

A group of preteachers sitting in a circle (minimum 10, maximum, 12).

> Preteacher A (to B): Well, B, what's going on with you?
> B: Some things are moving, I think I'm catching on about getting kids to help plan the unit. It seems to be working.
> A: O.K., that's fine, I take it everything else is perfect.
> C: Like what else is going on in your life at the school?
> D: Well, no real problems.

[17] This is a variation on a game used in the rehabilitation of drug addicts, the purpose of which is to give the members a "stay clean" reference group. See Louis Yablonsky, *Synanon: The Tunnel Back* (Baltimore: Penguin, 1967).

E: (to A): This joker is telling us that he can do everything he wants to do. Who does he think he's talking to, like we don't know the problems.

A: Isn't there anything else you want to tell us about?

B: Well, there is one thing.

C: Run it.

B: Well, I'm just not sure it's worth the effort, I mean I don't think I'm going to be able to do all the things I'm learning to do, or want to do.

D: Like what, what the hell are you talking about?

B: I can already see myself falling into certain patterns that I don't like, like yelling at the kids when they get noisy, becoming impatient for them to learn things, you know, wanting to prove things to everybody, like my supervising teacher, and the principal.

D: You poor thing, you don't like yourself, so why don't you do something about it?

E: You're an introspective type, aren't you, always thinking about what you'd like to do or be.

D: Always getting ready to get ready, you're a pussycat.

B: These things aren't easy, to change a school's way of looking at it.

A: That's tragic, it's not easy, a big cop out.

C: What are you doing about yourself, so you can live with it and not feel like an impotent child.

B: What do you expect me to do for Christ's sake.

C: You know as well as anybody, just do something, come back next week and tell us one step you've taken. O.K. A, you sound guilty about something what's your hangup?

Freedom and Autonomy

Freedom is the condition under which persons have the courage to choose their behavioral cues from among those they believe are the most directly congruent with the intention or desire of the self. At times they may feel that a cue emanating from the traditions of the institution are sound in terms of the belief system of the self. Here there is no conflict. When the cues for performance emanating from any source (any of the three systems) are in conflict with the self, the free man reserves the right to disregard such cues and appeal to one of the other sources which is more congruent with the self. But this kind of freedom, as Fromm's several works reiterate (see *Escape from Freedom*), is difficult for most people. It requires the strength to stand alone and to bear up under considerable isolation.

Empirically, although Fromm simply makes historical inference, most people run from this kind of aloneness and isolation and are usually forced to select a physician that meets the approval of others in his social world. This is probably the dynamic which explains the adaptive load selected by school teachers. The only solution to this dilemma would appear to be a concert of autonomous professionals, or those who want to be. We may start people down the road of commitment to professional autonomy, give them the desire to develop an integrative self and communicate this to others in all interpersonal relationships, but we may only be able to maintain this commitment by providing an ongoing experience such as the one described in the previous section. At a time when social machinery is molding man into a servant of the machine, and reducing the human condition to congeries of artificial relationships all in the interest of efficiency, our task is most difficult. Yet the task must be undertaken, for teachers can produce the future man. There is no necessity for the teachers of our future, the instructors of our progeny, to be alienated. Human intervention, on a new bureaucratized basis, is still theoretically possible.

5

Growth of a Flexible Self Through Creativity and Awareness

GEORGE ISAAC BROWN

George Brown's primary work has been in the affective domain—especially the affective responses of children and teachers. His work at the Esalen Institute and elsewhere has provided him with the opportunity to adopt Gestalt Therapy to both elementary and teacher education and he has done so with imagination and insight.

Like Hunt, he does not dichotomize the cognitive and the affective. Rather, he sees affective development as the key to personality development. Awareness training, by increasing the extent and richness of experience, improves the intellectual functioning of the individual. The creativity of the teacher is related to his general capacity to reason and to solve problems.

In several settings—at the University of Delaware, Howard University, the University of Santa Barbara, and at Esalen—George Brown has worked with teachers to free them for personal development and for more creative work with children. In this paper he describes this work, with theory and practice intertwined, as befits one who is comfortable with intellect and emotion.

Portions of this chapter are reprinted from "Teaching Creativity to Teachers and Others," *The Journal of Teacher Education,* 21, 2, Summer 1970; "Awareness Training and Creativity Based on Gestalt Therapy," *Journal of Contemporary Psychotherapy,* 2, 1, Summer 1969, 25–32.

This paper consists of three parts:

The first part discusses certain approaches to developing "readiness" for creativity or awareness. The development of readiness is a preliminary step to direct awareness training based on Gestalt Therapy.

The second part describes an existential approach to creativity and awareness based on the works of Dr. Frederick Perls, founder of Gestalt Therapy, work which I feel holds great promise for educational practices both in the classroom and in teacher education. Gestalt Therapy—as distinguished from Gestalt psychology—provides a body of theory and methodology which, although complex and difficult, has the advantage of usefulness even when applied in parts. That is, a portion of the theory, even a single Gestalt Therapy technique, can be used profitably by itself. The more theory and the greater the repertoire of techniques based on the theory available to the practitioner the greater the overall effectiveness of what is done and the greater the success of an individual technique, but many specific aspects and techniques can be profitably incorporated into schools or teacher education programs.

The concluding portion of the paper offers suggestions of possible models for the development of a flexible self within a range of teacher education programs.

Developing Readiness for Awareness and Creativity

As one becomes more aware, he admits the possible existence of alternatives to his ways of behavior or thinking, even to values he may have held dear; he allows for change *if* he judges and feels the new way is more appropriate for him at that moment. In contrast is the person who is unwilling to alter his status quo. Through the use of various concrete and psychological mechanisms and devices he refuses to move into new experiences or even consider alternatives.

Two significant points should be noted. First, the aware person *both* judges *and* feels. He not only "knows" in the conventional intellectual or cognitive sense, but he also senses or feels. He is in touch with his intuitive and emotional being. Secondly, he stays in the reality of the moment and only the moment. The developing use of intuition and comfort with the intuitive as well as the rational self and the acceptance of the existential position are crucial to Gestalt Therapy.

When one moves into new experiences, ultimately he does this himself. New situations do not equate with new experiences, for one can wall himself off from the new in any situation. Moving into new experiences involves risk in not knowing the consequences of the new experience. The person who struggles to maintain his status quo frequently does so just for this reason. He has catastrophic expectations of any change. Even though he may be miserable in his present existence, for him it is "best" because at least he knows what being miserable is and he can count on it. The problem then is to provide new experiences which to this person apparently involve only the tiniest of risks. Then, as the person is successful, i.e., experiences the change without disaster but instead with at least some slight feelings of personal satisfaction, the instructor, trainer, or group leader can gradually increase the intrinsic risk in each succeeding new experience to a degree for which the individual has become ready.

One shortcut in developing readiness for awareness training is to plunge people into a conventional encounter group situation. Here participants learn to "ventilate" their emotions. I am ambivalent about this approach. Although there are expressions of positive affect occurring in encounter groups it has been my experience that most of the time negative affect is expressed, such as anger, hostility, and fear. A disadvantage of many encounter contexts is that emotions feed upon themselves. Anger expressed toward someone stimulates anger in return, hostility directed at another creates counterhostility, etc., and these feelings are often not worked on. Little growth takes place relative to what might occur if the leader knew how to give feedback in ways that could help the participant become aware of what he was doing. Such feedback can occur with some leaders, but frequently the group leader is content just "to get feelings out."

The following description of a sequence of experiences in a creativity and awareness workshop is given as *one* example of how readiness for awareness training can be increased.

The workshop pattern suggested is one which provides a series of experiences that move from events characterized as relatively comfortable, didactic, with mostly cognitive content to those with increasingly less verbalization, greater risk-taking in terms of new experience, and an enlarging focus on affective adventure.

The workshop begins with conventional self-introduction of the participants which may include "What I do" or "What I am here for." This is followed by an overall sketch of the workshop (including the statement that no one has to do anything in this workshop he does not want to) and a lecture-discussion of creativity stressing philosophical as well as psychological dimensions. The first session usually concludes with the reading of a children's book, *The Very Nice Things* by Merill and Solbert,[1] which explicitly portrays a creative and a noncreative personality. The characters in the story, William Elephant and Old Owl, are used as symbols to trigger a "creative" subself and a "noncreative" subself in two studies in the teaching of creativity (Brown, 1964, 1965). The studies describe a procedure that may be considered a readiness approach. The participants in the workshops studied were juniors in elementary education who, in a semester course in teaching procedures, were provided with the symbols around which to construct two matrices of behavior, creative and noncreative. Practices developed by the instructor, and later to some extent taken over and reinforced by the students themselves, were used to develop a creative subself. The data from the studies indicate that the subselves could be developed and later triggered. Further unpublished preliminary findings of Dennis Ridley support the use of these symbols in contrast to direct brainstorming creativity training.

The second session is divided into three parts: moving from a completely verbal activity to a combined verbal and body activity to one which is essentially nonverbal. At first, small groups of about five participants are given slips of paper containing questions based on an Osborn brainstorming technique called object modification[2] except that "I" is substituted for the object. There are about twenty-five questions like, "What if you were made smaller?" "What if something were taken away from you and something else put in its place?" "What if you were multiplied?" Members of each group are told to respond spontaneously and to change to a new question the moment it is received. The leader allows only a minute or two for responses to each question. The second exercise is a kind of charade with talking. One member of the group is given a slip of paper which has written on it "A blade of grass from the point of view of a lawnmower" or "A mound of ice cream from the point of view of an ant," etc. The participants are instructed to act this out using words if they wish but without direct reference to what they are attempting to portray. Other members of the group then try to guess what they are doing. The direction "from the point of view of" is confusing, which is helpful in breaking down fixed definitions. The last exercise of the session involves pure acting with only grunts, groans, and other nonverbal exclamations allowed. Here items like "A balloon being released," "A girdle being taken off," and "An executioner pulling the switch," are given to persons in turn on slips of paper. The others in the group again try to guess what the actor is doing.

---

[1] Merill and Solbert, *The Very Nice Things* (New York: Harper and Row, 1959).

[2] E. P. Torrance, *Education and the Creativity Potential* (Minneapolis: The University of Minnesota Press, 1963).

Examining these exercises one can see that although the participants move into more and more nonverbal behavior, the nature of the experience becomes more and more novel, and the risk seems slight because of the fun game context.

In the third session the participants are requested to bring a number of objects from what is readily available. A series of experiences based on Synectics, developed by Gordon provide the structure of this session.[3] Synectics is a method used to train groups from industry in a group creative problem-solving process, based on three forms of analogical thinking: (1) *direct analogy*—an object is examined and "what it looks like," or "what it reminds you of," is used to have individuals generate names of other objects that are related, however obscurely—in fact, the more obscurely the better. (These exercises are also done in small groups with each person taking his turn at presenting an object.) Again, spontaneity is encouraged. Participants are encouraged to "Stop thinking too hard about it" and "Let it come, naturally." (2) *symbolic analogy*—the same or another object is examined and "What do its characteristics remind you of?" "What is its essence or symbolic meaning and what object can this be assigned to?" are used to encourage an analogical leap. (3) *personal analogy*—the participants are asked to focus on an object and through intense concentration or "attending to" to actually become the object. "How do you feel?" "What object comes to mind as you experience this feeling?" are used for this third form of analogical bridging between objects. A brief period of time is then spent in using any or all of the forms of analogical thinking with new objects.

In addition to the intrinsic value of Synectics as an increasingly new and risk-taking adventure, the experiences in the use of personal analogy act as a precursor and readiness training for the fourth workshop session. (Sometimes, depending upon the nature of the geographical setting and the ease with which it is possible, additional small leaderless encounter groups are set up for the evening. The workshop leader moves from group to group reinforcing initial instructions which are to "talk about how you feel now, avoid explanations and histories and stay with your feelings. Check one another on this. Remember, no one has to say anything unless he wants to.")

The unfinished past or anticipated future is often clearly described or, at the very least, implicitly hinted at in the life map painting. This is important because many people cover the present by using the past or the future. A major function of awareness training is to increase one's experiencing of the Now. The only reality that can truly be experienced is the reality of the moment. When a pseudoreality of the past or of the

---

[3] W. J. J. Gordon, *Synectics* (New York: Harper and Row, 1961).

future is substituted for the reality of the Now, the intensity of this fantasy determines the degree to which one cannot touch and experience reality as it presently exists. The fantasies we cling to, a product of the "computing" of our minds and the denial of what we feel or sense, often seem very real to us. They lead to what we think the world "should be" but must concurrently distort or even deny what the world "is."

SUMMARY OF READINESS APPROACHES

What has been described in this section is one series of experiences structured so that risk-taking in terms of moving into new experience or awareness is gradually increased. My assumption is that such a structure is more likely to be effective with a large group than abrupt encounters which immerse the student in the problem of finding the present and the reality of the self. The individual variance in most groups is usually broad, ranging from the individual who is immediately ready for direct awareness training at the very beginning of a workshop to the person who stubbornly resists change and who clings to the status quo by cleverly sabotaging every opportunity for new experience provided him throughout the workshop. Too abrupt an approach often results in an "in-group" of the most ready. This can block the progression of the less ready. A more gradual approach permits the readier to help the others by example, but consolidates *their* readiness, which does not happen if "ins" and "outs" develop.

There are a number of readiness approaches available that can be drawn from humanistic psychology and other behavioral sciences. What is important is (1) that these approaches be organized or structured in effective sequences, gradually increasing risk-taking; (2) that they be artistically used by the leader or trainer so that they become means for the individual members of the class or group and not ends unto themselves; and (3) that they be conceptualized as means toward the more direct goal of developing a flexible, creative, and aware person.

It is the position of this paper that the latter can be expeditiously achieved through awareness training based on Gestalt Therapy. The next section of the paper describes the theoretical background of awareness training.

Awareness Training and Creativity,
Based on Gestalt Therapy

Gestalt Therapy is a humanistic, existential approach in psychology. The therapist or trainer does not interpret but instead is directed toward helping an individual be aware of his here and now in feeling and sensory terms; not in terms of *why* he is behaving so, but rather *what* he is doing and *how* he is experiencing it. Central to Gestalt Therapy is the goal of helping the individual move from moment to moment, experiencing the freshness of each, rather than "covering" the present in an intellectual smog composed of remembrance of things past.

Gestalt Therapy has consequently sometimes been defined as awareness training. The definition is based on the existential nature of Gestalt Therapy, the concern for experiencing the reality of the instant and avoiding any involvement in the past or future which would replace or distort the awareness of the present. There appears to be a paradox in Gestalt Therapy in that as one works either as patient or therapist the only way to allow for change to occur is through the absence of a desire to change. A desire to change is directed toward some goal or ideal created or "computed" in a fantasy form by the intellect. To the degree the individual is caught up in his fantasized ideal "should" or "ought to", he cannot attend to or be aware of reality as it is. Gestalt Therapy affirms that natural and healthy growth can only occur as the individual is aware of and lives a here and now existence. The condition of anaesthetizing affect, of retreating to a fantasy existence in order to avoid altering the status quo of one's life, is directly related to the lack of realization of the creative potential of each individual. Gestalt Therapy offers a philosophy *and* methodology for moving from the maintenance of status quo and deadness toward creativity and life.

Change through flexibility is both an implicit and an explicit quality of creativity; this is true whether creativity is thought of as value or a process. As might be expected, what is explicit in change is more obvious. The creative act requires an overt search for that which is at first possible, new, original, better. Both the search and its consequences produce change. What is implicit in the relationship between change and creativity is a prerequisite to overt creative behavior. Once an individual accepts the responsibility for the consequence of living fully in each moment, a state which Gestalt Therapy can help bring about, he will experience each moment as fresh experience. He thereby accepts the implicit value that alternatives to what is may exist, that by being flexible (open to experience) one might experience one of these alternatives. The condition of being open to new experience, flexibility, is essential if one is to energetically engage in innovation.

Barron (1963) describes the creative person as one who seeks out complexity and chaos. The creative person is willing to experience the tension or frustration or pain of a temporarily unresolved chaotic condition in that part of the universe in which he intentionally places himself. According to Barron, he does this in anticipation of what satisfaction he will experience when through the creative process he creates order out of chaos, simplicity out of complexity, or meaning out of confusion. Barron's description is intriguing and there are dimensions of Perls' work that add much to it. The creative person is first *aware* that chaos exists. He is then willing to confront this chaos and to "stay with" it. The person who is busily engaged in maintaining his status quo is unwilling to move into new experience, chaotic or otherwise, for he never knows whether it will be chaotic or not. He is not only unwilling to move into new experience, but he cannot perceive the reality of new possibilities even when directly confronted with them. He is so actively engaged in defending his fantasies that he must substitute them for real perception and genuine experience. He thus rides a merry-go-round, remaining as he is, not even experiencing the deadness of his existence but instead combining the thinking about his pseudofeelings with his fantasies about his pseudoreality. This cardboard person replaces the reality of the world with clicked posters of washed-out colors all painted by himself. The posters are not creative because they do not meet the ultimate criterion of creativity: how does that which is created compare with what already exists and is experienced? This criterion holds whether the form be personal creativity, that which has primary meaning only to the individual, or social creativity, that which may involve more than one person. Though the comparative judgment may be purely subjective, as in the case of personal creativity (or pragmatic, empirical, aesthetic, ethical, etc., as in the case of social creativity), the criterion requires the existence of alternatives with which to compare what has been created. The cardboard person "knows" no alternatives; he is afraid even to admit their existence and thus is stuck on his merry-go-round, seeing only his posters.

Potentialities for the creative process continue to be unrealized because the cardboard person living in his computed fantasies persists in maintaining his separation from the real world. "Out of this world" he cannot experience, with either mind or feelings, that which is real. As a consequence, both his conscious knowledge and his intuitive and affective resources are denied enrichment. Both the cognitive and affective dimensions of the self are sources for the creative act and in the healthy, alive, creative individual the affective and cognitive domains are integrated. What one *thinks* coincides with one *feels*. He who denies change, the nonreal individual, either anaesthetizes his feelings when they conflict with his thought-produced, substituted-for-the-real-world fantasies, or is caught in a conflict between feelings and thoughts. When there is no integration of the affective and cognitive domains, not only is there no new data to enrich either conscious or intuitive processes, there is also no energy for the individual to spare for the creative process. This energy is instead directed by the cardboard person to preserving his anaesthetization so that feeling will not emerge, or dissipated in maintaining or intensifying the conflict between emotion and thought at the source of his impasse.

The meaning of "integration" between the affective domain and the cognitive domain can perhaps be clarified with the following examples:

(1) The cognitive domain functions but affect or feeling is anaesthetized. . . . A child sits on the floor playing with an Erector set, perhaps because his mother has told him to. He reads the directions and very carefully, step by step, puts the pieces together. There is little joy in the process. He then takes the pieces apart with the same lack of enthusiasm.

(2) The affective domain and the cognitive domain are harmoniously integrated. . . . The child, sometimes experiencing excitement and pleasure, sometimes frustration, puts the pieces together making his own design or invention. He stays with his process of construction—personal creativity— until he feels and knows he is finished. As he constructs he uses both his feelings about the pieces he is putting together and their new patterned relationships, and his knowledge about characteristics such as length, diameter and function of each piece. The child's energy is directed toward a personally *satisfying* process of independent creativity. He feels alert, excited, substantial, worthwhile, and capable of experiencing temporary frustration confident of his strength and ability; he feels alive. The only cardboard here is in the toy.

What then can Gestalt Therapy do for the cardboard person, or to help animate those parts of ourselves that are dry, stiff, weak, and like cardboard?

First, Gestalt Therapy can help the individual be aware of what is obvious, those parts of himself that are cardboard. This is done by helping him experience what "being cardboard" is like. Included here would be experiencing one's resistance to change—without falling into the trap of wanting to change. Gestalt Therapy can provide methods and techniques to help facilitate change and growth by enabling the individual to experience himself as he actually is. As he becomes more aware of his own reality, he will at the same time experience himself within reality, partaking of the universe. For as he more fully experiences himself, he will experience himself some place—probably with some people. At each moment he will become more aware of both himself and the world in which he finds himself. "Himself" includes both his intuitive reservoir and his conscious knowledge that he draws upon to merge "himself" with that which is new and fresh in his experience of the external world and thus create new patterns, relationships, ideas, and things.

The creative act as conventionally described comprises four stages. Although I have reservations about this four-stage structure because it implies a sequential time character which belies certain creative acts (Brown and Gaynor, 1967), and because it does not correspond to an existential understanding of behavior, there is some convenience in examining how awareness training through Gestalt Therapy can improve creative functioning at each stage.

The first stage, the preparation stage, involves the selection or differentiation of data available in the external environment which can be used in the process of creating. It is likely, however, that once differentiated, the data would be combined at conscious or below conscious levels with other meanings, understandings, or knowledge, remaining both in memory as experienced and also in these new combined forms until utilized in the act of creation. The preparation stage is really composed of three substages: (1) experiencing the data, (2) storing the data in pure or combined states at either conscious or below conscious levels, and (3) retrieval of the data for use in the creative act.

Gestalt Therapy can have direct relevance to sub-stages (1) and (3). A greater awareness of reality as fresh experience from moment to moment allows for richer perceptual and affective experience as one becomes aware of the universe. The individual becomes more in touch with himself including the below-conscious levels of his existence, therapy making available its content. Perhaps most important, however, is that the gestalt of the "person-universe" can be better experienced or sensed so that the meaning of each personal experience fits into this rich and more total context and is therefore much richer itself. The accumulation of these richer experiences (richer because of the broader and deeper meanings inherent in a person-universe unity as opposed to a dichotomous, person vs. universe context) should lead to a more creative act, there being richer data and experience from which to draw for creative activity.

In the second stage of the creative process, the incubation stage, the "data" mill, stew, and percolate about, combining and recombining into new patterns and relationships. Especially crucial is the importance of letting oneself be, staying with one's own life flow without straining to change direction, speed, or content including immersion in painful experience. A number of descriptions by creative persons of their own creative processes often describe the need to get away from their work through sleep, recreation, or in Poincare's case, riding streetcars. Whether this nonpressure situation allows the incubation stage to flourish or permits the next stage to emerge is a moot question. In either case, the ability to let oneself be seems essential.

The next stage is called the illumination stage. It is here where the new concept, idea, invention, etc., emerges into consciousness, usually accompanied by expressions of "Aha," "Eureka," "I've got it," or pictured in comic strips by an electric bulb shining over some character's head. The willingness to tune into one's feelings is especially important. A phenomenon, called the "hedonic impulse," is sometimes described as a vague pleasurable feeling occurring just before illumination takes place. It is not the same joyful burst or glow of feeling which occurs at illumination, but precedes this more obvious sensation. Creative individuals, having learned to trust this feeling, apparently are able both to allow illumination to take place more readily and to know when it is coming. Most people have in some way repressed the hedonic impulse. Although little attention has been directed to the hedonic impulse in research and little evidence has been published to support the following thesis, it is quite possible that repression of the feelings involved in the hedonic impulse could also tend to repress the emergence of the illumination stage. The acceptance of one's feelings as a general mode of existence for the individual who has achieved some increased health through Gestalt Therapy should directly facilitate both phenomena, the hedonic impulse and the illumination stage.

The hedonic impulse has recently also been described by Brown and Melchoir (1967) as a precursor to synchronicity, meaningful chance, or coincidence. Synchronicity occurs in a condition or situation where things just seem to fit together, the right people in the right place at the right time, without planning. The spontaneous quality of these occurrences often seems mysterious in its beyond random chance nature. I believe that the relationship between synchronicity and creativity will one day be more clearly delineated and the common quality touching both will be the ability of the experiencer through extreme flexibility to move into the flow of the universe at that moment.

The final stage in the creative process is called the verification or elaboration stage. Here, whatever has been brought into consciousness in the illumination stage has to be given form in reality—the painting is painted, the music written and played, the invention constructed, the idea written, spoken or elaborated—and in this form tested or compared with what has previously existed to see if it is more desirable, beautiful, elegant, worthwhile, etc. Training in Gestalt Therapy can obviously be helpful here. What is real can more likely be perceived and experienced, making the testing or comparison more valid. This perception contrasts with the blindness to reality or the distortion of reality which can occur in those who use fantasy as the foundation of their existence. Getting in touch with what is and staying with what is, brings one closer to the only reality one can experience, the reality of the moment.

Gestalt Therapy can provide another kind of teaching to help the individual become more creative. This has to do with his belief he is capable of being flexible. In order to experience the possibility of selecting alternatives or new experiences for himself, the individual must (1) assimilate, digest and integrate this possibility of change, of altering his status quo into his being, and (2) alone must assume responsibility for himself and his behavior. If he can assume responsibility for his behavior including the possibility of growth through new experiences he moves closer to the state of being creative.

At the risk of seeming simplistic I repeat that to be creative is to be aware of, to discover what already exists in the universe. Polanyi (1966) states that research is successful and original only if the problem is good and original. The point is to see the problem. The problem is hidden. "To see a problem that will lead to a great discovery is not just to see something hidden, but to see something of which the rest of humanity cannot have even an inkling." Polanyi goes on to say that it is through tacit knowing, including "intimations of something hidden, which we may yet discover," that we reveal the problem.

It is possible then to hold that nothing is ever created. It is rather discovered in the moment of experience. And it is discovered through the individual's awareness of the universe, an awareness which includes intuitions, intimations, and tacit sensings as well as conscious and explicit perceivings and knowings. When I imply that everything to be discovered or created already exists, this does not mean that what is discovered may necessarily exist in a concrete form. It may exist only in terms of an idea or an essence or even derive its meaning from previously undetected relationships between concrete things that already do exist.

Furthermore, this does not negative the existence of the conventional four stages of the creative process. They all may well be involved at the same time or in different proportions in the moment of discovery. They could singly or in combination be descriptions of what might be going on in the individual as he becomes aware of this new thing that is already in existence.

The awareness trainer, using principles of Gestalt Therapy (Perls, 1947, 1961, 1967, 1968; Perls, Hefferline, and Goddman, 1965; Simkin, 1965; Naranjo, 1966) can, by skillfully giving feedback to the student or teacher, help him to experience himself at the moment—including perhaps his avoidance of this act—help him to become more in touch with the Now, especially that part of the Now that is himself. As he becomes more aware of himself, he becomes increasingly aware of the universe as a part of a special Gestalt, the "person-universe." Of course, the increased awareness of the universe would include that of other humans with whom he lives, including his pupils.

Sometimes an impediment to awareness and creativity is a common yet major split of the individual self into two selves. One is an authoritarian, intellectual self which insists on perfection, ideals, all the "shoulds." The other self is primarily hedonistic and emotional, and through cunning and clever ways attempts to avoid all the demands of the first self. The two selves can be in desperate conflict. The first self bullies, threatening all sorts of dire consequences if the person does not shape up. The second self professes weakness, promises to try harder, but always tomrrow, meanwhile slyly sabotaging the bully's demands. The individual remains in an unproductive bind. Until the two can be integrated into a whole person, another Gestalt, much energy will be worthlessly dissipated in the conflict, energy which cannot be directed at experiencing reality.

The awareness trainer, again using principles and techniques of Gestalt Therapy, can help individual become aware of the split in himself and the nature, strengths, and weaknesses of these polarities. He can then help the polarized selves to become conscious of each other and, hopefully, bring about some integration of the two selves into an individual person-self.

Awareness training based on Gestalt Therapy not only can increase the creativity and flexibility of one's life style, it can also be invaluable in other ways for teachers and others who work with human beings. Awareness training teaches one really to listen to and to see who is there. Too often teachers see and hear a *concept* of an individual child, one they have "computed" for themselves, rather than the child as he actually is *at the moment*. The learning experiences they provide as a consequence of this concept often have little relevance to the child as he is. Being aware of a child as he really is half the battle toward effective and creative teaching, especially in terms of relevant curriculum content and teacher behavior.

We have only one relevant reality available to us. Through an increasing awareness of this reality we can become more creative. As we become more creative, more in touch with reality, it consequently follows that we become more flexible and thus we become more alive.

References

BARRON, F., *Creativity and psychological health*. New York: Van Nostrand Rheinhold, 1963.

BROWN, G., A second study in the teaching of creativity. *Harvard Educational Review*, 35, 1965, 1, 39–54.

BROWN, G., Operational creativity: a strategy for teacher change. *Journal of Creative Behavior*, Fall 1968.

BROWN, G., and D. GAYNOR, Athletic action as creativity. *Journal of Creative Behavior*, 1, 1967, 2, 155–62.

BROWN, G. and P. Melchior, Informal discussion at Esalen Institute, April 1967.

GORDON, W. J. J., *Synectics*. New York: Harper and Row, 1961.

HOBBS, N., Sources of gain in psychotherapy. *American Psychologist*, 17, November 1962, 11, 741–47.

Naranjo, C., *I and thou: here and now.* Esalen Monograph No. 2.Esalen Institute, Big Sur, California, 1966.

Perls, F. S., *Ego, hunger and aggression: a revision of Freud's theory and method.* New York: Random House, Fall 1968.

Perls, F. S., *Gestalt therapy and human potentialities.* In H. A. Otto, Ed., *Explorations in Human Personalities.* Springfield, Ill.: Charles C Thomas, 1966.

Perls, F. S., Workshop vs. individual therapy. *Journal of Long Island Consultation Center,* 5, Fall 1967, 2, 13–17.

Perls, F. S., R. F., Hefferline, and P. Goodman,*Gestalt therapy: excitement and growth in the human personality.* New York: Dell, 1965.

Polanyi, M., *The tacit dimension.* Garden City, N.Y.: Doubleday, 1966, pp. 21–22.

Simkin, J. S., "Introduction to Gestalt therapy." Gestalt Therapy Institute, Los Angeles, 1965 (Mimeo).

Torrance, E. P., Education and the creative potential. Minneapolis: The University of Minnesota Press, 1963, pp. 137–38.

How should George Brown's ideas be implemented? We can think of no way to say how which would be as effective as to present a sample of his own work. Hence, with permission we include the experiment which he mentioned and which he carried out as one of his own early attempts to take risks with his own venture into new awareness. (Ed.)

A Second Study in the Teaching of Creativity

"Creativity is a gift." Like good looks or wealthy parents, creativity is often thought to be something one has or has not. Although occasionally there is a grudging admission that possibly creativity can be learned, this learning process is believed to be an arduous one, usually encompassing a magnificent total change in both behavior and behavior's antecedent, personality.

Here we posit that creativity can be learned through the use of a strategy that contrasts with the grand attack aimed at overall change. Creativity can be taught even if not in a way that permeates for all time every dimension of the subject's personality. Instead, attempts are made in this study to develop a personality structure, a subself built around a focus on creativity. A "creativity symbol," part of the focus on creativity, is used to trigger the creative subself. When triggered from the welter of total personality or total self, the newly developed creative subself emerges as the major and crucial rubric which governs the functioning of the subject. Antithetical or inappropriate elements, patterns, or subselves within the subject's total personality fade into background and have for the time being little or no influence on the individual's perceiving or consequent behavior. A hypothesis of the study is that when a triggered creative subself is thus brought from ground into figure—in terms of Gestalt psychology—the subject's perceptual frame of reference will be altered significantly so that the subject will perceive in a way similar to populations previously designated by others as creative, a designation which is based on evaluations of productivity.

The study is a replication of an original investigation reported at the 1963 meeting of the American Educational Research Association. In the first study an attempt was made to develop what was then called an aspect of the total self built around a number of creativity symbols. When triggered through the use of one of the symbols, this aspect of self would be capable of acting from a creative frame of reference. The procedure was carried on with an experimental group in a semester university course required of junior elementary education majors. Two additional groups were used to control for both the experimental method and instructor variable. A detailed description of both the experimental and control group procedures may be found in Brown (1965). Analysis of covariance comparing the test results of the experimental group with the control groups resulted in significant F values. The second study is also an amplification of the original study. In addition to further theoretical treatment in the procedure, there are attempts at developing a noncreative subself along with a creative subself which, when triggered, will come into figure and have a perceptual frame of reference in many ways antithetical to that of the creative subself. This is similarly crystallized about a noncreativity symbol which can be used as a trigger for the subself. It is hypothesized that the subjects will then perceive in a manner similar to populations designated as noncreative, extrapolated from known creative and "normal" populations. The second study also makes use of additional instruments for measuring perceptual alteration.

In this study the total personality is equated with what Combs and

Snygg (1959) call the phenomenal self. This includes "those aspects of the perceptual field to which we refer when we say 'I' or 'me.'" The dynamic nature of the phenomenal self is a consequence of continual modifications of the figure-ground relationship. Behavior at the instant of action is solely determined by the perceptions of the individual. Figure-ground relationships govern the process of differentiation, the searching of one's perceptual field or perceived universe.

As the individual finds himself in a different role or situation and as these roles and situations become familiar, a relatively predictable corresponding organization of the phenomenal self takes place. This organization is that which the individual has found appropriate for the role or situation. As the organization becomes more and more crystallized and predictable, it can be conceptualized as a subself, brought, in a sense, from ground into figure within the total phenomenal self. The total phenomenal self, then, contains a multitude of subselves. These all overlap to some extent. The degree of overlap is probably influenced by similarity between the determining roles or situations perceived by the individual. The total self may be thought of as a kind of multidimensional psychological mosaic which continually changes in characteristics and organization as subselves, moving from ground to figure, replace other subselves, only to fade in turn into ground as each is itself replaced.

The preconscious is defined by Kubie (1961) as the level of mentation or symbolic process whose function is to express "by implication the nuances of thought and feeling, those collateral and emotional references" which form a kind of coded language essential for all creative thinking. The eclectic theory of this study includes the preconscious as part of the total phenomenal self; also included are the conscious and the unconscious betwixt which lies the locus of the preconscious. Little attention is given to the unconscious in the theory, not from a de-emphasis of its power, but because attempts at considering its influence within the experimental procedures were not deemed possible.

Subselves slice through a kind of layer cake of the conscious and the preconscious. The analogy is imperfect because the division between layers in a cake is precise and distinct. The division between conscious and preconscious might more aptly be conceptualized as similar to that between colors in a rainbow. Another imperfection of the analogy is the static nature of the concept "slice." What is more probable is that as the phenomenal self palpitates in its uneven way, bumping against the universe, the imprecise dimensions of the subself are subject to variance when more than one instant of behavior is considered. This variance includes the relative proportions of the conscious and preconscious as well as the nature of the two levels. Relative to its occupancy of figure, however, the subself becomes prominent and dominant in terms of operational aspects of the individual: his perceiving, his differentiating, his behavior. The duration of a subself's occupation of figure would be determined by the role, situation, or context perceived and differentiated by the individual.

Just as roles and situations can be determining factors in the bringing of subselves into figure, it is theorized that symbols, too, can perform this function. A symbol may be used to trigger a subself, to bring it from ground into figure if the subself is crystallized around the symbol. The symbol might be a central core of meaning for the individual about which a subself has been organized. It should then be possible for the symbol to perform two functions, a kind of skeletal function in which the symbol becomes the bones about which the subself is built, and a triggering function so that when the symbol is encountered and differentiated by the individual, the related subself, as a consequence, moves into figure and becomes prominent within the total self.

The theory of this study maintains that through deliberate structuring, a symbol for creativity itself can be developed. Along with it, or rather about it, can be constructed a subself of perception and consequent behavior, which is characterized by originality, inventiveness, spontaneity, uniqueness, experimentality, etc. Furthermore, the creativity symbol operates at both the preconscious and conscious levels, becoming both a symbol for the symbols at the preconscious level and, within the total self including the conscious level, a trigger for a subself which is relaxed yet eager for novelty —a creative subself. This is a subself which feels a minimum of threat and guilt and has available perhaps the widest perceptual field or personal universe that can be experienced by the individual. The creativity symbol also forms a strong tensile link between the preconscious and the conscious, performing what Kubie calls bipolar anchorage of the symbolic process with roots existing simultaneously in the external perceptual experiences of the outer world (conscious) and the internal perceptual experience of the body (preconscious). This is needed if the results of the preconscious symbolic process are to be transmuted into the conscious world.

METHOD

Subjects

The experimental group consisted of 24 females and one male, all junior elementary education majors. The group met from four to six hours per week as students in a course entitled Elementary School Procedure, which covered the teaching of language arts, social studies, reading, and principles of education. Two control groups of 23 and 15 girls, also junior elementary education majors, were used.

Procedure

Each student was asked to keep a journal. This was to include a record of what the students felt were significant experiences, insights, values, reactions, questions, etc., occurring in class or outside the class if the student perceived these as being related to the context or the goals of the course. Because these journals are extensive in both range and length, they will be published together elsewhere. However, it is the summation of the student perceptions of "what happened," as expressed in the journals, which probably most accurately describes the experimental procedure. The description which follows is solely that of the instructor and is inadequate to the degree that it is reporting from an external frame of reference what is essentially number of internal personal processes.

Emphasis in the first stage of the procedure, a period of approximately three weeks, was on the discussion of the following books: *Lord of the Flies, 1984,* and *The Stranger,* in that order. The intent of the discussion was to develop an internalized need for stressing the creative process in both a professional and personal context. Questions discussed included: What is the nature of the world? What are the capabilities and potentialities of humans? How does one feel about and resolve conflict between status quo and change?

A film, Visual Perception, was shown to help in the acceptance of a concept of learning through the making of mistakes and thus to help eradicate the fear of risking mistakes. The film also clarified the perceptual prcoess, especially concerning that which is required to alter perception and consequently change behavior.

During this initial stage the instructor maintained a dominant classroom role, sometimes acting as a devil's advocate, often challenging cliché responses, and frequently providing support and encouragement as a student began to risk new perceptions, ideas, and values. The instructor tried to help the students to become personally involved in and committed to exploring ways they could become more creative in their approaches to teaching, and more effective in developing the creative potential of their future students.

The next step was to introduce the creativity symbol and the non-creativity symbol. This was done in the fourth week by reading to the class a children's book, *The Very Nice Things.* In the story William Elephant and Old Owl find the clothes of a man who apparently has gone swimming. William Elephant finds unique ways to use these very nice things; for example, he makes a bird bath for his bird friends with the pith helmet. Old Owl's chronic plaint, even when the man appears and puts the clothes on, is, "I don't think that's what these things are for." The two characters were continually referred to by both instructor and students throughout the remainder of the course. William Elephant became a symbol for willingness to think and act in new, unique, inventive, original ways, while Old Owl represented antithetical behaviors such as conformity, resisting innovation, clinging to the conventional, and fearing to make mistakes. This is not to say that novelty became the sole criterion of student behavior in and out of class. The solutions, ideas, or teaching approaches which emerged during the procedure that followed had to be operational. These had to "work" in real or simulated classroom situations. Thus the instructor held as his responsibility from here on a double function of facilitating the flow of creative process while also encouraging an accompanying kind of reality testing, which at the same time would not inhibit the creative process.

As in the first study, no special instructions were given as to how these two characters, William Elephant and Old Owl, might perceive. The characters as symbols subsequently came into increasing use, apparently because of their appropriateness, attractiveness, availability, and capability as symbols for integrating the contributions to and refinement of the concept of the evolving creative process.

After the introduction of the creativity and noncreativity symbols, in keeping with some of the conditions hypothesized as facilitating creativity—emotional involvement, an open system, lack of threat, provision for individual daring—the instructor moved from a position of relative dominance toward one of shared authority. The class gradually accepted more responsibility for deciding what was to be covered in future class sessions—when, how much, and how. Committees were set up in each of the curriculum areas to draft these plans. There was also a coordinating committee. All plans were submitted to the class for approval or modification, and were then activated. The instructor made himself available. Sometimes he continued the challenging or supporting role, but generally he tried to act as just a member of the total group. Even in an infrequent dominant role, rather than take the position of one in authority who was filling a vacuum created by a group's inadequacy, the instructor endeavored to communicate the feeling that his behavior was quite temporary, intended only to help clarify thinking. He attempted to impute his confidence in the ability of the group to quickly reassume responsibility.

The amount of work the class required of itself was more than equal to that conventionally covered in the course. This included lesson plans, teaching units, research papers, etc. in the areas of reading, language arts, and social studies. In addition, the class decided to continue reading and discussing "nonprofessional" books because of the stimulating effect on their thinking. Selected were *Catcher in the Rye, Black Like Me, The Genius and the Goddess,* and *Mrs. Bridge.*

There was no emphasis on grades and none were given until the end of the course. This was done in conference with each student. The students had been encouraged to present suggestions for evaluating individual achievement; for the most part, however, students seemed to ignore grades as a problem, apparently wanting instead to get on with what they were planning and doing.

It was decided to substitute for one class session per week, a morning in a teacher's-aide-student-teaching situation. This was to help provide a context of reality for the students' work in educational theory; it would also provide opportunity to try out ideas and lesson plans on how to work with children toward, among other goals, more creative behavior. Ten mornings were given to this activity.

Students conducted many of the university class sessions. This responsibility was distributed among all the students. At the students' initiative, planning and teaching strategy meetings were held with the instructor. The instructor made use of these highly informal sessions to expand concepts of creativity and noncreativity and to reinforce the creativity and noncreativity symbols. This was also done in the many individual conferences requested by students. Although the instructor attempted similar structuring in class sessions, the opportunities for so doing without being obtrusive seemed to decrease as the students took over more and more responsibility for the class operation. This was offset, however, both by increased use by the students of the two symbols in the dialogue of the class sessions and by consistent attention to creativity as a foundation for nearly everything related to the course.

A statement of qualification should be made here lest the reader assume that for any reasonable length of time during the experiment change was constant, even, or linear. In actuality there were uneven leaps, depressions, regressions, and, most important, extreme individual variances. The procedural description above is fundamentally nomothetic. A more valid description will be found in the collection of individual journals kept by the students.

Testing

The experimental group was given the Welsh Figure Preference Test which includes the 62-item Barron-Welsh Art Scale[4], a measure of aesthetic sensitivity and preference for complexity. This scale has been used with some success by the Institute for Personality Assessment and Research at Berkeley to differentiate between groups previously categorized as to rela-

4 A relevant discussion of the scale may be found in Frank Barron, *Creativity and Psychological Health* (New York: Van Nostrand Rheinhold, 1963).

tive high, average, and low creativity, based on a productivity criterion. The test was administered in February during the first week of the course. The test was given again on Monday of the fifteenth week of class meetings. On Tuesday the experimental group was asked to retake the test and was given the following instructions: "This time I want you to be William Elephant, or let that part of you that is William Elephant take the test and shut the rest of you off." On Wednesday the test and instructions were repeated with Old Owl substituted for William Elephant.

Also used was the Barron Complexity Scale (Barron, 1963), a 50-statement true-false instrument based on the work of Paul Heist, Center for the Study of Higher Education, University of California, Berkeley. This is similar to a scale included in the Omnibus Personality Inventory published by that institution. The instrument was encountered by the investigator after the second study was under way, so there was no February testing. The experimental group was given this instrument on Monday of

TABLE 5-1 Means and Standard Deviations of the Barron-Welsh Art Scale and Barron Complexity Scale Scores in Two Studies

Group	February	May	May (triggered creativity)	May (triggered non-creativity)
		Barron-Welsh Art Scale Scores		
Study #2				
Experimental	M 25.56	28.12	44.36	10.44
(N = 25)	SD 12.18	13.12	10.76	8.19
Control				
(N = 23)		M 27.09	24.70	
		SD 13.29	8.85	
Study #2				
Experimental	M 29.67	30.94	38.72	
(N = 18)	SD 10.00	12.73	10.54	
Control A				
(N = 24)	M 32.71	35.04	30.58	
	SD 10.58	11.14	12.61	
Control B	M 25.18	27.41		
(N = 22)	SD 11.05	12.12		
		Barron Complexity Scale Scores		
Study #2				
Experimental				
(N = 25)		M 22.32	32.16	
		SD 4.49	6.18	
Control				
(N = 15)		M 25.47	26.00	
		SD 7.65	7.92	

the fifteenth week with no special instructions, and on Tuesday with instructions to take the test as William Elephant, etc. There was no opportunity for the group to take the test again as Old Owl.

One control group was given the Welsh Figure Preference Test. The book, *The Very Nice Things,* was later read to the group. There was opportunity to react to the story and discuss any personal implications the story might have for members of the group. After being given the instructions to take the test as William Elephant, etc. the group was retested. Another control group was administered the Barron Complexity Scale, and the same procedure of reading, discussing, and retesting followed.

RESULTS

Table 5-1 shows an increase of over 18 points on the Barron-Welsh Art Scale for the experimental group from the mean in February to the mean in the Tuesday (May) retesting when the group was asked to take the test as William Elephant (triggered creativity). The increase is over twice that of the first study. There is a decrease of over 15 points when comparing the February mean with that of the retest (triggered noncreativity) when the group was asked to take the test as Old Owl. When the mean of the May (triggered creativity) retest scores is compared with the mean of the test taken Monday, the day before, when no special instructions were given, the increase is over 16 points, which is also more than twice that of the first study. For a control group there is a slight decrease in comparable means. When the Wednesday retest (May, triggered noncreativity) scores of the experimental group are compared with those of Monday, the decrease between means is almost 18 points.

There is an increase of about 10 points on the Barron Complexity Scale mean score from Monday's testing to Tuesday's retesting (triggered creativity) when the experimental group was asked to take the instrument as William Elephant. This contrasts with almost no gain after following similar testing procedures with a control group.

In the first study, covariance analyses of the gains comparing experimental and control groups (including a group used to control influence of the instructor variable) and test-retest results were significant beyond the .05 level.

The Barron-Welsh Art Scale can be accepted with some confidence as a measure of aesthetic sensitivity. It discriminates between groups of artists, a standardization group (M, 40.3), and a first cross-validation group (M, 39.1), compared with an unselected adult population (M, 13.9). Furthermore, the nature of the items on the scale is evidence that a high score indicates preference for asymmetry and complexity, while a low score suggests preference for symmetry and simplicity. This simplicity dimension

TABLE 5-2 Analyses of Variance and t Tests of Differences in Tests and Retest Scores on the Barron-Welsh Art Scale and the Barron Complexity Scale For Experimental and Control Groups in Study #2

Comparisons

Group and Tests	*Source*	*df*	*Variance Estimate*	*F*	*t*
Experimental, Barron-Welsh	Between	1	3296.7	22.0*	4.7*
May and May (triggered creativity)	Within	48	149.9		
Experimental, Barron-Welsh	Between	1	3907.3	31.4*	5.6*
May and May (triggered non-creativity)	Within	48	124.6		
Experimental, Barron-Welsh	Between	1	2858.0	25.4*	5.1*
February and May (triggered non-creativity)	Within	48	112.3		
Experimental, Barron Complexity	Between	1	1210.3	39.7*	6.3*
May and May (triggered creativity)	Within	48	30.5		
Control, Barron Complexity	Between	1	2.0	—	—
May and May (triggered creativity)	Within	28	65.1		

* significant at .001 level

is not to be confused with the possible simplicity in the elegance of a creative solution. Preference for simplicity in this dimension is rather a reflection of an intolerance for conditions of complexity prevailing *during* the problem-solving process. The Barron Complexity Scale is also, as the title suggests, a measure of complexity. Heist reports statistically significant differences between interviewer adjective descriptions of high and low scorers on this scale when interviewers, not knowing complexity scale scores, rate complexity. These and other data are reported by Barron (1963). In view of these data it may be concluded that in both studies experimental procedures developed high preference for complexity by the subjects, in contrast with those in the control groups, when tested as triggered creative subselves (William Elephant). Use of the Barron-Welsh Art Scale indicates that low preference for complexity, when the subjects were tested as triggered non-creative subselves (Old Owls), is also a consequence of the experimental procedure.

The possibility that a creative mental set, provided just by an introduction to the creativity and noncreativity symbols through familiarity with *The Very Nice Things,* might be responsible for the results may be discounted because of the analysis of the data for the control groups. The story simply and clearly tells of an encounter between a creativity-oriented character and a conformity-oriented character, with the former cast in a highly positive light. Yet when asked to take the tests as William Elephant, that is, to think as the creativity symbol, the results for these groups reveal no "creative" perceptual frame of reference under triggered conditions. No significant gain is reported. In fact, in the case of the Barron-Welsh Art Scale scores, the mean decreases and the standard deviation also becomes considerably smaller. These results would indicate that just knowing how William Elephant and Old Owl viewed things is not enough to alter perception. Apparently there must be a critical change within the subject, here postulated as the development of a subself, for a perceptual dimension such as preference for complexity to be significantly modified.

The findings for the experimental group are of interest when one considers that there was no direct teaching of aesthetic sensitivity or preference for complexity, the consideration or even mention of complexity or aesthetic sensitivity being carefully avoided in the experimental procedure.

The question remains: How good are these instruments as measures of creativity? Barron (1963) reports that the Barron-Welsh Art Scale has been found to have significant validities against criteria of originality and creativity. Examples of the range of samplings are as follows: Groups of architects—"creative," "control sample," and "representative"—have means of 37.1, 29.5, and 26.1 respectively. Groups of research scientists—"creative," "less creative," and "least creative"—have means of 30.7, 22.1, and 19.2 respectively. Similar comparisons are made with groups of writers, mathematicians, and others. Barron also reports that the Barron Complexity Scale apparently discriminates between creative and less creative groups. A sample of 22 college females nominated by the faculty for outstanding creative potential have a mean of 27.14 as compared with a mean of 23.9 for a sample of 113 classmates, a mean difference significant at the .01 level of confidence. Commercial writers who successfully write to sell have a mean of 23.9 as compared with a mean of 31.3 for creative writers whose major concern is "to create a work of art," again reported by Barron as a highly significant difference. Barron does report, however, a comparison of female mathematicians on the scale as not resulting in similar findings.

Inasmuch as the statistical concern of the studies is with a hypothesized increase or hypothesized decrease in experimental group means when tests are taken as the triggered creative or noncreative subselves, the significant difference between groups described by Barron in terms of degree of creativity, and the significant differences found between means in the two studies, suggest the passibility that creativity and noncreativity, as evidenced by preference for complexity and simplicity within perceptual frames of reference, may have been taught. More precisely, creative subselves may have been developed which, when triggered, have characteristics of perception similar to those for groups defined as comparatively creative; and in the case of the second study, noncreative subselves, which have characteristics interpolated as being expected of groups with creativity at a level below that of an unselected population, may have been developed and triggered. Both subselves, creative and noncreative, reside within the same total self.

One might assume that preference for complexity and asymmetry would reflect conditions characteristic of preconscious activity, where analogical, allegorical, and metaphorical symbolic processes would more likely occur than where there existed a preference for symmetry and simplicity. Such can only be inferred from evidence that creative people seem to prefer complexity and asymmetry. There may be, however, a circularity in this argument. Perhaps a more comfortable assumption is that complexity and asymmetry are related to open systems while simplicity and symmetry more likely fit into closed systems. Furthermore, open systems will tolerate preconscious activity; closed systems will not. This is supported by Kubie's description of the repressive effect on preconscious activity of the kind of consciousness which has characteristics of closed systems. That there is more preconscious activity in the creative subself or less in the noncreative subself, however, cannot be directly demonstrated in this study. Yet a need remains for the "preconscious" construct in the conceptualization of the creative subself in order to distinguish between the nonthreatened conscious functioning characterized by lassitude and laissez faire, and the open-systemed, also nonthreatened, creative conscious functioning which delights in new experience, new perception, and new relationships between symbols. Although the existence of the preconscious or its degree of activity in a subself defies precise validation, as a theoretical construct it helps explain properties of the creative subself and provides a locus for the subself's process sources.

If members of the experimental group do, in a triggered condition, perceive "in a creative way," it should follow that consequent behavior would also be creative. Taking a test is, of course, only limited evidence of such behavior, especially when the test measures only certain dimensions ascribed to creativity. It would be of great interest to structure situations which would test the triggered creative subself in problem-solving or productivity circumstances. It would also be of interest to examine the effect of other variables such as time, and/or various types of reinforcement, such as nurturance, on the strength of the subself. Also of general interest is the question of influence of the subself in the process of transfer to other subselves and thus on the overall personality.

Comparing the results of the two studies raises the question of why gains in the second study increased so dramatically. A partial explanation may be that only one creativity symbol was used here in contrast with at least two in the first study. There was, therefore, much more emphasis on the development and use of the one symbol in the second study. Moreover, the instructor felt more secure in the use of the William Elephant symbol— perhaps it now had more meaning for him—and more confident in the experimental situation. It is also possible that the introduction, development, and use of noncreativity symbol in the second study enriched the utility and meaning of the creativity symbol.

The choice of William Elephant and Old Owl as creativity and non- creativity symbols was intentional. Because the two are characters in a book for children, they present a minimum of striction for a reorientation from a wholly rational "adult" context to the sometimes playful, childlike, or innovative context which may be a condition of creativity. They also func- tion as an integral part of the developing subselves, their behavior in the story launching skeletons, essential parts about which the subselves may be crystallized. This combination of childlike quality and an operational frame- work for a new subself further contributes a bridge in the experimental procedure for moving from the context of "university student, under guid- ance of an instructor, seeking personal meaning for a concept of a creativity," to "human being and new teacher in process of becoming more open and innovative in perception and action, and more personally responsible for this process." Consequently, since William Elephant and Old Owl are at the core of the experimentally developed subselves, they become the ap- propriate symbols to be used to trigger the subselves under testing conditions.

In his chapter, "Play and Irrelevance," Gordon (1961) states, "the childlike and intuitive 'plasticity of vision' necessary to creativity on an adult level involves a paradox; it is childlike, but it is also childlike trans- posed, informed by an adult sense of responsibility and purposiveness." (p. 131) Although Gordon's work was encountered by the investigator after the completion of the second study, this statement buttresses the rationale for the initial stage of the experimental procedure. The development of "purposiveness" through discussion of the novels was intended at the initial stage. A goal was the establishment, personally and professionally, of an intrinsic need for and commitment to creativity. The "sense of responsibility" mentioned by Gordon may have been somewhat accomplished by the emphasis in the procedure on continual reality-testing of the ideas, teaching approaches, etc. which emerged from the experimental context of emphasis on creativity.

In discussing part of the Synectic technique of developing creative capacity, Gordon describes some individuals as "so wed to rigid inner control and rational behavior that any alternative behavior is anxiety-producing." (p. 46) He says that this kind of person needs to see someone else let go first and then he will "hesitatingly and finally with relaxed confidence" begin. This, too, might be a partial explanation for "what happened" in the two studies. If the students perceived the instructor as a model worthy of identification or creative behavior as an important value—it could be learned, to be creative was good—then they, too, could relax and become confident participants in the creative process during the experimental procedure.

The psychological and educational implications of this and the original study are many. The concept of subselves has utility for a number of areas of investigation and practice. It is an encouraging concept because it holds promise of significant behavioral change without the necessity for emphasis on total personality or overall behavior. The use of symbols to trigger the subselves has pedagogical import in many areas of the curriculum and in methodology. And the findings do suggest that something more can be done about creativity than just to have, like motherhood, everyone in favor of it.

References

BARRON, F. X., Discovering the Creative Personality. *College Admissions 10: The Behavioral Sciences and Education.* New York: College Entrance Examination Board, 1963.

BROWN, G. I., An Experiment in the Teaching of Creativity. *School Review,* 73, 4, Winter, 1965.

CAMUS, A., *The Stranger.* New York: Knopf, 1946.

COMBS, A., and D. SNYGG, *Individual Behavior* (Rev. Ed.) New York: Harper and Row, 1959.

CONNELL, E. S., *Mrs. Bridge.* New York: Viking, 1963.

GOLDING, W., *Lord of the Flies.* New York: Putnam's, 1959.

GORDON, W. J. J., *Synectics.* New York: Harper and Row, 1961.

GRIFFEN, J. H., *Black Like Me.* New York: Signet, 1962.

HUXLEY, A., *The Genius and the Goddess.* New York: Bantam, 1955.

KUBIE, L. S., *Neurotic Distortion of the Creative Process.* Lawrence: University of Kansas Press, 1958.

MERRILL, J. and R. SOLBERT, *The Very Nice Things.* New York: Harper and Row, 1959.

MILLER, N. and J. DOLLARD, *Social Learning and Imitation.* New Haven: Yale University Press, 1941.

ORWELL, G., *1984.* New York: Harcourt Brace Jovanovich, 1949.

SALINGER, J. S., *The Catcher in the Rye.* New York: Little, Brown, 1945.

WELSH, G. S., *Welsh Figure Preference Test.* Palo Alto: Consulting Psychologists Press, 1959.

6

Classroom Social Systems in Teacher Education

LOUIS M. SMITH

Louis Smith has addressed himself imaginatvely to the study of teaching and, reflecting on the products of his studies, has created a number of substantive ideas for the reform of teacher education. These ideas can be categorized in two areas. One is that, by virtue of his study of the classroom, Smith has come to a considerable understanding of the processes which teachers go through in order to manage and to teach creatively and effectively in the real world. He is therefore prepared to suggest the kinds of tasks that teachers need to master in order to cope successfully in the classroom and in order to teach vigorously and imaginatively. Second, he has developed conceptualizations and procedures which the young teacher can use in order to study classrooms (others and his own) in order to comprehend them more fully and to diagnose and recommend solutions to their problems.

Smith's primary method for the study of the classroom is derived from the microethnographic techniques of the research anthropologists. Especially, he has employed techniques which involve the researcher as a participant-observer in the situation to be studied. In other words, in order to study a classroom, Smith made a place for himself within a classroom and studied it, with his continued presence involving him gradually, but only partially, in a participant status. The observer, in other words, is on site and stays on site. While there, he observes what is going on and develops a running account of the activity. He conceptualizes these activities in terms of the developmental patterns of the classroom and tries to understand them. To organize and interpret his data, Smith employed conceptualizations drawn from the sociology of small groups in an effort to understand the dynamics of the flow of activities. To collect and conceptualize data, he spent a year in the classroom of an inner-city teacher; he and that teacher both kept a running account of the activities. They were able to conceptualize those activities in terms of control, instructional activities, the dynamics of the group, leadership patterns, and other concepts drawn from small-group sociology.

On another occasion, he spent more than one year in a single school studying the flow of activites of a group of teachers who were attempting to conceptualize and carry out instruction. This group of teachers had been placed in a very unusual open-plan school and the dynamics of their group was greatly affected by the kinds of activities that they were encouraged to try within that very structure. (This has been reported in *Anatomy of Educational Innovating,* Smith and Keith, 1971.)

The third piece of work to which he refers is a semester-long study of apprentices in an unusual teacher training program (Connor and Smith, 1967). The special problems encountered in the "two by two" program are dealt with in some detail.

The flow of activities which he has been able to describe by these methods have given Smith the understanding of the classroom which we referred to earlier. He is able to suggest the kinds of dynamics that occur during the early weeks of a class as the members and the teacher are trying to figure each other out and the group is forming norms and developing the work patterns that will carry them through the year. He has developed an understanding of the activity structure which the teacher develops and the kinds of techniques he uses to maintain that activity structure.

Smith recommends that the flow of activities which he has described be used as clues for teacher education. Young teachers can be taught how to engage in those activities in order to give them "survival skills" and, far beyond survival, to enable them to manage the classroom to afford creative and ingenious happenings. Second, he recommends that young teachers be taught the micro-ethnological techniques and how to apply these to the study of classrooms including their own. He imagines the young teacher as a kind of anthropologist, first visiting the classrooms of others, conceptualizing the activities he finds and gaining an understanding of the roles that the teacher and students play in relation to one another. He then imagines that same young teacher as an anthropologist in his own classroom, a participant-observer in the group which he has helped to make, studying his own group and using the knowledge he gains to guide his activities.

Louis Smith's work is creative and careful; he is one of the few psychologists who has been able to turn the study of teaching into clearly practical recommendations for teacher education. In the substance for his paper we find clues for the structure of a teacher education program and we find a strong methodology which can be taught to young teachers to help them understand the world of education and its institutions and to help them gain control of their own behavior as teachers. Thus, Smith provides us with a methodology we can use to develop teachers who will be able to function effectively in a school which is a center of inquiry.

Introduction

The purpose of this presentation is to analyze the conception of "the classroom as a social system" and develop implications for teacher training. The rather obvious but implicit assumption is that the particular perspective from which the teacher educator views the classroom determines, in part, his conception of the teacher's role and his conception of the necessary ingredients for the prospective teacher's preparation. The chapter is divided into four sections. The first describes in some detail several elements of the social system concept as they operate in the classroom. The second section relates this conception of the classroom to the concerns and training procedures for the preservice trainee. Section three presents briefly an account of inservice teachers' exposure and reaction to the social system notion. Finally, section four sets forth a further context, the phases and emphases in a program for teacher development.

While reference will be made to a variety of research and theory, the major ingredients will be generated by the author's own recent research (Smith and Geoffrey, 1968; Connor and Smith, 1967). Because we will cite at length aspects of these documents, we need to introduce them further. The Smith and Geoffrey (1968) monograph is a report of a semester-long observational study of a seventh-grade classroom in a slum neighborhood. Geoffrey was the teacher. He also kept notes of the events of the classroom. Smith was the outside observer who attended "all day-every day," sat at a table in the back of the classroom, and took careful field notes of the events of the classroom. From these "inside-outside" records the two investigators developed a description and conceptualization of the classroom structure and processes, or what they called "an analysis toward a general theory of teaching." The Connor and Smith monograph is similar in objective, description and conceptualization, but studies the apprentice teaching program at City Teachers College. (C.T.C.). The program was novel in that the apprentices spent two weeks at each grade level (K-8), i.e., two weeks in kindergarten, two in first, two in third, and so forth, in what Connor and Smith labeled a "two by two" program. Within the two-week period the apprentices observed the first day, taught one lesson the second day, two the third day, and so on. On Wednesday of the second week they taught all day with the teacher in the classroom; on Thursday they taught all day, but alone. This proved to be a climactic event. Participant observation was used to understand the behavioral and experiential dimensions of the program in the lives of a small group (twelve) of the apprentices.

Although of less significance for this document, we have used these research techniques in several other settings: an innovative elementary school (Smith and Keith, 1971), a high school science class (Smith and Brock, 1970), and a computer-assisted instruction program (Smith and Pohland, 1971). At times we will quote or refer to these works.

A second strand of experience on which the chapter is based is the author's teaching. An undergraduate educational psychology course and a general text (Smith and Hudgins, 1964) reflect some of his early biases. At the graduate level, he began teaching a course entitled, "The Classroom as a Social System," from which many of the present ideas have taken shape. In a sense, the ideas have been tried, revised, and retested against groups of experienced teachers. Finally, in a seminar of the same title, doctoral students have worked through research issues and topics related to the topic under consideration. Such is the context and basis of the analysis.

The Conceptual Framework

The most useful general statement of the social system position is that of sociologist George C. Homans in his book *The Human Group*. He introduces a number of concepts—group, environment, internal system, external system, social rank, norms, activities, sentiments, and interaction—which are useful in analyzing any particular social system. He builds his conception inductively by sequentially considering case studies of several groups: industrial, street corner, primitive society and rural community. He does not deal with an educational group. Smith and Geoffrey (1968) quite deliberately adopted the Homanian perspective and extended it to an elementary school classroom in an urban slum. In addition to the Homanian concepts, they accented concepts such as decision-making, initial teacher roles, teacher-pupil interaction, pupil beliefs, and pupil role structure. These seemed important in their data and useful for analysis of other educational settings. The conceptual framework presented here focuses on three major elements: (1) the conception of the classroom as a social system; (2) a decision-making model of teaching; and (3) a conception of initial teacher roles in the development of classroom social structure.

THE CLASSROOM AS A SOCIAL SYSTEM

In a brief presentation it is very difficult to review the wealth of ideas currently encompassed in the social system point of view. By "system" we mean an interdependent set of elements; by "social" we have reference to people. In a sense this is a redundancy, or an accent, because people are one of the elements. By classroom we refer to a unit of the school—usually, but not necessarily, the 30′ × 30′ cubicle with a teacher and 25 pupils.

Manifestly, the social system conception seems important because: (1) it accents a limited part of reality with which a teacher must deal; (2) it is important phenomenally, for principals, parents, pupils, and other teachers view it as an entity and consequently act with this, i.e., Miss Brown's class, as a determinant of their own behavior; (3) it has boundaries both physically and psychologically; and (4) typically, it has a time dimension, that is, a beginning in September, a development through the first few days and weeks of the fall, an equilibrium which carries through most of the year, and then a termination in the late spring.

For the teacher, system analysis has several other very important, if less obvious, qualities. In discussing the theoretical requirements of applied social science Gouldner (1961) extends the implications of a systems perspective:

1. System models forewarn the applied social scientist of the possibility that a change in one part of the system may yield unforeseen and undesirable changes in another part of the system, due to the interdependence of its elements.
2. System models indicate that changes may be secured in one element, not only by a frontal attack upon it but also by a circumspect and indirect manipulation of more distantly removed variables. These, because of system interdependence, may ultimately produce the desired changes in the target variable.
3. ...system analysis therefore directs attention to the multiple possibilities of intervention with respect to a single problem. (p. 90)

Another manner of labelling these implications is that of anticipated and unanticipated consequences. These terms grow out of Merton's (1957) more general functional theory. For our use it is important to realize that in a purposeful action system, such as a classroom, individuals take action toward goals. The actions have "anticipated consequences" which are sub-goals or steps toward the more remote goals. However, the action, because of the interdependence of the elements, often will have an array of social consequences which the actor did not intend or anticipate. These unanticipated consequences become part of the structure of the system and later are often highlighted as future problems, about which decisions must be made and action then be taken.

In short, the social system concept has a potency for a teacher who must work with and influence a totality such as a classroom. The interdependency or mutual dependency of elements is its major thrust.

TEACHER DECISION MAKING[1]

Introductory Considerations

For a number of years, we have wrestled with the problem of the teacher's relationship to her group of children (Smith, 1959; Smith and Hudgins, 1964). To pose the issue as a critical one for educational psychology, methods of teaching, and teacher training seems obvious, if not fatuous. Nonetheless, we have found it troublesome on at least two levels. First, a serious discontinuity exists within educational psychology. The language of learning theory—Hull, Mowrer, Skinner, or other behaviorists—used to analyze the behavior of children cannot be used easily by the teacher to analyze and alter his own behavior. In the learn theory tradition the child's "rationality" and autonomy are minimized as the program and the reinforcing contingencies are accented. The teacher, however, usually is implored to be rational, to plan carefully, and to meet the child's needs, as though the locus of control lay within himself. Teacher training materials emanating from these sources tend to be didactic and prescriptive rather than shaping, approximating, and reinforcing. Goals and objectives are givens rather than problems for analysis. The forces of the school culture—"the downtown office," the faculty peer groups, the textbooks, and the prescribed curriculum —all seem to be ignored, if not discounted. The teacher who thinks about his own behavior as a series of operants and respondents has difficulty in synthesizing these positions. We believe the issue lies fundamentally in the heart of contemporary social science theory, and we do not propose anything like a basic solution, but it remains troublesome.

In addition, our observations of what teachers actually do in classrooms and schools were incongruent with the discussions most psychological theorists were raising. Jackson's (1968) position was refreshingly different, and

[1] These materials draw heavily on Smith and Geoffrey, 1968, pp. 87–96.

we found ourselves in essential agreement with his point of view on the realities of classroom life:

> From a clinical perspective the central "causes" of behavior reside within the individual. A person does what he does, in this view, because of interests, needs, motives, values, and other internal motivational structures. Therefore, to understand behavior, the argument continues, it is necessary to reveal these hidden springs of action.... But the view of behavior gained from standing in front of a class is of quite a different order. From the teacher's perspective much of the behavior he witnesses seems to be "caused" not by some set of mysterious driving forces hidden within his students but by his own actions as a teacher. If he tells his students to take out their spelling books, the spelling books appear, if he asks a question, hands go up, if he calls for silence, he usually gets it. In other words, many obvious and dramatic shifts in students' behavior are largely under his control. This is not to say that his students are merely marionettes who twitch on command.... But for the most part, classrooms, like churches and cafeterias, are such highly structured and coercive environments that the observer does not need a detailed knowledge of the internal states of the participants in order to understand what is going on there. Motives, interests, needs, and other psychic mechanisms surely affect behavior in these settings but the influence of these idiosyncratic motivational structures is greatly tempered and restrained by situational demands. The clarification and management of these demands make up a central part of the teacher's work. As he seeks ways of trying to do his job better, the teacher who turns to an intensive study of personality dynamics or psychological pathology may discover that he has learned more about alligators than he needs to know. (Jackson, 1968, p. 172)

In part, these observations and dilemmas have led us toward the alternative of a broad social system conception of the classroom. Also, and as an extension of the Homans' stance, it has led us to a purposive framework, the perspective of the teacher as a decision-maker.

As we looked to more general theory on decision making, we found discussions of choices, fact-and-value propositions, rationality, alternatives, consequences, and effectiveness. Teaching often involves doing or not doing something such as tossing or not tossing a chalkboard eraser to a child as a dramatic illustration of a direct object in language arts teaching. "Choice behavior" is part of the decision-maker's conceptual repertory. It is also part of the teacher's schema. Lying behind such a choice are the teacher's objectives in language arts for the morning. Objectives are goals and values to the decision-maker. The teacher suspects that such action on his part will startle a few children, provide a concrete illustration of an important concept, and will give him a chance to compliment lightly or tease gently one of the boys for his skill or lack thereof. The decision-maker, conceptually, refers to these suspicions as subjective probabilities. The several events that might occur are, to the theorist, consequences. Later, when the children report such an incident to their friends, within earshot of another teacher, other events may occur. In addition to throwing or not throwing an eraser, the teacher also may dramatically snap a new Board of Education pencil into pieces, call a child up front and rap him lightly on the head with a flourish, or he may draw humorous stick figure cartoons on the board. In the theorist's terms, each of these are alternatives. They, too, have consequences. The consequences have probabilities both objective and subjective. We might phrase the teacher's behavior as "subjctively rational."

The Prediction System

The two most central concepts in decision theory are prediction system and value system. Analytically they can be separated; practically they become intertwined quickly and continuously. The prediction system refers to the causal chain of events: A leads to B, B leads to C, C leads to D, and so forth. The system may be phrased concretely in terms of specific events or abstractly as a set of conceptual relationships. In the illustration from Jackson's account, the statements "take out your spelling books" followed by "the books appear" is quite concrete and specific. Authoritative command and compliance phrases the illustration more abstractly. Presumably subsequent events—spelling, recitation, and pupil learning—follow sequentially. The events may be conceived in short time intervals, a 15-second episode, beginning the above lesson, or in larger intervals, "This week in spelling we'll emphasize prefixes, next week suffixes, and then combinations. Later in the semester we'll relate this to the general language arts lessons."

Other illustrations occur. Early in the semester, as reported by Smith and Geoffrey (1968), consideration was given to the concept of "pacing" and the slow speed with which the children were introduced to academic content. The field notes contained the teacher's rationale:

> His [Geoffrey's] statement concerned earlier experience in which he tried to rush the children (and rush probably would be defined as moving them along faster than they would want to be moved by themselves). Moving more rapidly, in his experience, has often resulted in not getting very much farther in the long run, and at the same time, frustrating everyone, the children and himself, and creating, as a consequence, several emotional problems in the group. (p. 90)

In this illustration, the teacher was at a choice point which he conceptualized as a two-alternative problem—slow pace versus fast pace (rushing). His experience suggested that increased pace did not increase materially pupil academic progress and did result in frustration and then emotional problems. In essence, he possessed a simple prediction system based on "clinical" evidence. The more general truth of the system might be ascertained experimentally.

The Value System

The value system in its "pure" and perhaps "ultimate" form is not a series of scientific cause-effect statements. It is a statement of preferences, desires, and values. When conceived as ends in themselves they are nonarguable. For instance, my preference for or valuing of vanilla ice cream as opposed to chocolate ice cream is at that nonarguable level. Or my preference for a hedonistic life style versus a contemplative life style, versus a "balanced one," so long as considered an end in itself is noncontrovertible. However, when arguments appear that these preferences and values lead— or supposedly lead—to higher or more distant ends, then arguments of fact and truth enter. To return to our illustrations, one can argue that pupil compliance in opening spelling books is "good" if it does in fact lead to recitations that result in "cognitive pupil learning" and if no alternative means gets there more easily. How much and what kind of cognitive learning is necessary for what pupils becomes a later set of decisions. Similarly, in Geoffrey's case, his experience is arguing that "no getting very much farther in the long run" on the road to an accepted goal and producing "frustration" and "emotional problems" are important consequences. The latter are implicitly viewed as undesirable in and of themselves or because they lead to other undesirable conditions.

The value system has presented us with a number of difficulties. In most situations requiring a decision it is impossible to determine the desirability of each alternative, compare these desirabilities and undesirabilities, and combine them into a meaningful summary. Among the many reasons for this, the lack of scales with common meaningful zero points and units is the most important. In wrestling with this problem and attempting to order our data, we have found that a model involving a "conception of the ideal" makes a more satisfactory point of departure. In the vernacular this might be phrased, "If you had your druthers how would you like things to be?" or "What do you see as the optimal equilibrium?" or "What is the best of all possible worlds?"

In the educational setting, the resolution frequently involves strong priority to goals of cognitive learning. Within that general position, however, considerable disagreement exists in the valuation of factual information, conceptual structure, or intellectual skills such as problem solving, critical thinking and creativity. Within the affective domain the consensus is far less. In addition, the problems of definitions, meaning, and measurement are entangled almost hopelessly. The mention of tolerance, alienation, anxiety, and mental health provide sufficient illustration. For our purposes in a discussion of classroom social systems the problem is complicated further because we want to argue that the social processes which the teacher engages in and the social structure he tries to create are intermediary goals which are valued because they lead to varying amounts and kinds of pupil learning—both cognitive and affective. A class which is attentive, involved, and active is very different from one which is inattentive, noninvolved, and inactive. It is our strong contention that educational psychology has paid too little attention to these social structures as intermediate objectives.[2]

Combining the Prediction and Value System

While there are number of principles regarding the combination of prediction and value systems (e.g., minimax), in one sense, decision-making involves a very simple judgment as to whether the prediction system surrounding one alternative or chain of alternatives corresponds more closely to the ideal conception than does the prediction system following the selection of another alternative. Obviously, decisions are not that easy.

For example, Smith and Geoffrey (1968) report an incident when the teacher had to decide, after a month of school, which children would be sent to another teacher and which children would remain with him. The problem arose because a room in the school was closed. As the teacher commented later on the decision, the prediction and value elements stand out dramatically:

> I decided to send to her the group I had received at the beginning of the year—mostly repeats from Rooms 13 and 14 and new students who had come in. I kept the other natural group—those who had come to me from Room 16 group, and I felt the seventh-grade group would fit better with the sixth graders than would the other group . . . . the numbers were okay per the instructions from the office . . . . I was sensitive to what had happened the previous year. I chose the simplest way administratively and one which I thought she would have the least complaint about.

And in regard to the complications arising from the fact that several groups of siblings were involved:

> Some of these kids had been together anyway. Since I made the decision by groups I saw no particular reason to make any exceptions. . . . After all, I had both Allison and Edwin together anyway, and she (another teacher) had both Patty and Rose together. All-in-all, again, I took the simplest way to a decision—by the groups in which the children came to me.

Strategically, we would hypothesize that the process proceeds more effectively when one frames his ideal or value system *first*. By asking for an organized statement of ends, conditioned by the time, place, and circum-

---

2 Examples to the contrary are Dewey's (1909) early work on moral education, Friedenberg's (1965) caustic analysis of the social structure of the high school, and Kounin's (1970) tour de force on group management and discipline.

stances in which decisions must be made, one introduces what is usually called flexibility and rationality. Then, as soon as alternatives are raised at any choice point, one can compute probabilities of an alternative aiding the attainment of a goal or subgoal. Future research is needed to verify hypotheses in teacher attempts to combine prediction and value systems.

Operationalizing the Decision-Making Model

To make the conceptual models viable, operational techniques become mandatory. For a long period of time we had considerable difficulty in thinking through concrete ways in which we could implement the model in field research with ongoing classes. While our discovery, if it be that, sounds simple as hindsight, the process of arrival was slow and difficult. However, we finally outlined the following steps.

First, one must establish several "natural" units in teaching—the lesson, the day, the week, the unit or the semester. It is our belief that the unit will vary with a number of conditions. For instance, some spelling programs have basically a weekly rhythm within which there are also daily regularities. Some activities, independent reading, library books, and book reports have a semester unit as the rhythm. If we select a single lesson in a subject such as geography we can illustrate the second step. The model requires that the teacher be quizzed via questionnaires or interviews concerning his goals (the value system) and the means (the prediction system) for reaching the goals in the geography lesson. An alternative, which has the beauty of objectivity and ease of access, is to make the age-old "lesson plan" into a functioning research tool.[3] In the case of many an experienced teacher, the lesson plans, in geography for instance, lay in his head, in the text, and in assignments registered in his plan book, which many teachers are supposed to keep up to date. After selecting the unit and obtaining quantifiable statements of plans and intentions, the third step, careful observation of the lesson—with a move toward reliable quantifiable schedules —would then occur. Post-lesson interviews or questionnaires could be obtained concerning altered goals and means and concerning cues that suggested to the teacher the need for instructional alterations.[4] Finally, as a number of teachers in varying situations are studied, verifiable principles should be generated.

Additional Implications

With the model in hand, we began to see a number of additional implications in difficult problems relevant to a general theory of teaching

---

[3] Incidentally, the research literature on lesson plans is almost barren.

[4] Currently we are underway with this kind of research (Smith and Brock, 1970; Smith and Brock, in process).

and to a miniature theory of classroom social systems. These include items such as legitimizing the "What do I do?" question, the best of a bad situation, and treating the children as decision-makers. Briefly, we raise half a dozen implications to indicate the potency of the possibilities rather than to carry out the necessary exhaustive analysis.

THE PRODUCT OF TEACHER EDUCATION. The decision-making model provides, for us, a clearer image of the product of a teacher education program and suggests some experiences, i.e., role playing, simulation, and skill training in classroom behavior, as vital, but not currently prevalent. The last two sections of this chapter are based upon and amplify this implication.

CONGRUENCE WITH TEACHER SCHEMA. Congruence with teacher schema concerns the consequence of making the model conscious and explicit. If it can be established that teachers implicitly operate within this framework, then we have an important vehicle for moving from the "real world" to one we might call, on some grounds, more ideal. Specifically, we are thinking here of long, involved discussions that we have had with students who reject Skinner's image of man as it is presented in *Walden II, Science and Human Behavior, and The Technology of Teaching,* and who have difficulty thinking of classroom problems in behavioristic terms. Some early field notes cast it this way:

> The model that keeps getting reiterated in the discussions of teachers and the discussions of the pupils and the threats and warnings, the pleading, the arguing, is almost universally a responsibility model. In effect, it goes something like this: You as pupil are responsible for your own behavior, for getting your lessons, for getting to school, for doing the homework, and so forth. When you don't do these things, then you are liable to certain kinds of consequences that follow directly from not doing these things. You should be able to perceive these consequences, you should be able to alter your own behavior to handle the contingencies as they arise. This model seems to pervade everything that goes on in schools. It is the kind of model that the Skinnerian approach has put into considerable doubt. (Smith and Geoffrey, 1968, p. 94)

If the changes the teacher educator is trying to make do not demand reorganization of the basic dimensions of teachers' conceptual systems, the probability for learning should be higher. Such an hypothesis in a psychology of teaching needs evidence.

THE WHAT-DO-I-DO? QUESTION. By legitimizing the what-do-I-do question we refer to our many years experience with teachers who have been asking the question, "What do I do with this child, this situation, or this problem?" For as many years, in our experience, psychologists and teacher educators have parried the question by remarking "It's impossible to respond to such a question; answers aren't that simple." The teachers complain to their colleagues about unhelpful experts. The psychologists and teacher educators talk to their colleagues about the teachers wanting "something practical," "wanting a push-button psychology," or "wanting recipes." The hypothesis we would offer is that the decision-making model legitimizes the teacher's question. By this we mean there is basic psychological theory where such a question is not heresy, but in its more abstract form holds a central position. For instance, in a literature lesson, what goals do I have? What are the specific ways I can present the material? What probabilities of success exist for changed attitudes? For increased information? For improved reading skills? A research-supported theory of teaching will indicate the probabilities of these relationships.

THE BEST OF A BAD SITUATION. The best of a bad situation suggests another group of difficult problems faced by the teacher. For example, a teacher may be faced with the dilemma of giving or not giving homework assignments. Part of his thinking may be predicated on such propositions as: (1) these children are academically behind for their age and grade; (2) additional work beyond class time is necessary to maintain progress as well as to cancel the increasing discrepancy; (3) the students are apathetic and will do little homework; (4) the parents are disinterested in school and will not support the teacher's efforts; (5) assignments which are made but not carried out will weaken the teacher's power and control in future situations. As one analyzes such complexities in assignment making, one might ask what the "good teacher" would do in this instance. The solution rests in picking an alternative which, while not desirable in some absolute sense, is relatively more desirable than other alternatives. In the teacher's terms, you "make the best of a bad situation." Such an analysis fosters rationality, suggests pertinent research problems, and lessens the load of guilt carried by the teacher. Obviously, one must guard against restriction in alternatives considered and rationalization in logical analysis.

THE PROCESS OF TEACHING.[5] Finally, the model stresses a time dimension, and consequently accents classroom processes as well as classroom structure. Each decision, each action, and each interaction rests upon a past and has implications for the future. Further, events outside the class and outside the teacher's immediate control influence the system and, as time moves on, this environment changes. As a consequence the class situation will be different and must be reanalyzed by the thoughtful inquiring teacher.

THE CHILD AS DECISION-MAKER. Another implication involves the congruency in the child as a decision-maker as well as the teacher as a decision-

---

[5] Smith and Brock (1970) provide an extended analysis of the methodological problems this creates for research on classroom systems.

maker. In some contexts, teachers treat the children as decision-makers. As we have illustrated, they act, both verbally and nonverbally, as if the children have choices, for instance, to attend or not attend school, to behave or not behave, to do their work or not. Pupils are held responsible, accountable for their actions. Often the teacher indicates the consequences that follow such choices on their part and which consequences he has control over—that is, which alternatives are in his own repertory. The theoretical excitement we find here resides in the synthesis of a number of educational and psychological positions. White and Lippitt's (1960) early ideas of democratic social climates can be rephrased without the emotionally toned labels. De Charms (1968) presents a sophisticated reanalysis and extension of motivation theory in terms of personal causation and the pupil as an "origin" or "pawn." If the child perceives himself as an origin, that is, his behavior is determined by his own choosing, a number of significant consequences result. Ojemann's (1961) causality training seems primarily an attempt to teach children complex prediction systems while ignoring the value system. Finally, one of the recent attempts to alter social studies curriculum (Oliver and Shaver, 1966) explicitly attacks the value dilemma problem in the context of ethics and political science—explicit and implicit values in the Constitution, the law, and governmental institutions. This kind of conceptual "fit" has the possibility of markedly increasing the potency of a theory of teaching.

ORGANIZATIONAL DIMENSIONS OF TEACHING. In recent years the world of the public school pupil, teacher, administrator has been overwhelmed by educational innovation: nongradedness, individualized instruction, team teaching, open space, new technology, and so forth. The integration of such practices into school life is exceedingly difficult. Even more difficult is the conceptual codification of such points of view. A major reason for this is the implicit theoretical position within the broader organization of teaching. By definition, a major ingredient in most innovations is "planned change." Organizations, at least at the formal level, are purposeful systems. As such, innovative theory, organizational theory, and decision-making thery have fundamental congruencies (Smith and Keith, 1971). Such generality over several domains is a major purpose of scientific abstraction.

Professional Responsibility

The decision making model is congruent with the far-reaching issue of professional responsibility. The issue is illustrated most dramatically in medical education. In the Becker et al. study (1961), the most essential "outcome" or "acquisition" of the physician trainee is learning the full significance of medical responsibility. On occasion, the physician holds the patient's life in his hands. They illustrate this with an episode from their notes. In the presence of a group of medical students, a patient died of a perforated ulcer. The post-mortem involved serious discussion regarding the decision and alternatives—operate immediately with low blood pressure and volume and risk death during the operation or wait and administer transfusions. As one of the staff physicians commented:

> You see, a case like this, you're damned if you do and damned if you don't. ...I'm not trying to attach any blame to anyone, nor am I trying to say it was anyone's fault...I think that you have to realize that it was a touchy situation either way. (p. 225)

In Becker and others' words, "The physician is most a physician when he exercises this responsibility." This issue, as in the illustration we cited above, comes through in concrete cases.

In the Connor and Smith (1967) data, the responsibility theme received considerable accent, although not quite in the terms of *Boys in White*. The critical experience was "Thursday alone." As stated earlier, each two-week episode culminated in total responsibility. The preceding days were targeted toward this. The apprentices had to know enough about the children and the cooperating teacher's program, had to have worked out a stance with the pupils which would permit survival, and had to integrate skills well enough to produce a visible product—teaching the children. While this was an anxiety producing phenomenon to most of the apprentices it was also a positive opportunity to test oneself and to see the progress one was making on the road to becoming a professionally responsible teacher. The decision-making model is readily integrated with this aspect of teaching.

INITIAL TEACHER ROLES [6]

One of the most understudied phenomena in the psychology of teaching is the way in which teachers begin the school year. How do classroom systems get started? What are the problems teachers face? What consequences occur from different initial decisions and the tentative stances teachers take? As we have indicated, very little data exist. For our comments here we will appeal again to the analysis made by Smith and Geoffrey (1968). They argue that the teacher faces two major problems that bear on the development of the classroom social system: initiation of the activity structure and development of classroom control. By the former they mean that an instructional program must begin and that the teacher has major responsibility for this beginning. By establishing control they mean that the pupils comply with requests, instructions, and directions given by the teacher. The Smith and Geoffrey data are limited by the fact that the children were

---

[6] This discussion is based on Smith and Geoffrey (1968), pages 83–86 and 67–72.

from a low SES area, and it can be argued are much less receptive to the teacher's usual efforts in each role. Further, limits exist since the data are derived from a case study of a single teacher. Consequently, while the issues are general the tactics suggested may be more illustrative than compelling.

Establishing the Activity Structure

In the beginning of school the teacher has many problems. From the organization's perspective, the key directive for the teacher concerns the establishment of the activity structure. As we have understood sociologists such as Homans (1950), an important part of the social structure of a group is the activity of the group, the transactions of the group with the physical facilities and environment. In the classroom, it is the "work" to be done. A major and often neglected part of the classroom social system analysis is the structure of activities. Activity is one of the basic dimensions of a group. In most elementary classrooms the children do a "variety of things" and this variety has special patterns. In the words of the teachers and the children, they study a number of subjects. This simple taxonomy of the curricular areas—reading, writing, arithmetic, and so forth—represents the public schools' attempt to order the "structure of knowledge" that has been accumulated in Western Civilization and to which the growing child must be socialized. In Big City, the school says there are eight of these areas for the seventh-grade teacher and their varying importance requires a set distribution of time.

The official form for the activity structure is the "teacher's program." The school system gives explicit directions for each of the three parts of the form. In Part A the teacher is instructed to:

> Give the curricular area or subject studied in each period. Show your full school day including recess.[7]

The several columns require the teacher, as we have indicated in Table 6-1, to indicate time of day, length of period, and subject taught each day of the week.

In Part B, the directions read:

> Summarize under the proper area the approximate number of minutes per week devoted to each area as shown in Part A of the program. Total each curricular area.

Geoffrey did this. The areas include fine arts (composed of music and art), language arts (which includes reading, language, spelling, and writing),

---

[7] These quotes and the following are from the official record forms used at the Washington School (Smith and Geoffrey, 1968).

TABLE 6-1   Mr. Geoffrey's Teaching Program (as filed in the permanent records)

Time of Day	Length of Period	M	T	W	T	F
8:30– 8:35	5			Organization		
8:35– 9:30	55			Reading		Language
9:30–10:15	45	Gym	Science	Gym	Science	Social Studies
10:15–10:30	15			Recess		
10:30–10:35	5			Organization		
10:35–11:15	40			Language		
11:15–12:00	45			Social Studies		
1:00– 1:05	5			Organization		
1:05– 2:00	55			Arithmetic		
2:00– 2:30	30			Spelling and Writing		
2:30– 3:30	60	Music	Art	Music	Art	Health

mathematics, social studies, science, physical well-being (including recess and physical education), practical arts (not given in the fall in the seventh grade) and organization. The latter are those minutes at the beginning of each day in the morning and just after recess and lunch when "chores" are to be done.

The final part of the form, Part C, operates by implication and assumption. Its directions are:

> Copy the time allotment for each area from the *Superintendent's Circular* or from the *Handbook for Beginning Teachers and Substitutes*.

Geoffrey did this. The form included: fine arts, 180 (minutes); language arts, 520; mathematics, 240; social studies, 300; science 90; physical well-being, 260; practical arts, 110; and organization, 100.

Interpretively we are saying several things at this point. First, a major part of classroom structure has its origins in the organization's primary purpose—fostering academic learning. Second, some degree of goal displacement occurs with the emphasis on the time allotments teachers spend in each category of activities. The system does test, at regular intervals, the achievement of pupils, but these results are "confounded" by pupil abilities and social class factors that vary significantly across the city. Third, the implication exists in Part C that the teacher's program should be similar to the time allotments in the *Superintendent's Circular*. Fourth, the actual time of various activities varied markedly from the program as filed. For the moment, we would note that the pupils seldom were in the class before 8:37 in the morning and it was almost always 8:45 or later before attendance and lunch money collections had been completed. Also, organizational problems arose all semester. Considerable variation existed in a heavy 3

R's orientation, especially in language arts, which went far beyond the stated time allotments. Fifth, the teacher has freedom to arrange these areas into the day and the week as he desires. Similarly, organizational limits exist in the degree to which the pupils have a voice in what activities are to be studied. Sixth, within the activity a large number of options exist in the sequence one might use in the presentation or the discovering of the accumulated knowledge. In the Washington School generally and in Mr. Geoffrey's case in particular, this part of the sequence was determined by the authors of the texts. In effect, Mr. Geoffrey and the children moved through the text page by page and, usually, problem by problem. Presumably this is one set of meanings to such phrases as "textbook-oriented curriculum," "systematic teaching," "traditional teaching," and so forth. Insofar as the text authors can clearly see their domain, this puts meaning into the activities. Insofar as one follows regularly through the text, this puts a procedural clarity into the activities. Pupils know what to expect. Most teachers at the Washington School believe that this is especially important for children with limited ability, with limited auxiliary skills (for instance, use of reference materials and related reading techniques), with limited motivation, and with limited self-control, all of which are alleged to be part of the syndrome of "cultural deprivation".

In short, as the semester begins, one of the teacher's responsibilities involves the establishment of an activity structure. We have phrased this as an important initial teacher role. The first few days contain the teacher's gambits into several curricular areas. Prior experience "in school" has long since developed pupil beliefs and norms regarding the activities to be undertaken. The major novelty resides in a particular teacher's idiosyncratic ways of structuring the activities. As we have indicated, the central office directives and the faculty norms to which he must be sensitive often make his choices reasonably uniform.

Establishing Control

Frequently teachers refer to a phenomenon which they label classroom control. Most educational psychology discussions do not make clear what teachers mean by this term. Instead, they move into discussions of discipline problems, mental health outcomes, and terminological confusion centering on "democracy" in the classroom. The thesis we wish to state is quite simple: classroom control refers to the relationship between teacher direction, usually verbal, and a high probability of pupil compliance. If we separate teachers into those who have control and those who do not, then we have situations where pupils acquiesce and follow direction or they do not. The dichotomy may be thought of as a continuum. Questions may be raised concerning compliance by the total class, various subportions of the class, and individual pupils. Further, we can subdivide according to situations which range from the imperative of the fire alarm to chewing gum. And we may distinguish between responses to direct commands by the teacher and responses mediated by an activity suggested or imposed by the teacher; for example, does the child answer questions and carry out exercises in spelling as these were outlined and set in motion three weeks before? It is important when discussing classroom control to distinguish norms from beliefs. A norm is a generalized or group expectation of what ought to exist while a belief is a generalized perception of what exists, i.e., these are the class rules. Part of the teacher's task is not only to have people know what they "should" do but be "willing" to do it. In other words, the teacher tries to build emotional sentiment and commitment into the belief. In this way, "acceptance of belief" is equivalent to the concept of norms and becomes part of the process of shaping the normative structure.

Those, then, are the elements in the debate regarding the concept of classroom control, a necessary prelude to the issue we need to address, the teacher's efforts to establish that state in the classroom. These efforts constitute the second teacher role, establishing control.

Once again, for illustrative purposes, we appeal to examples from the Smith and Geoffrey monograph in which they describe how classroom life occurred in a particular slum school. The particular approach of Geoffrey's might well serve as one defined position against which to contrast other defined positions. We do not present it as the only nor the best way of achieving control. It is *a* way. Except for the exploratory work of Kounin and Gump (1958), the scholarly community has produced little knowledge of this phenomenon. Smith and Geoffrey develop a four step model from their data.

GROOVING THE CHILDREN: ACHIEVING CLARITY IN THE ROLE. They called the first step "grooving the children." Specifically, during the first few days Geoffrey gave literally dozens of orders—to individuals and to the total group—which involved a number of trivial items. For instance, he handled the distribution of books by assigning each person a number, then calling out the number of the books from the storage cabinet, and having each child walk up and get his book. Later he modified this with "runners," children who distributed books to those children who raised their hands as he had instructed them. Next, he utilized the word "permission" over and over again. In the field notes, recorded before 9:00 A.M. on the first morning, "permission phrase appears and reappears." Interestingly, Geoffrey's statements showed situations requiring permission differentiated from those not requiring permission: "If you wish to leave the room to go downstairs, you must ask permission." And later, "For occasional borrowing, you don't need my permission."

Theoretically, we would argue that these interactions moved within the pupil group, towards a belief system: "The teacher gives directions and the pupils follow them." The immediate consequence of such a belief is the additional belief that future order-giving-and-following will occur in the same fashion. This eliminates questioning by the pupils and extended teacher explanations. It also eliminates rewards for compliance as well as punishments for noncompliance. This point is important for discussions of bureaucratic versus personal authority. Implications exist also for critical and creative thinking, activities that demand that one doubt and question before one acts.

Finally, the development of this belief system capitalizes on several aspects: (1) the requests themselves were individually quite insignificant; (2) they dealt mostly with activities in which teachers are expected to be involved; (3) they were asked of all pupils—consequently, to refuse would be to cast oneself in a special light; (4) the situations were cloaked with individual attention, warmth, and humor; (5) they often involved activities such as getting up and moving about, which was a pleasurable alternative to being seated for a long period of time; and (6) many of the requests involved volunteering and special, favorable attention. Some of these points are seen in the following episode:

"Do I have any good pencil sharpeners?" Several boys raised their hands. He picks two who didn't pass out books. He directs them, "Out in the hall."

Beyond the development of the belief system as a relatively emotionless organization of cause-effect relationships, the association with conditions of positive emotion moves toward what we call a classroom norm containing both beliefs and sentiments.

I MEAN IT: SECOND STEPS IN ESTABLISHING BELIEF SYSTEMS. So far, we have emphasized clarity of presentation of those aspects of behavior that Geoffrey wanted built into the belief and normative system of the classroom. Beyond clarity, Geoffrey's behavior contained an "I mean it" quality, which one might interpret as a threat or as a statement of cause-effect relationship. Our interpretation suggests that this dimension of a teacher's performance needs analysis for implications in establishing the social structure of the classroom; in other words, threats must be distinguished as to whether they suggest cause-effect consequences that may or may not be punishing, or those that reflect punishment per se. The former seems evident in Geoffrey's interaction with Susan:

"Who's been eating sunflower seeds?" Susan says she has. "Don't dine on them in the school room. I'll confiscate them. Who knows what confiscate means?" (Keep them.) "Anytime I collect food you'll be lucky to see it again." Geoffrey moves about checking papers. (9/10)

FOLLOWING THROUGH: A THIRD STEP IN ESTABLISHING BELIEFS. What we call "following through" is another dimension of teacher performance. Its meaning lies in the combination of an earlier statement of intent, frequently a warning or test situation (as in the sunflower seed episode), and now a demand that the pupil behave in accord with the rule. In a way, the simple behavior of Eileen's walking to the board carries considerable import for the classroom system:

> Few questions about letters. Sarah asks about "trachery," Geoffrey sends Eileen up to correct and to make it "treachery." (LMS—This seems very critical also. Without fanfare Geoffrey always sends the erring one back to correct his or her own mistakes. Implicit rule—if you don't do it right you'll do it again. Expand and interrelate.) (9/10)

A similar situation occurs with Sam. At approximately 11:25 during a language arts lesson:

> "How many are through? Those who are please wait patiently and quietly. Sam!" Geoffrey walks around the room, gives Allison a look. Stops to talk to Sam. (Can't pick up conversation except some about staying busy, book report. Sam protests that he has finished and is ready to give report.) Discussion—not quite banter—occurs between Geoffrey and Sam. (9/10)

Three minutes later:

> "Sam! All right, that's enough. Turn around. All the way." He does. (9/10)

On occasion, more severe punitive following through behavior occurred.

THE SHIFT FROM BELIEFS TO NORMS: SOFTENING THE TONE OF CLASSROOM MANAGEMENT. Geoffrey's humor seemed to be a major instrument for bringing about an "acceptance of belief." For example, late one afternoon, he received a memorandum from the office regarding some insurance forms to be taken home. In the course of the discussion the following notes were made:

> "Let me have your attention. I have some material for you." Raises accident insurance materials. Indicates parents are to make decisions about materials and not the kids. "Don't mutilate. Stop work and listen. Know what I have done on occasions with someone who wouldn't stop working? Don't guess. Ask someone who knows me." Geoffrey goes through insurance form carefully. (9/10)

A similar illustration, the incident with Susan and the sunflower seeds to which we have already referred, applies to "softening the tone of classroom management." It indicates Geoffrey's concern for establishing not only a belief but a norm as well. Many times he seemed to feel the need to make rules and regulations clear. He often did this dramatically. However, when his point was made, he usually softened the criticism and maintained the task-oriented quality of the group through drama, humor, and incidental learning.

In short, classroom control may be viewed as an important aspect of classroom social structure. In this sense it becomes a goal the teacher strives to reach. Our analysis has suggested that the teacher is faced with the problem of developing such a belief and normative system within the classroom. In this instance, the beliefs and norms center about his own role in the classroom. As Smith and Geoffrey analyzed their data, they described a number of interactional sequences in which Geoffrey gave orders and obtained compliance in a variety of mundane and critical situations. As these accumulated, they developed into belief systems—"this is the way it's done"—and ultimately into normative systems—"this is the way it should be done." Achievement of this goal had a number of positive and negative consequences for further long-term goals.

ADDITIONAL ELEMENTS IN A THEORY OF CLASSROOM SOCIAL SYSTEMS

While the concepts of system, teacher decision-making, and initial teacher roles are very critical—and we have tried to clarify them in some detail—they are only illustrative of the theoretical position. A number of additional elements of classroom social systems need to be developed and we can mention them only. Further aspects of teacher-pupil interaction include such important ideas as awareness (Smith and Kleine, 1969), continuity, banter, and drama. The social structure of the pupil world can be discussed as conceptually independent of the teacher, even though he is a major figure in its actual determination. We are convinced of the potency of such concepts as "pupil roles" and identify such important ones as monitor roles, sex roles, and individual roles.[8] The latter would include such phenomena as "court jester," "nonworker: troubled or troublesome," and "on contract." The sentiment structure (acceptance and rejection) and the subgroup interaction structure are also important conceptions.

In conclusion, our conceptual stance of the classroom as a social system is reflected most completely in two volumes *The Human Group* and *The Complexities of an Urban Classroom*. It is impossible to indicate briefly and adequately here the breadth and depth of the position taken in those discussions. The assumption we make is that increased sophistication in the ideas and accompanying practices produces consequences the majority of teachers would consider "good."

[8] See Smith and Geoffrey, pp. 54–58, 58–65, 151–53.

The Preservice Training Problem [9]

We have considered in detail several of the intellectual threads of the conceptual position, "the classroom as a social system," and have indicated rather briefly other necessary aspects of the position. At this point our purpose moves into issues in teacher training relevant to the social system stance. We raise some of the special problems of the preservice teacher and suggest several programmatic tasks which focus specifically on the interdependencies of the social system position and the characteristics of the individuals in the preservice program.

THE SPECIAL PROBLEMS OF THE PRESERVICE TRAINEE

Concrete Perceptual Images

Several interconnected major problems face the preservice teacher. Much of the dissatisfaction often attributed to teacher education seems to occur because the major efforts of teacher trainers focus elsewhere than on these problems. First, most preservice teachers have very limited perceptual backgrounds and images of classroom life—especially as these images occur from the position of teacher. Attempts to talk and theorize about classroom events without building such images are fruitless. This point arose vividly in our apprenticeship study (Connor and Smith, 1967).

The "two by two" program of City Teachers College had a number of latent consequences which were not anticipated before our inductive approach to the program. The concrete perceptual images dimension arose from an early observation of one of the apprentice's logs and from a conversation with a principal. The field notes stated it this way.

> To this point I've made arrangements to see two of the apprentices at City Teachers College on Friday morning. They seem most willing and cooperative in this endeavor. Both of those that I've had a chance to talk to and make such arrangements have also carried out several of the daily writing assignments. As I scan briefly a couple of Miss Frank's it is very interesting the mundane kind of percepts that are getting built. One of them, for instance, centers around the frequency of the kindergarten kids crying and the advice of the teachers not to pay any attention to it or otherwise you'll have a whole lot of it. How we will eventually categorize and organize these remains a very interesting kinds of question. (9/16)

Our notes are replete with the filling in of the vague, the general, the abstract with the specific, the particular, and the concrete. Our apprentices absorbed these details as does the proverbial sponge.

---

[9] This section draws heavily upon the discussion in Connor and Smith (1967) and upon conversations with faculty colleagues at Washington University.

The Principal used also the word "smattering" to describe the City program. Apparently she has some questions about what is accomplished more long-term wise in this short "two by two" program. Part of the argument we might make here concerns the state of the apprentice and what might and should be learned. The high number of varying raw perceptions that are created as you go through the whole school in various styles may be most appropriate as a sort of "background experience" with the necessity of the long-term apprenticeship coming later. It could be argued that the longer term experience would then be handled something more like a paid internship. Similarly, it might be argued that the "two by two" experience could well be in the form of a teacher's aide. You do what you can and you pick up what you can and in between that experience, or concurrent with it, you take the related courses in the theory of pedagogy. (9/21)

Presumably ways of measuring such experiences could be evolved, and if one decided the experience was important, then ways could be developed to phase apprentices through the total process.

In the October field notes (Connor and Smith, 1967), items with a sensational dimension appeared as the apprentices traded stories:

It's now 11:10 and I'm on my way back from my usual Friday morning meeting with the four apprentices. They are all full of vitality and excitement about what they are learning and the experiences they are having.
While I'm beginning to sound like a broken record, it seems to me that many of the ideas that we've generated about the importance of concrete images and the trying one's wings in the role of teacher, these seem to keep coming through very strongly. For instance, Miss Charles mentioned with some feeling of having missed an important event, the fact that one of the boys in her class had a seizure this Monday, the morning after Miss Charles had left the room. There was no question that she felt strong sympathy and feeling for the boy who has epilepsy; at the same time, this kind of unique new experience was one that she hadn't had and she wondered what one would do about the child to keep him from biting and swallowing his tongue, etc. Similarly, Miss Frank commented about the fact that she probably will get playground duty this next week, even though she's not supposed to have it. Some of this arose in the discussion with a young man, not part of the sample, who reported the same kind of "jungle" occurring at the north side Roosevelt School, wherein one kid stepped on another kid's face. The apprentice had to break it up. The senior lounge is a haven for this kind of discussion on Friday mornings when the apprentices come in from the schools. (10/8)

Need and Desire for Skills

Our experience has been that productive thinking in a field often proceeds through the use of analogies. By this we mean that the knotty problems in one area often are unraveled a bit by using concepts and modes of approach from a more highly developed field. As we observed our apprentices, we were impressed with what looked like the development and learning of a skill. Hypothetically, if one poses the problem of teaching as a skill, then the literature and mode of approach from the skill learning area might provide a fruitful way of exploring what it means to learn to teach. In the apprentice study, the first meeting we attended reintegrated earlier and related ideas on such a possibility. The field notes relate this early reaction.

> The supervisor has an elaborately worked out document which she passes out to each apprentice. This includes the schedules, three forms, and a variety of general advice. There are long lists of do's and don't's. She picked out and highlighted a few of these. Some of them as mundane as handwriting, penmanship and talking to the class rather than to the chalk board. One of my major impressions here was the notion that teaching is really a craft or a trade and that the apprenticeship is a very relevant word. All of this carries overtones of Dan Lortie's analysis of teaching as a sub-profession, a craft. Another way of putting the issue is that teaching is considered a complex, psychological, social and psychomotor skill. As in many skills, there are a whole variety of very small, mundane things that one has to do, to coordinate, and to attend to if one is to do it correctly. Within this same analogue there seems also to be a pretty clear criterion statement of performance. In a sense, I would guess that the cooperating teacher and Big City School District have a pretty clear idea of what it considers to be good teaching. Whether this image relates significantly to any or all kinds of pupil learning is an open question. In some sense, however, from the teachers' and the apprentices' points of view it's an irrelevant question. One of the issues that seems to me to be a good problem at this point is the characterization of this image of "the good teacher." (9/14)

On occasion, as one observes in a naturalistic setting, the seed of an idea which has the potential of providing a framework or theses for ordering a series of phenomena continues to develop. This occurred in the analogy of teaching as a psychomotor skill during the apprenticeship study. The idea bloomed most dramatically late in September. The field notes summarizing an hour with Miss Charles, one of the apprentices, carry the idea.

> As this discussion went on I was struck again by the analogy of teaching and psychomotor skills. This, it seems to me, is a very good lead and one that warrants considerable attention. As the cooperating teacher was describing the way things went, there were overtones of sequencing, coordination, perception of minimal cues, of behaving in kind of an intuitive free and easy style with much less of a cognitive component. I am reminded here of John E. Anderson's old comment that once you get a psychomotor skill, such as a well-learned golf swing, then you don't want to think about it at all. You just want to do it. This was very heavily the kind of thing that the cooperating teacher was saying about teaching. Specifically, she thought Miss Charles wrote very beautiful lesson plans but was perhaps too fixated, and that's my word, on the plan so that she couldn't move easily and improvise as other situations arose. She was most clear in stating that you had to have an idea of what you wanted to do and where you wanted to go and have that clearly in mind,

but that you shouldn't be bound to it. She had a good bit of difficulty putting this into words as she tried to say it. Another illustration that she gave concerned the break between each lesson and the fact that they should "melt," and that was her word, together. In her words also, some of this would "come with practice." In short, a good bit of this ties in with the notion of teaching as a craft or a skilled trade or an artistic performance.

Another concept that came up repeatedly was that of "losing the pupils." This was in reference to a long reading lesson, approximately 45 minutes, which Miss Charles taught. The cooperating teacher was willing to entertain the reasons that the lesson was so long, and Miss Charles had really very few reasons except that she wanted to finish one section and hadn't really noticed how long it was taking. At the same time, she commented that part of teaching is knowing when to stop and the "losing them" perception is one of those times. She indicated also that it is important to have "something tucked away" that the teacher can move into in such circumstances.

Around the "losing them" phenomenon were further images of the artistry and the notion of teaching as a skill.

Another comment that the cooperating teacher made concerned the "lack of confidence" and fearfulness which she thought Miss Charles had. Again, she saw this as perfectly normal and one of the things that apprentices have to get over. This sort of inhibition continually gets in the way of the smooth performance of any kind of sequenced skill. This also seems to be a part of the cooperating teacher's general position on the development of apprentices. She sees these issues as a series of problems that the apprentice must face and must work with and that over a period of time, and what she would describe as the normal processes of learning, one comes to overcome. She, herself, doesn't seem much agitated or much in a rush for the problems to be mastered for once and for all, but rather she acts much like some of the child development people when they talk about a young child gradually maturing and coming to take his place as a well socialized being in the group. She would fit, I think, quite nicely as an illustration of Stephen's conception of spontaneous schooling as this might apply to the learning problems of the apprentice. (9/29)

In short, our field notes and interpretations suggest a number of implications concerning the "performance" or "skill" dimensions of teacher training.

Confidence and Anxiety

Most teacher trainees possess strong adient-avoidant motivations regarding their ability to carry out the day-to-day planning, processes and skills of teaching a group of children. In the adient sense, the trainees want to try their hand at "making the animal behave." By this we mean they are eager to plan and to teach lessons in reading, arithmetic, and the other curricular areas and they are eager to test their abilities in what we have called the core interpersonal skills of teaching. On the avoidant side of the motivational coin, almost all are at least somewhat fearful that they will not succeed—at least not as well as they would like—and some are extremely anxious about any success whatsoever. In this situation, extended discourse about teaching bores those who are essentially adient and frightens those who are essentially avoidant. With some trainees, the usual education course —be it methods, psychology, or foundations—does some of each. In our apprenticeship study, we accented what we called the "psychomotor analogy." The psychomotor literature suggests that confidence in one's self is a most necessary ingredient in performance of a skill. As one "loses confidence," becomes anxious, the collapse of even well-practiced habits can occur. Similarly, the physical educator speaks of the individuals and teams which are beaten before they start.

Anxiety is an emotional reaction characterized by experiential components of discomfort, general malaise, inadequacy and dread of unknown consequences. Physiologically, the reactions include accelerated heart beat, perspiration, tremor, and muscular tenseness. Some people (and at least one of our apprentices seems to qualify in this regard) carry a good bit of this reaction with them all the time. Most people experience some of the reactions in new situations for which they have few available responses. This seemed to be true of almost all of our apprentices as they moved into teaching.

As we have indicated, some persons carry with them what the psychiatrists call basic anxiety or free floating anxiety. As such, it is readily available to be attached, associated or conditioned to any aspect of the environment which comes along. In addition, we have alluded to the fact that the demands of any new and difficult task for which one does not have readily available and appropriate responses produce stress, frustration and generalized emotional reactions. In addition, the individual, as the educationists are prone to say, brings his total personality to the learning situation. Specifically, he brings his good standing with his peer group. To maintain his standing—and peers means a society of equals—the individual must perform in that range of tolerable behavior which the norm defines as acceptable. The potency of this for the child with his gang or the adult with his social group is not to be scoffed at nor denied by disparaging references to fallacies in "other-directedness" or "conformity." All of us have our reference groups and even though one may be different from another and the other's group does not seem so important, one should not be misled. It is there and it is important. Without elaborating, one's family —parents, siblings, spouse, etc.—provide for most learners a significant reference group, and for our argument here, a source of anxiety if one does not perform and accomplish to the degree the group defines as adequate.

Phrased more positively, confidence spirals into permitting one to try the unusual, the novel or the difficult. It gives clarity to one's action and a flair to one's performance. It has a self-fulfilling quality about itself.

These factors lead to success and to increments in confidence. Connor and Smith (1967) have diagrammed these relationships which we reproduce as Figure 6-1.

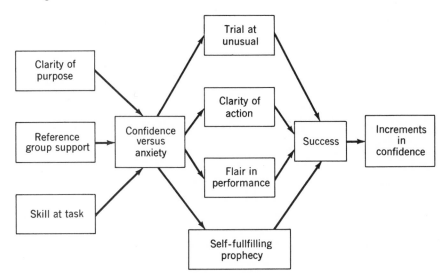

FIGURE 6-1 Antecedents and Consequences of "Confidence" in Teaching (After Connor and Smith, 1967, p. 241).

The teacher-pupil relationship literature is cluttered with emotional appeals for the need of warmth and pupil centeredness. The essence of this, as we look at the psychomotor phenomenon, is that failure and unsuccessful trials are going to occur. The child misses the ball with the bat and strikes out, or a ball is hit and dropped in the field. He does not need someone to tell him he erred or to harangue him for erring. All that is very clear. In our judgment, what the child needs is someone to be there, to support him and to localize the issue to that time and place and that particular skill and episode. The key issue reflects the demand that the failure and lack of success does not generalize to the total activity and precipitate the child's quitting, or engaging in any one of a variety of defense mechanisms (e.g., "She's a lousy teacher," or "She yells at us," or "Who cares?"). It is in this sense—the pervasiveness of anxiety, fear, and negative emotions—that the principle of warmth and supportiveness becomes very apparent. Connor and Smith, as accepting observers outside the authority structure of the program, found themselves playing a major and unanticipated role in the lives of the apprentices. The cooperating teachers, supervisors, and principals played similar roles in varying degrees; they often were hampered by status differentials and evaluation responsibilities. Ultimately training programs must recognize these dimensions of the system and build mechanisms to alter the more debilitating consequences.

THE MICROETHNOGRAPHY OF THE CLASSROOM: AN APPROACH TO THE IMAGE PROBLEM[10]

Perhaps we are committing the error of the cultist who perceives his own limited perspective to be the panacea which will solve all problems, but our own teaching experience—not our research—suggests that preservice students become highly involved both motivationally and cognitively in becoming "microethnographers."

Initially we had tried having teachers make a brief observation of an elementary or secondary classroom as a prelude to discussions in educational psychology. More recently we have elevated such a task to a major focus in the program. Roughly, the trainee spends four or five clock hours over several consecutive days in the classroom. During his stay he collects careful field notes of the events of each hour. His primary purposes are to produce a description of the classroom in what we have called the everyday or "lay" language and to produce an initial set of concepts and hypotheses which will help him explain what he has seen. While this sounds simple, it can be extraordinarily difficult and challenging to trainees of varying abilities, backgrounds and interests.

To facilitate independent work on such an observational project, we have concurrently described and analyzed in detail some of our own experiences as they have been reported in Smith and Geoffrey (1968), especially Chapter One and the Appendix. We raise our conception of theoretical models and a variety of suggestions for making the approach productive. The major aspect of our model building is to urge upon our trainees the need to focus upon antecedents and consequences. In part, this is an elaboration of such widely accepted general positions as searching for causes and the multiple causation of educational and psychological events. The concern for consequences has been a much less accented point of view in educational psychology (in contrast to sociological functionalism). Finally, we have urged our students to present their ideas figuratively, in diagrams, much like those presented elsewhere in this chapter. The ability to scan a system this way seems most helpful in making meaningful the more linear prose.

Several interrelated phenomena seem to be critical if one is to find microethnography a productive approach for classroom analysis. Lying behind the deceptively simple appearance of the method, several conditions have been found to be important.

[10] These materials draw heavily upon Smith (1967).

Descriptive and Theoretical Foci

Perhaps the most significant aspect is the simple direction, "come to know your observed class well enough to be able to describe it to your colleagues in your educational psychology course." This usually includes the children, the teacher, the physical aspects of the room, the materials, ideas, and so on. Moving to the more general or abstract ideas is usually a more difficult individual assignment. But in the students reporting back to their college peers the abstractions and interpretations begin to enter. The observed teacher was "too stern" or "too lax," the materials were "too hard," "too easy," or "irrelevant," the children were "excited" or "bored" or "hostile." At that point, the abstractions flow rapidly, and the problem becomes one of ordering the interrelationships, probing for evidence, and assessing contradictory experiences. Integrating these materials into the more general educational psychology literature and into a beginning theory of teaching becomes the next problem.

Foreshadowed Problems

Foreshadowed problems are those knotty questions, the toughest ones you can find which you keep asking the data to answer. In his monograph, *Argonauts of the Western Pacific,* Malinowski (1922) states his perception of the issue:

> The ethnographer has not only to spread his nets in the right place, and wait for what will fall into them. He must be an active huntsman, and drive his quarry into them and follow it up to its most inaccessible lairs. And that leads to the more active methods of pursuing ethnographic evidence. . . . The ethnographer has to be inspired by the knowledge of the most modern results of scientific study, by its principles and aims. I shall not enlarge upon this subject, except by way of one remark, to avoid the possibility of misunderstanding. Good training in theory, and acquaintance with its latest results, is not identical with being burdened with "preconceived ideas." If a man sets out on an expedition, determined to prove certain hypotheses, if he is incapable of changing his views constantly and casting them off ungrudgingly under the pressure of evidence, needless to say his work will be worthless. But the more problems he brings with him into the field, the more he is in the habit of moulding his theories according to facts, and of seeing facts in their bearing upon theory, the better he is equipped for the work. Preconceived ideas are pernicious in any scientific work, but foreshadowed problems are the main endowment of a scientific thinker, and these problems are first revealed to the observer by his theoretical studies. (pp. 8–9)

The central thrust of the "foreshadowed problem" is that it selectively guides one's perception and thought while one is in the field. For instance, the Washington School Study I was continuously asking myself, "How does one manage the children? How do you get them to listen to you? What's it like to be in the class hour after hour, day after day? What are the satisfactions and the frustrations?" As these questions keep turning over and over in one's thoughts one is continually jotting down the concrete overt behavior of the teacher and children. "Who said what? Who is where? Who is moving about, talking, playing, reading, and so forth?" Such fore-shadowed problems, whether cast in lay language or in more abstract for-mulations, are different from having preconceived ideas or solutions. The "preconceived ideas," in one instance, were cast as a standing joke between Geoffrey and me. When he was faced with difficult choices he would ask, with a twinkle in his eye, "How does the 'good teacher' handle that?", or "What does Education 101, The Principles of Teaching, say about that?" For stu-dents learning and using the methods, the important issue is convincing them that introspection is important and that their relatively vague initial notions have merit and are worthy of pursuit in the context of the events that they are witnessing.

The Attentive Ear

As one has unanswered questions lying in the novel setting which one is observing, it seems to create a listening set in the observer, an attentive ear. Not only as one observes the processes of interaction, but while talking with the persons involved in the organization, one asks them in a myriad of ways to "tell me what it's really like here." We have found that the attentive ear is a major reinforcer to participants. It is also a gold mine for "classical solutions" to one's foreshadowed problems. And even more critically, the attentive ear elicits new definitions of those problems as well as many more problems worthy of being foreshadowed but which the field has not begun to analyze. These may be serendipic or latent and unanticipated to use the "good" words of the field. For instance, an upper-grade teacher, one of the most gracious women I've ever met, told me about the difficulties she had in learning to live in a slum school. She related the disbelief held by her physician that one so gentle and shy as she could handle a group of youngsters with reputations such as those at the Washington School. On one occasion, a time of serious crises in the school, we observed her discipline a big, rough 15-year-old who was six inches taller and 50 pounds heavier than she. She verbally went through him like a flame-throwing tank. Such incidents raise issues for a personality theory which will handle the integra-tion of such divergent components of self, for social theory which will provide conceptions to describe the settings when such behavior is "necessary," and conceptions to understand the degree to which the latter is a norm or a rationalization within the faculty group. These issues also provide a starting point for involved discussions of teaching both in the school faculty lounge and in the university classroom.

The Interpretive Asides

As we observed we found that aspects of our foreshadowed problems kept arising as insights, guesses, and hunches. We tried to jot these, in parentheses, into the notes. These turned out to be invaluable points of departure, key concepts which later were to carry a heavy burden in the analysis. For instance, we have puzzled for some time over aspects of teacher directiveness and indirectiveness—the Anderson, Withall, and Flanders tradition—and we had been asking ourselves, "How does this fit in the Washington School?" Our notes contained an episode surrounding Geoffrey's setting up a recess coffee table for teachers. Quoting from the notes:

> Billy and Edwin bring in a table.... Geoffrey tells Sandy to move assignment board sometime during the day—to accommodate the coffee table. Looks for a coffee monitor...No volunteers. Geoffrey comments: "Don't everyone volunteer at once." Oliver suggests that Mr. Geoffrey volunteer. Geoffrey goes along moving materials. He *does not* push, ask, or plead. (LMS—This seems very significant. Pick up later in the notes as to how it works out. This is part of his aloofness, powerfulness, or autonomy.)

Out of this came such hypotheses as: Within a traditional self-contained classroom, teachers who solicit volunteers rather than direct pupils in those situations outside the commonly accepted province of the teacher's role *qua* instructor are held in higher esteem than those who do not. The interpretive aside in the note helped us in our later conceptualizing the complex phenomena in teacher-pupil interaction. Most students find similar challenges.

Vivid and Concrete Data

One of the most fascinating aspects of the methodology has been the vividness and concreteness of the raw data. As one moves into problems at this level, beneath the glittering abstractions and the prescriptive generalizations so characteristic of education and psychology, we have a strong emotional reaction of being involved with a kind of "bed rock reality." While that may be true or false, the data have a hard quality which we have found most engaging and productive as we have tried to build back to more abstract formulations. The consistent attempt to stay away from prescriptive generalizations and to talk about antecedents and consequences has been aided by the flow of the data, by the processes, and by the complexities of the problems as we have looked at the concreteness of this part of the world. For instance, during an early morning reading lesson on word analysis, the observer made the following notes:

> Geoffrey offers the general principle: syllabicate to help us read words we know in our speaking. Geoffrey presents "unmanliness." Asks Joe K. about the word; he's stuck. Has Harry analyze it into syllables, then has Joe K. pronounce it. He comes very close. Then enters into "manly" to get "like a man" and "un" as not. Through most of this Harry is most helpful. He knows root and prefix as conceptual labels. (LMS—The trick here, in part, is using the able kids to start discussions and to use on rough and difficult points. As the others can respond (easier points, continuity, etc.) you call on them. If the lesson has appropriate difficulty level, you have got to tax the average student and gradually extend him to be differentiated and shaped. The responses of able kids serve as prompts to less able; start the processes and permit reinforcement. This is pertinent to group structure, its development and its use.) (10/21)

In short, grappling with the concrete has seemed most provocative, for it gives the general issues a flint-like response. One cannot conceptually slip and slide about so easily when one translates into who said what to whom, in a particular sequence, and in a known context. Trainees find this to be exciting when it is their images, ideas, and conceptualizations which are up for analysis.

In short, the problem of concrete perceptual images about classroom systems—teachers, pupils, activities, interactions—receives strong emphasis in this kind of training task. Further, the student is impressed immediately with theoretical problems, that is, the need for a clear, consistent, fruitful language to utilize in analyzing his own data and in communicating with his fellows who have not observed the same episodes. Putting the responsibility upon the student to construct his own models, congruent with his data and his reading, seems appropriate also in the climate of our undergraduate times in which high student involvement is the *sine qua non* of instruction.

THE EDUCATIONAL PSYCHOLOGICAL LABORATORY: ELABORATING IMAGES AND IDEAS

In moving from initial images and ideas of the classroom as a social system to further refine and extend them we have aspirations toward setting up an Educational Psychology Laboratory; since time and financing have not enabled us to institute this aspect, our comments in this section will be brief and speculative. The core of the idea is to make a second part of the educational psychology and principles of teaching block of work into an experimental laboratory experience.[11] Social psychology has moved in

---

[11] In contrast to the naturalistic laboratory of the ongoing classroom described in the microethnography discussion.

recent years to more and more sophistication in laboratory experimentation. Aspects of this work can be introduced into the teacher training program. To this point we have utilized materials in classroom exercises but not to the desired point of actual experimentation by the students.

Ideally, as concepts and hypotheses are generated from the micro-ethnography activities, the trainees would extend their knowledge by trying to examine their positions in laboratory experiments and to emulate the mode of inquiry of the laboratory psychologist. For instance, considerable interest among students exists in teacher styles and classroom discussions. As class experiments we have replicated a number of N.R.F. Maier's multiple role playing experiments (Maier and Solem, 1956; Maier, Solem and Maier, 1957) in which techniques for handling minority opinions, developmental discussions, and creative solutions were central issues.[12] Involving students in designing and carrying out simple experiments as part of their training program will hopefully make some of their reading less an exercise of verbalisms and more a meaningful way of extending images and ideas about classroom social systems.[13]

SIMULATION OF CLASSROOMS

Another major technique which we see as important in developing an understanding of classroom processes with teacher trainees is through complex simulation activities. Our particular intent, and once again we have not implemented our approach, accents the decision-making skills of the teacher trainee. The format seems exceedingly important for developing sophistication in making the student aware of multiple consequences of action and in moving many issues from the "latent and unanticipated" category to that of manifest and manageable.

Our interest in this part of the training sequence also grows out of the data which we have accumulated in our research. For instance, our long sojourn at the Washington School left us with a richness of specific detail and a breadth of events in the classroom, the school, and the district. From these we could build real problems with real and reasonable alternatives and consequences which would prove difficult and interesting to the most sophisticated trainees. Further, it would permit the sequencing and development of alternative structures which would extend over the several months of the semester. For instance, the attention that is paid to careful records would have implications for the grading one does, for the occasional visits by central office supervisors, and for interviews with hostile

12 Similarly, Luchins' (1957) work on first impressions has been a provocative class experiment for another set of issues.

13 The fruitfulness of this in discussion of children's learning and intellectual development seems even more impressive.

parents. Each of these consequences would intertwine with the social roles pupils play in the class, the classroom authority structure, control, the faculty social structure and one's position in it, and ultimately the learning, promotion, and retention of individual children.

The momentary resolutions but ultimate cul-de-sacs, the momentary unpleasantness but long-term resolutions, etc. seemingly could be programmed so well that a wiser and more rational teacher could be developed in the preservice period. As one teacher expressed it, these are the kinds of things one usually finds out painfully by experience. With the advances being made in computer technology the exercises could well be instrumented in the form of computer assisted instruction. The implementation problems are those of time, money and technical knowledge, all of which can be resolved.

In summary, the technique (simulation) relates to a fundamental conception (decision-making) in the social system model. At the same time, it has a practical cast to it. This blending of theory and specific training tasks toward relevant goals seems to be a much needed integration in conceptualizations of teacher training programs.

MICROTEACHING: SKILLS BASED UPON CONFIDENCE AND DECISIONS

The reports emanating from the Stanford University program on microteaching suggest that the technique of building microexperiences into teaching is quite fruitful (Allen and Ryan, 1969). Micro in this sense means limited purposes, limited time, and limited class size. I have had no personal experience with the technique, but find it theoretically very compatible with our analysis of teacher decision-making, with the issues of confidence and anxiety in apprentices, and with the conception of skill components in teaching.

The major weakness in the approach at this point seems to lie in the kinds of skills upon which the microlessons focus. From our analyses (Smith and Geoffrey, 1968; Smith and Keith, 1971; Smith and Brock, 1970; Connor and Smith, 1967) we think we have developed ideas susceptible to microteaching, but which have higher potency as variables within the classroom as a social system. We are in the process of trying to build situations involving ringmastership (a dimension of teacher behavior reflecting an ability to handle multiple and simultaneous strands of interaction); continuity (a dimension of activity and interaction referring to connections with a past and a future); drama (a dimension of teacher behavior characterized by the unexpected, the theatrical); personalized interaction (a dyadic interaction between the teacher and one pupil); and so forth.

Further, a possible sequencing of tasks might involve first the intensive microethnography experience. Each trainee then selects from his conceptual analysis an important teaching skill which he then develops into a micro-teaching lesson. The usual possibilities of video taping, discussion with instructors and classmates, and reteaching would be integrated. If the idea remains important and the trainee is so inclined, further exploration could be made in the experimental educational psychology laboratory. Or, the trainee could move into specially selected sequences of the total battery of microteaching problems on file in the training program library. Obvious advantages occur in furthering general objectives of inquiry about teaching, images of the teaching process and skill and confidence in teaching. Opening several options seems a most important aspect of dealing with the varying interests and abilities of the trainees. Again, we have not yet tried to implement such a program; at the speculative stage it seems very intriguing.

A MODIFIED "TWO BY TWO" APPRENTICESHIP

As our analysis has progressed we have been concerned with a social system stance in teaching and with a total training program which develops, at least hypothetically, the teacher into the kind of person to carry out successfully the task demanded. In recent years, as on many occasions in the past, these issues are not only in debate among teachers, teacher educators and members of the more general establishment, but also within the general public.

It has long been recognized, in the field of teacher education, that the practice teaching or clinical aspect is crucial. In fact, historically, the methods of teaching, observation and demonstration, and practice in teaching have been the most dominant elements of the preparation for teaching. The practice in teaching has occurred under a number of formats known variously as practice teaching, apprentice teaching, and the internship. In all instances the emphasis appears to be on "practice" in "realistic" situations with increasing responsibility being given to the student for the conduct of teaching. The nature of the organizational pattern for "practice in teaching" does not necessarily tell us what is, or ought to be, the major focus of the experience. The format does not tell us what is to be learned; what kind of a teacher we wish to develop through time; what outcomes are to be desired concerning continued growth in teaching; what conceptions of teaching behavior and resulting pupil behavior are deemed to be desirable as a consequence of engaging in the deliberate education of the young. An answer to these latter queries may help us to give more nearly effective structure to the practice experience; it may aid us in defining the kinds of activities we wish practice teachers to engage in; and it may aid us in better defining the roles of the multiple persons (and the interrelationship of roles) as they converge in the total educative process for pupils, student teachers, cooperating teachers, administrators, and college personnel concerned with both the clinical and theoretical aspects of the education of teachers and pupils in the schools.

The many advantages and limitations of the "two by two" apprenticeship have been recounted in Connor and Smith (1967). At this point, we will be concerned with only one aspect, the "nine trials" phenomenon. The reader will recall that the apprentices spent an intensive two weeks teaching each of nine grade levels (K-8) during his semester's practicum. One of the latent aspects of the "two by two" program is the ability to practice skills and apply generalizations since the apprentice has nine trials at new groups of children. In that analysis, one focus was on the problems of learning elements of discipline, especially setting up an authority structure. As we reflected on the experience of one of our apprentices, Greg Jennings, the field notes conveyed it this way:

> One of the morning-after residual impressions I have of Greg Jennings centers on the phenomenon of "discipline." He seemed to be saying to me...that the apprentice's problem was to work out a means whereby when he gave a verbal order, command, suggestion, or as he or a teacher would probably put it, a simple direction, the pupils would follow it with a high degree of probability. Initially he seemed to operate on the assumption that if the kids liked him they would follow these orders. In the kindergarten he made it a point of individually getting to know, and be friendly with the kids. This didn't work. His move toward the collectivity and toward firmness was his attempt to set up the intervening condition that would establish the authority structure....
>
> An additional aspect of the "two by two" program is the experience that it provides not only as we were pointing out yesterday, with new groups to start on when you have difficulty with past groups, but it also provides an attempt to practice any growing generalizations and points of view such as this one. In effect, the apprentices get nine shots at trying to establish an authority structure. This is a tremendous amount of experience, literally nine year's worth, in contrast to the experience of apprentices from other programs. The potential kicker in this is that the "two by two" may force the individual, because of the brevity of the period of time the system operates, into very directive techniques which then will inhibit certain kinds of academic learning, particularly intellectual skills such as critical and creative thinking, and potentially some of the affective goals of self-discipline and group responsibility and consequently have some very negative long-run consequences. (9/23)

While we have illustrated the "2 × 2" program with data related to establishing an authority structure, a variety of other aspects grew out of our analysis. Briefly, as shown in Figure 6-2, we would indicate some of those points which integrate with the more general arguments in the present paper.

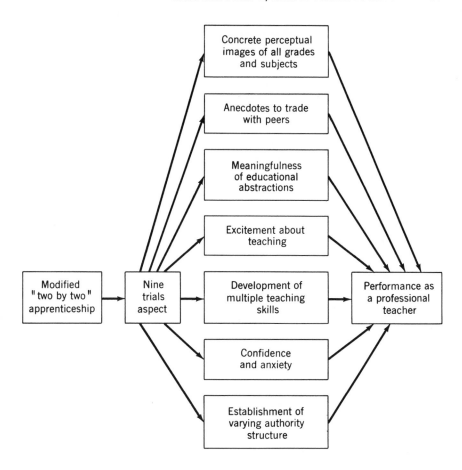

FIGURE 6-2 Aspects of the Modified "Two by Two" Apprenticeship.

The possibilities of blending this kind of student teaching format with the more typical extended exposure to one teacher and one group of children have not been explored. Similarly, the phasing of ethnographic analysis and microteaching with this kind of student teaching has not been carried out. Such concepts are open to exciting verifying experiments across programs and institutions. Finally, a synthesis with the internship type program, which is in some vogue in professional education today, has not been carried out.

CONCLUSION

The preservice program regarding classroom social systems has been based on the conceptual elements within this theoretical domain and the special characteristics which seem to typify many inexperienced teacher trainees. In the usual instructional sequences of teacher training many of the tasks fall within the educational psychology and principles of teaching block of courses. That this should remain the format is not a necessary assumption in the present analysis. In fact, our growing belief is that the conservative forces of established professional disciplines, course definitions and descriptions, and hallowed textbooks represent major entrenched special interests with which the broader reformulation of teacher training must deal.

Inservice Teacher Training

Neither time nor space permit an extended essay on problems of inservice teacher training in the social system area. However, we will touch briefly upon several items that have grown out of our experience at Washington University. Many of these have been made concrete in the form of a graduate course, "The Classroom as a Social System," taught by the author for about ten years.

The students have been masters and doctoral students in a variety of programs: educational psychology, elementary education, secondary education, and administration. The intellectual content of the course was developed along two interweaving strands—those of social psychology, and educational theory and research. The social psychological ideas were carried in part by two texts, Cartwright and Zander's *Group Dynamics* and Homans' *The Human Group*. These materials gave emphasis to the experimental verification tradition and to the model building field tradition. The educational ideas were developed out of general research in educational psychology and, more specifically, *The Complexities of an Urban Classroom*. In sum, the several sources provided a theoretical context to which we could continually refer.

The Homans' book provided the additional thrust of showing the teachers how to think in case study terms and how to move from the descriptive to the conceptual levels. This served as background for the major "applied" aspect of the course, the description and analysis of one's own class. To implement these aspects we devised a series of probes demanding that the teachers examine their own teaching and the setting in which the teaching occurred. Problem 1, "The environment of the classroom" presents one such problem. This exercise carries the students into the heart of the "external system" concept and makes relevant and meaningful a host of illustrative material from the text (factories, boys' gangs, South Sea island life). It permits development of concepts of bureaucracy, social norms of the faculty, reference groups, and so forth.

Problem 1   The Environment of the Classroom.

The unique dynamics and structure of a particular group are, in part, a function of the particular environment in which it resides. This is a basic

principle which is often ignored by parents, teachers, and supervisory personnel. Homans (1950) uses the concept external system to help organize observations relevant to the principle. I would like you to develop an essay
indicating your observations of the applications of this principle in your own
setting. While there are many ways in which responses to this assignment may
be organized, and I would hope you would respond as inventively and originally
as possible, please attend to these points as a minimum: 1) the physical
layout of the school building, 2) general system-wide school policy, 3) the
principal of your school, 4) the group of teachers in your building, especially
those who teach the same grade level as you and those immediately below
and above you, and 5) the student body of the school.

Illustrative of the attempt to blend our own research into teaching are
the probes in Problems 2 and 3. Earlier in this chapter we described issues
from Smith and Geoffrey (1968) regarding the establishment of the authority structure and the initiation of the activity structure. In the essays
stimulated by "The first few days" we have very successfully brought forth
an array of alternative approaches which can be analyzed, evaluated and
synthesized. Parenthetically, it should be mentioned that one agreement
between the course instructor and the experienced teachers in the class is
that the content of the essays are confidential. The instructor does not raise
any specific point or illustration in class discussion until it has been introduced first by the individual class member who reported it.[14] This understanding is made in the context of reporting what "teaching's really like"
rather than what some text or ideology says teaching ought to be. We have
had no difficulty in maintaining such confidences nor in engendering productive class discussion. Most students find their peers accepting and respectful
of diverse positions and interested in the "whys and wherefores" of these
approaches.

The probe in Problem 2 asks the student to discuss his views on the
importance of the first few days of school. In addition to illustrating our
general concern for "initiation of the activity" structure, the assignment
implicitly illustrates our basic intellectual concern for the decision-making
concept within the social system stance. The essay also enables us to see
the activity structure as a process with changes over time.

Problem 2   The First Few Days.

Many teachers have commented to me, "The first few days of school are
the most important, you've got to get off on the right foot." The explicit
meaning attached to the proposition is generally not clear in the educational

---

14 While it has not been stressed in this essay, the problems of anonymity and
the keeping of confidence in field work, such as participant observation or microethnography of the classroom, are very important, and not to be underestimated nor
ignored.

and psychological literature. Essentially, the intent of this paper is an analysis of what you think about this statement. I would like you to tell me in as practical and as specific a manner as possible how you stand on this issue. While you may organize your paper in any fashion you desire, I would like for you to comment at some point on 1) the goals you have for the first few days or weeks of school; 2) the plans you have for reaching the goals; 3) anything about the school where you teach or the children you teach which are special or important to keep in mind as you set your goals and plans; 4) the specific aspects of the class which you keep alert to during this time which serve as cues for modifying plans or goals.

The issue in Problem 3 concerns a phenomenon of the authority structure in which some teachers establish an informal contract with certain students, agreeing not to demand anything of each other nor to bother each other.[15]

Problem 3   The Contract.

Recently, in the course of observing several classrooms, I have noted that some teachers have established an informal contract with certain pupils. "If you don't bother me or the class, I won't bother you," describes the relationship. Essentially, the pupil attends class and does little or none of the assigned work; the teacher does not call on him nor get involved with him in any extended way. I am interested in your experience regarding such a relationship. Have you ever been involved in such a "contract" or have you known teachers in such a relationship? What consequences do you see for the pupil and the classroom as a unit? I would like you to describe in as much detail as possible such a phenomenon.

Our final illustration, Problem 4, the teacher's concept of power, is an attempt to reach several goals in helping teachers inquire about social systems. First, the essay stresses more careful definitions and the move toward more rigorous propositions. Zetterberg (1965) has been our model here. Second, the essay enabled us to move into a provocative discussion of the quite technical French and Ravens bases of power paper in Cartwright and Zander. Third, the focus is upon the teacher as an agent in the system utilizing concepts which have analytical power in molding the system.

Problem 4   The Teacher's Concept of Power.

Consider the following concepts and their definitions: 1) Psychological change is the alteration of an individual's behavior, opinions, goals, values, etc., or the alteration in the elements of a group or social system. 2) Influence is the process by which an individual or group brings about the change in another individual or group. 3) Power is the potential ability of one individual or group to influence another.

[15] Smith and Geoffrey (1968, pp. 151–53).

In the teacher-pupil relationship these concepts might be applied in this manner. Frequently teachers engage in altering—in directions they see as desirable—pupil cognitive behavior and pupil social behavior. To carry out such influence attempts requires power. Although I do not have data, it seems to me that a reasonable case can be made for these propositions: 1) Teachers vary in the amount of power they possess. 2) Teachers differ in their conceptions of the bases or sources of their power. 3) Teachers utilize different strategies to augment or increase their social power.

I would like you to write an essay making reference to 1) the relevance of the concept of power in teacher-pupil relationships; 2) your conception of your power as a teacher; 3) your conception of the sources of this power; 4) the strategies you have found successful and unsuccessful in increasing power in your particular situation(s) past or present; 5) other aspects of the problem which seem relevant to you.

In conclusion, most of the students (experienced teachers) find the inquiry emphasis stimulating. Most find the readings novel and highly interesting. The problems we pose for analysis of their own situations and experience are very time consuming as they become entranced with making the nuances clear and understandable. The several problems presented here are just a sample of several dozen on file from which we can select depending on the particular group and the kind of focus which grows out of the discussion. Such a reservoir permits capitalizing on the momentary issues and the uniqueness of any one group of students and prevents the instructor or class from getting bored with a routine set of exercises.[16]

While the experience seems to have been very successful in terms of student interest, conceptual development, and analytical skills (that is, helping teachers inquire into social system dimensions of education), the major limitation lies in advanced skill training. For instance, we have not had a "teaching hospital" (Knowles, 1966; Bolster, 1967) type of facility with children and technical equipment (such as video recording) available. To be able to move from some of the new concepts to their utilization in day-to-day activities would add a powerful increment to the experience.

Also, and at a more general level in teacher training, we have not invented a mechanism to maintain contact longer than one semester with the experienced teachers. The advantages of direct extended contact into new groups of children and new kinds of problems seems very important. As illustrations, both Geoffrey and Brock, with whom I've collaborated intensively over several years, were met originally in class. The benefits seem mutual and very great in both instances. A means of maintaining a contact similar in kind if not in intensity with larger numbers of students

[16] It should be noted that building and teaching this course has been the author's most exciting teaching experience. The reader can discount the hyperbole and encomium.

would seem very desirable. The usual university courses and degree programs have minimal flexibility in this regard.

General Conclusions[17]

Various teacher educators have made comments, proposals and critiques relevant to some of the ideas presented in our analysis. For instance, in his monograph, *The Professional Education of Teachers,* Combs (1965) makes a telling comment as he criticizes the "competency" approach to developing a teacher education program. He states:

> . . .it is a fallacy to assume that the method of the experts either can or should be taught directly to beginners. It is seldom that we can determine what should be done for the beginner by examining what the expert does well. (pp. 4–5)

In general, the implications of this specific point seem far-reaching and underestimated in teacher education. In his comment regarding the "static affair" of teaching, Schaefer (1967) offers a different critique in the consideration of the competencies approach and suggests the inquiry model in the context of the long-range development of the professional teacher.

> If teaching is an essentially static affair, the various pedagogical skills required are best learned by apprenticeship under a master teacher. A particular preparing institution, if it wished to cater even further to the vocational motivations of its students, might also provide an orientation to the job through a historical or sociological look at the school as a social institution, a "practical" review of human development and of learning principles, and a repertoire of techniques and procedures proved useful by experience.
>
> If, on the other hand, preservice teacher education is intended to provide a foundation for career-long development as an inquiring scholar-teacher, initial training must emphasize ways of knowing. There must be less concern for job information already discovered and far more interest in the strategies for acquiring new knowledge. Philosophy of education would include epistemology and an introduction to the philosophy of science. Studies in psychology might furnish a working knowledge of research methodology and of experimental design, observational categories for observing and recording the behavior of children, and an introduction to the complex problems of measurement and evaluation. Courses in educational sociology would develop analytical tools for understanding student sub-cultures and the characteristics of pupils in a particular school. Courses in methods of teaching would eschew talk about techniques and procedures—laboratory experience and apprenticeships would be relied upon to develop these skills—and would focus upon the critical analysis of teaching behavior and a beginning approach to the logic of pedagogical strategies. In short, teacher education must seek to prepare teachers not as complete and polished practitioners but as beginning professionals

[17] These conclusions draw heavily upon Connor and Smith (1967), especially pages 278–82.

who possess the trained capacity and the attitudes requisite to lifelong learning. (pp. 69–70)

Such thoughts as the above, our developing research, and our experience in teacher education have led us toward a process analysis—teacher training with a time dimension. This might be phrased as "phases and emphases in teacher training."

If a teaching career is spread over a time line and units struck off at the prepracticum period, the apprenticeship, the first year of teaching, the probationary period, and finally the long span of the professional career, it is possible to view teacher training in a larger context. If we trace across this time line half a dozen categories of events important to teaching, perhaps we can lay the groundwork for the richer analysis of teaching. In Figure 6-3, the abscissa is the time line focusing on the college and career years. The ordinate represents the amount of emphasis, roughly gauged from low to high, of six threads within teacher training. The six threads are: (1) general liberal arts education and academic specialization; (2) concrete images of teaching; (3) core interpersonal survival skills; (4) idiosyncratic style of teaching; (5) analysis, conceptualization, and inquiry about teaching; and (6) nonclassroom roles in teaching.

In effect, we are placing our social system concerns into two larger contexts. First, there are the additional substantive strands important in a general conception of teaching. Second, we are trying to face the reality that teaching is a career which encompasses a lifetime. Such contexts have been ignored too frequently and, as a consequence, have produced irrelevant if not impotent analyses.

More specifically, we have engaged in little discussion of the liberal arts and substantive knowledge, strand one in Figure 8, in this paper. However, our belief is that the high school and first years of college must be devoted heavily to such training. This emphasis in the first few years drops off sharply at the time of the apprenticeship and presumably remains low through the probationary period. Training for higher degrees, general maturation, travel, and experience should see it rise again and presumably level off during the long years of the professional career. The varied possibilities in extending the knowledge and intellectual competencies of teachers are under development in local inservice programs and in federally financed institutes. The latent functions and dysfunctions seem ripe for analysis.

We have made a strong point regarding the development of concrete perceptual images during the apprenticeship, strand two in Figure 6-3. Presumably this begins before the apprenticeship, reaches a maximum in the practicum and the first year or two of teaching, and drops off over

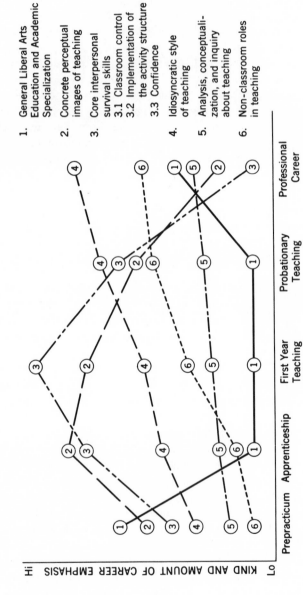

1. General Liberal Arts Education and Academic Specialization
2. Concrete perceptual images of teaching
3. Core interpersonal survival skills
   3.1 Classroom control
   3.2 Implementation of the activity structure
   3.3 Confidence
4. Idiosyncratic style of teaching
5. Analysis, conceptualization, and inquiry about teaching
6. Non-classroom roles in teaching

KIND AND AMOUNT OF CAREER EMPHASIS

Hi

Lo

Prepracticum   Apprenticeship   First Year Teaching   Probationary Teaching   Professional Career

T_1 T_2 T_3 T_4 T_5

FIGURE 6-3 A Preliminary Model of Phases and Emphases in Developing a Professional Teacher

time. In our research the apprentices kept reporting the mundane and the significant events which they had not been privy to before. The perceptions were of children and their families, teachers and classrooms, principals and school organizations. They were many and varied.

A broad category of "core interpersonal survival skills," strand three, seems a major component of the apprenticeship: less important in the prior years, most important in the first year of teaching and hypothetically solved in the probationary period, and of little importance in terms of new learning over the long career period. We analyzed these in great detail earlier and we accented such items as classroom control (the authority structure), implementing the activity structure (initiating and maintaining the instructional program) and the development of confidence in playing the teaching role. These are particularly relevant to the classroom as a social system.

The idiosyncratic styles of teaching, which we have not emphasized explicitly but which we hope are implicit throughout this paper, would be in gradual development from the first experiences in teaching and should continue to blossom long into one's career as new emphases in curriculum, in instructional processes, and in the psychological and social foundations arise on the broader scene and as one builds them into or reformulates one's practices. In a fundamental sense the artistry of teaching should be a major focus and satisfaction in the profession of teaching. In our research we obviously do not have direct data on this from our dozen apprentices. More indirectly, the cooperating teachers seemed quite varied in this regard, although our data are not good in that we did not observe them teach to any great extent. Further examination of idiosyncracy as a means and as an objective in a psychology of teaching seems very important.

The analysis and conceptualization of teaching stressed throughout this paper was not accented by the apprentices in our research. The scholar-teacher conception, for good or ill, seemed foreign to many of the people and settings in which our apprentices interacted. The schools seemed to have too many children, too many immediate problems, and too little time for reflection about teaching or curricular innovations. Our apprentices were not inclined in this direction. They defined the task of the semester to get as much practical experience in teaching—presenting lessons—as possible so that they would be prepared for Thursday, and eventually for next year. The degree to which it is possible—or desirable—to alter the system is, at this point, a matter of speculation, debate, and exhortation. Little data exist. Still less data are available when juxtaposed against the value statements.

Finally, strand six, the nonclassroom roles in teaching—conferring with parents, working on curriculum committees, playing a role in school and educational organizations—are parts of the career which become important, presumably only as one is a practicing professional. We have suggested that such roles are important in teaching and that social system concepts such as environment, reference groups, external system, normative structure, and teacher decision-making aid in the theoretical analysis of those day-to-day problems.

The manifest substance of this chapter has been the interrelationship of classroom social systems and teacher education. The latent thesis is that each is a complex, fascinating, and perhaps even tractable set of issues. An unanalyzed assumption is that the field of professional education can have a unity, integrity and commonality for practitioners, researchers, and theorists. The implicit value stance is that involvement in professional education in varying ways and at varying levels can be a rich and meaningful experience.

References

1. ALLEN, D. W., and K. RYAN, *Micro-teaching.* Reading, Mass.: Addison-Wesley, 1969.
2. BECKER, H., et al., *Boys in White.* Chicago: University of Chicago Press, 1961.
3. BOLSTER, A. S., JR., Review of *The Teaching Hospital. Harvard Educational Review,* 1967, 37, 273–81.
4. BROSS, I. D., *Design for Decision.* New York: Macmillan, 1953.
5. CARTWRIGHT, D., and A. ZANDER eds., *Group Dynamics.* (2nd ed.). New York: Harper and Row, 1960.
6. COMBS, A. W., *The Professional Education of Teachers.* Boston: Allyn and Bacon, 1965.
7. CONNOR, W. H., and L. M. SMITH, *Analysis of Patterns of Student Teaching.* Washington, D.C.: U.S. Office of Education, Bureau of Research, Final Report 5–8204, 1967.
8. DEWEY, J., *Moral Principles in Education.* Boston: Houghton Mifflin, 1909.
9. FRIEDENBERG, E. Z., *Coming of Age in America.* New York: Random House, 1965.
10. GOULDNER, A. W., Theoretical requirements of the applied social sciences. In W. BENNIS, et al., eds., *The Planning of Change.* New York: Holt, Rinehart and Winston, 1961.
11. HOMANS, G. C., *The Human Group.* New York: Harcourt, Brace Jovanovich, 1950.
12. JACKSON, P., *Life in Classrooms.* New York: Holt, Rinehart and Winston, 1968.
13. KNOWLES, J. H. (Ed.), *The Teaching Hospital: Evolution and Contemporary Issues.* Cambridge, Mass.: Harvard University Press, 1966.
14. KOUNIN, J. S., *Discipline and Group Management in Classrooms.* New York: Holt, Rinehart and Winston, 1970.
15. KOUNIN, J. S., and P. V. GUMP, The ripple effect in discipline. *Elementary School Journal,* 1958, 158–62.

16. LUCHINS, A. S., Experimental attempts to minimize the impact of first impressions. In C. I. Hovland, et al., eds., *Order of Presentation in Persuasion.* New Haven: Yale University Press, 1957.

17. MAIER, N. R. F., and A. R. SOLEM, The contribution of discussion leader to the quality of group thinking: The effective use of minority opinions. *Human Relations,* 1952, 5, 277–88.

18. MAIER, N. R. F., A. R. SOLEM, and A. MAIER, *Supervisory and Executive Development.* New York: Wiley, 1957.

19. MALINOWSKI, B., *Argonauts of the Western Pacific.* New York: Dutton, 1922.

20. MERTON, R. K., *Social Theory and Social Structure* (Rev. ed.). New York: Free Press, 1957.

21. OJEMANN, R. H., The human relations program at S. U. I. *Personnel and Guidance Journal,* 1958, 37, 199–206.

22. OLIVER, D. W., and J. P. SHAVER, *Teaching Public Issues in the High School.* Boston: Houghton Mifflin, 1966.

23. REDL, F., and D. WINEMAN, *The Aggressive Child.* New York: Free Press, 1957.

24. SCHAEFER, R. J., *The School as a Center of Inquiry.* New York: Harper and Row, 1967.

25. SHAPLIN, J. T., and A. G. POWELL, A comparison of internship programs. *Journal of Teacher Education,* 1964.

26. SIMON, H., *Administrative Behavior* (2nd ed.). New York: Macmillan, 1961.

27. SMITH, L. M., Classroom social systems and pupil personality. *Psychology in the Schools,* 1964, 1, 118–29.

28. SMITH, L. M., *Group Processes in Elementary and Secondary Schools.* Washington, D.C.: National Education Association, 1959.

29. SMITH, L. M., The microethnography of the classroom. *Psychology in the Schools,* 1967, 4, 216–21.

30. SMITH, L. M., and J. A. M. BROCK, *"Go, Bug, Go!": Methodological Issues in Classroom Observational Research.* Occasional Paper Series No. 5. St. Ann, Mo.: CEMREL, 1970.

31. SMITH, L. M., and J. A. M. BROCK, *Teacher Plans and Classroom Interaction.* St. Ann, Mo.: CEMREL (in process).

32. SMITH, L. M. and W. GEOFFREY, *The Complexities of an Urban Classroom.* New York: Holt, Rinehart and Winston, 1968.

33. SMITH, L. M. and B. B. HUDGINS, *Educational Psychology.* New York: Knopf, 1964.

34. SMITH, L. M., and P. M. KEITH, *Anatomy of Educational Innovation.* New York: Wiley, 1971.

35. WHITE, R., and R. LIPPITT, Leader behavior and member reaction in three social climates. In D. Cartwright and A. Zander, eds., *Group Dynamics.* New York: Harper and Row, 1960.

36. ZETTERBERG, H. L., *On Theory and Verification in Sociology* (3rd ed.). Totowa, N. J.: Bedminster Press, 1965.

7

Developmental and Contemporaneous Individual Differences and Their Role in Curriculum Decision Making and Teacher Training

EDMUND V. SULLIVAN

Professor Sullivan has searched for a structure to conceptualize psychology in terms which are operationally relevant to education. His search has been guided by two definitions of the operation of the teacher. One of these is that the teacher operates professionally by creating (or radiating) particular educational environments. These environments consist of interpersonal climates which can vary along several dimensions, notably those of structure, nature and type of feedback provided to the learner, and mutuality. In addition, environments consist of tasks or activities which vary by type, complexity, origin (learner or teacher), etc. The potential range of environments available to a teacher is very great, although in reality any human being is limited in his operational range. Sullivan's second definition is related to the first: If the teacher operates by generating a variety of environments, his central decision-making task consists of distinguishing among learners, and identifying their individual differences in terms which indicate what environments are optimal for their growth. In other words, if the growth of the individual is a product of his personality times his environment, then teaching becomes a process of matching environments to individuals.

164

The chief substance of Sullivan's paper is his exploration of ways to describe individual differences in educationally relevant terms—that is, in terms which enable the hypothetical specification of appropriate environments.

In the resulting excursion into psychology, Professor Sullivan takes us into research and theory on cognitive and affective development and functioning, and works out a conceptual framework which speaks directly to the educators' work as defined above.

His work is exciting; it generates highly operational ways of developing models to guide educators, greatly affecting the shape of the interactive teaching component of the teacher innovators program described in Chapter 1. Now, however, his work provides us with a conceptual framework which can be used to structure the teaching of psychology to teachers in terms that have relevance for action. For many years educational psychologists have tried to help teachers to "see" individual differences. What has been difficult is to help them "see" what to do about individual differences. Sullivan has gone far toward a solution to this problem.

In addition, he has considered the very serious questions in educational planning: What are the human limitations in providing optimal environments for groups of different children? Are the needed environments for any group likely to be more than one teacher can provide? In our emphasis on the classroom and the teacher we have avoided this question much too long, assuming that the teacher, working alone, could do the job. Sullivan's analysis suggests that we may have asked too much of the teacher; his work points the way to a better definition of teaching and ways to effect teacher improvement.

Psychologists have historically focused on the differences among people in distinct ways. Two of these broad categories or dimensions of individual differences will be discussed in this chapter and their educational relevance explored. Developmental individual differences are differences among individuals that can be dimensionalized over age. In other words, they are differences that can be detected as the organism grows older. Contemporaneous individual differences, in contrast, are differences among individuals that can be dimensionalized within a specified age category. They are, therefore, differences that can be detected in people who are contemporaries as far as age is concerned. In many instances this distinction between developmental and contemporaneous differences disappears if the theorist does not consider age as an important dimension in his theory.

It is evident that there is no problem in demonstrating these types of individual differences. As every psychologist has seen for himself each time he puts his measuring instruments to a population, there are, inevitably, individual differences within that population. The practical educational question is, "What differences in the population should make a difference in teacher programming?" This inevitably takes us outside of the domain of descriptive psychology, since the question is a prescriptive moral one. In a democratic society, our moral prescriptions for certain types of educational outcomes should help us determine what types of individual differences should make a difference in teaching programs. I do not, by this, wish to sidestep the question but simply put it in its correct perspective. It must be kept in mind that developmental psychology is a *pure* as opposed to an *applied* science and its normative findings may yield a variety of educational prescriptions. Psychological research is a takeoff point or springboard for educational innovations (Hartup and Smothergill, 1967). It would be futile for educational practitioners to look for recipes in basic psychological research (Hartup and Smothergill, 1967). A word of caution is in order concerning the interpretation of psychological findings. In many instances, research shapes expectations about children, suggests teaching procedures, and assists in the selection of curriculum content (Hartup and Smothergill, 1967). However, this may actually serve as a binder upon the way teaching may be done, since there are probably many instances where research indicates strategies different from the ones that are initially thought appropriate. Thus, it could be argued, for example, in the case of Piaget's normative data, that stages are partial reflections of the present school practices and should not necessarily provide prescriptions for future educational planning.

Orientation of the Field of Psychology to Issues Involving Individual Differences

The history of the study of individual differences reveals two major orientations which have competed with one another during the first half of our century. The early mental testing movement proceeded under the basic assumption that individual differences were *genetically determined* and that development of these differences was predetermined (Hunt, 1961). Concomitant with a strong emphasis on genetic factors, there was a serious underplaying of the role of the environment in effecting the course of development. This view received support, in the area of child development, in the theorizing of Gesell and his followers (Gesell and Ilg, 1943). Gesell theorized that developmental sequences are relatively invariable in all areas of growth, evolve more or less spontaneously and inevitably, and show basic uniformities even in striking different cultural settings (Ausubel and Sullivan, 1970).

In the early twenties, this viewpoint of individual differences was directly challenged by the behaviorists (Watson, 1919). In brief, this school of thought treated the organism as a *tabula rasa* (i.e., blank slate), minimizing the contributions of genic endowment and of directional factors coming from within the individual and concomitantly emphasizing the preeminent role of the environment in determining the outcome of development (Ausubel and Sullivan, 1970). Individual differences from a behaviorist's viewpoint occurred because of differences in the environment rather than genic endowment.

The disparity between these competing orientations prevailed in general until the mid 1950s, when a general convergence of these viewpoints led to an articulation of an *interactionist* approach to *individual differences* which is now the prevailing orientation in the school setting. This approach prescribes *differential* training environments for individuals with different personality, motivational, and cognitive traits. Because of its importance within the context of the present chapter, the interaction model will now be considered in more detail.

The Interactionist Model

The model to be set down has been advanced by many other authors (e.g., Cronbach, 1957, 1967; Gagné, 1967; Jensen, 1967, 1968; Hunt, 1966a; Thelen, 1967; etc.). In its simplest form, it states that an individual's responses are a result of the *interaction* between the environment and the predispositional state of the organism (see Figure 7-1). In the present discussion, the components of the model will be illustrated by educational examples because this will aid in understanding subsequent actions. As can be seen, the predispositions of the organism can be specified by focusing on either developmental or contemporaneous individual differences or on both. The environment can also be specified in a variety of ways, moving distally from the more impersonal environmental aspects of the school structure (e.g., open plan, nongraded) to the more proximal interpersonal environment that is radiated by teachers and peers. The assumption is that educational outcomes at the far right of the figure are resultants of this complex interaction of the organism with its environment. This model has led to a variety of educational statements centering around the tailoring of specific types of teaching environments to fit individual differences in pre-dispositional states of the students. Several examples are given here to illustrate the practical educational import of the model.

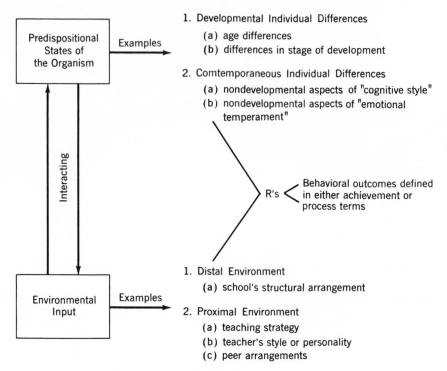

FIGURE 7-1 Interaction Model

1. High-anxious students function better under a *structured* teaching situation, whereas low-anxious students function better in an *unstructured* teaching situation.

2. Children in the Piagetian stage of *preoperational* thought learn more when the material is presented in *concrete* terms whereas children in the stage of *formal operations* profit best with more *abstract* presentations of the learning material.

3. Compulsive children do better than less compulsive children under structured conditions.

4. Children with low conceptual ability function better under a *controlling* teacher style, whereas children of high-conceptual level function better under a *reflective* teacher style.

For purposes of clarity of presentation, the interaction model will be treated separately for developmental and contemporaneous individual differences.

Developmental Individual Differences

The importance of age differences as an initial consideration for the recognition of individual differences appears to be a universal fact in all cultures. Age is a primary factor for treating growing individuals differently at different segments of the life cycle and is clearly seen in the different societal expectations that the culture imposes on an individual when considering his age. Thus, in such areas as social, moral, cognitive and emotional development, etc., the culture normally places different expectations in these areas if the individual is an infant as opposed to a middle-years child.

THE STAGE THEORY APPROACH TO DEVELOPMENTAL DIFFERENCES

The educational question to be asked in this context is, "When is a difference in age important enough to dictate a different type(s) of educational environment(s)?" Historically, the importance of the age variable has been recognized in education by the grouping of individuals according to their age level. From the point of view of developmental psychology, however, age is a rough first approximation for some interesting scientific observations. The fact is that in all cultures, as children grow older, they demonstrate different quantitative and qualitative changes in behavior. The attempts to move to more sophisticated explanations for these changes over age have led to the development of *stage* theoretical constructs. The notion of *stage* is not unique to developmental psychology and has a long scientific and philosophical history. In many instances (for example, in the work of Gesell and Ilg, 1943) its use in developmental psychology has simply been as a *substitute* term for age (Kessen, 1962). This type of usage, of course, gets us no further than the use of the term age. Although there are many stage theories that could be relevant for education (e.g., Harvey, Hunt and Schroder, 1961; Kohlberg, 1964), we will take as our prototype Piaget's stage theory of intellectual development.

The term *stage* is a structural concept which in some way attempts to account for the different quantitative and qualitative behavior changes with age. Piaget (1960) describes cognitive development in terms of stages; this means that changes in this area of development are due to qualitatively different structures (stages) which are changing as the individual grows older. In contrast to somatic and perceptual development, cognitive development seems more amenable to a stage theory formulation. The criteria for stages have been defined by Inhelder (1962) and are as follows: (1) each stage involves a period of formation (genesis) and a period of attainment. Attainment is characterized by the progressive organization of a composite structure of mental operations; (2) each structure constitutes at the same time, the attainment of one stage and the starting point of the next, of a new evolutionary process. Thus, structures can be said to be in a *stable* state and a *transitional* state at the same time; (3) the order of succession of stages is constant (e.g., the preoperational stage always occurs before the concrete operational stage). Ages of attainment can vary within certain limits as a function of factors of motivation, exercise, cultural milieu, etc.; and finally (4) the transition from an earlier to a later stage follows a law of implication analogous to the process of integration—preceding structures are subsumed and integrated into later structures. Thus, each stage is a necessity in the framework of the more advanced stages.

As pointed out previously, a stage is an attempt to assess the structural characteristics of the organism which appears to change in ontogenesis. Age becomes a superficial variable in this dispensation, with the underlying structural changes taking on greater prominence for explaining the changes which appear with age. We turn now to a description of Piaget's stage theory of intellectual development to make this discussion more concrete.

Basic Concepts

Piaget defines intelligence as a process of adaptation and organization. Adaptation is seen as an equilibration (equilibrium)[1] in the organism's interaction with its environment. Organization is a concept which is structural and this involves the constant organization, reorganization, and integration of what Piaget calls *schemas*. Schemas are defined as essentially repeatable, psychological units of intelligent action (Piaget, 1960). The best interpretation of this definition is that schemas are types of "programs" or "strategies" that the individual has at his disposal when interacting with the environment (Sullivan, 1967a).

Adaptation involves the two invariant processes of assimilation and accommodation. Assimilation is the incorporation of environment into present patterns of behavior (schemas). Accommodation is the change in the intellectual structures (schemas) which is necessary for the person to adjust to the demands made on him by the external environment. Equilibration involves a balance between the two invariant processes of assimilation and accommodation. When imbalance occurs, the organism is forced to change its schemas (i.e., strategies) in order to adjust to the demands of the external environment (adaptation). When the organism attempts to adapt to the environment with the already existing schemas, assimilation

---

[1] In a more recent article Piaget has expressed a preference for "equilibration" over "equilibrium" which he feels has a static connotation. For purposes of consistency, we will use the word equilibration (Piaget, 1965).

is said to be in operation. The postulation of *schemas* as mental processes by which past experiences are stored and made partial determinants of present behavior is significant, because it implies that the organism perceives the environment in terms of its existing organization. Disequilibration or imbalance exists when assimilation is unsuccessful. Accommodation occurs as a result of disequilibration and the alteration or emergence of new schemas ensues. Cognitive development is marked by a series of equilibration-disequilibration states. Stages in Piaget's theory may be considered as particular sets of strategies (schemas) which are in a relative state of equilibration at some point in the child's development. The development from one stage to the next in Piaget's framework involves a hierarchical organization of preceding and successive stages. Simply stated, the lower stage is coordinated and integrated into the next higher stage.

Stages

Piaget has delineated intellectual development as emerging through three main stages and also through various substages:[2]

SENSORIMOTOR STAGE. This first stage (birth to approximately two years) involves simple structures (schemas) starting with the inborn reflex mechanisms which increasingly become altered and complicated by the child's interaction with his environment. Characteristically, the sensorimotor period is exemplified in those behaviors which are preverbal and are not mediated by signs and symbols. At birth, the child mediates with the world with inborn reflex schemas and has no conception of object permanence. The fact that the child lacks object permanence is an indication that he lacks at birth *representative* symbolic activity. During this period, the child is concerned with objects as objects. Thus, when a toy is hidden from his view, he shows no searching movements, since he has no internal representation of the objective world (i.e., object schemas) when not directly perceiving it. Gradually, object permanence develops through repeated experience with the environment. As the child constructs object permanence through experience, primitive concepts of space, time, causality, and intentionality, which were not present at birth, develop and are incorporated into present patterns of behavior.

PREOPERATIONAL STAGE. This stage (2 to 7 years) is subdivided into the substages of preconceptual thought (2 to 4 years) and intuitive thought (4 to 7 years). In contrast to sensorimotor intelligence, adaptations during *preconceptual thought* appear to be mediated by structures (schemas) that

---

[2] There are several summaries of Piaget's theory of intellectual development available by Piaget and by others. Flavell's (1963) work is an excellent treatment for English-speaking readers.

indicate the presence of symbolic representative activity. This symbolic activity is seen in the child's "symbolic play", as well as in his use of language. With the appearance of language, the objective world is now symbolized by a thought process which can be retained by the mind (i.e., primitive symbolic structures). Despite the fact that the child's world is mediated by signs and symbols in the form of words and images, the child nevertheless operates in a world of preconcepts. In contrast to adult thought, which is characterized by inductive and deductive reasoning, the child's reasoning is transductive (preconceptual) since he makes no distinction between the general and the particular which is an essential part of time concepts. Transduction is a logic which moves from particular to particular instances. *Intuitive thought* appears at approximately age four and marks the half-way house between preconceptual thought and the more advanced stage of concrete operations. During this stage children begin intuitively to comprehend problems related to class-inclusion, certain conservation principles and principles of ordination and seriation. The stage is called *intuitive* because the child cannot at this time give rational articulate explanations for the correctness of his intuitions. The stage of concrete operations adds to correct problem solving, the rationale which is lacking during this stage.

OPERATIONAL THOUGHT. The operational thought stage (7 through 16 years) commences with what Piaget (1965) regards as the advent of rational activity in the child. Up to this time, the child demonstrates a logic (transductive) which is quite different from the adult members of his species (i.e., induction and deduction). The ability to reason inductively and deductively is due to the presence of thought structures (schemas) which are labelled operations. *Operations* are defined as internalized actions which can return to their starting point, and which can be integrated with other actions also possessing this feature of reversibility (Piaget, 1960). Stated simply, operations are "mental acts" which were formerly actions which had reversible properties.

Concrete operational thought (7 through 11 years) is characterized as "concrete" because the starting point of the operation is always some real system of objects and relations that the child perceives; that is, the operations are carried out on concrete objects. The emergence of concrete operations is often a sudden phenomenon in development. Piaget (1960) attributes these operations to a sudden thawing out of intuitive structures which were up to now more rigid despite their progressive articulation. Concrete operational structures (schemas) are analogous to particular operations which have been identified in mathematical and logical disciplines. Briefly, these structures are described as the logico-mathematical operations of reversibility, combinativity, associativity, identity, tautology, etc. (Piaget, 1960). Piaget identifies these operations in the verbal explanations that children give in solving class inclusion problems, seriation and ordination dilemmas, and conservation problems.

Formal operations (11 to 16 years) marks the completion of the child's emancipation from perception and action. In contrast to the concrete action-oriented thought of the child, the adolescent thinker goes beyond the present and forms theories about everything. This thought is considered "reflective" since the adolescent reasons on the basis of purely formal assumptions. He can consider hypotheses as either true or false and work out inferences which would follow if they were true.

The formal operational adolescent can make "logical experiments", not merely factual ones. Propositional logic enables the child to test the validity of statements by reference to their purely logical properties, rather than to their correspondence with the concrete empirical world. In other words, the adolescent is able to deal with the form of a proposition rather than with the content.

Contrasting formal operations with concrete operations, Piaget (1960) points out that concrete reasoning concerns action or reality of first degree groupings of operations (i.e., internalized actions that have become capable of combination or reversal), whereas formal reasoning consists of reflecting on operations or on their results and consequently effecting a second degree grouping of operations (i.e., operations on operations). At the stage of formal operational thought, the adolescent is able to manipulate the hypothetical intellectually, and systematically to evaluate a lengthy set of alternatives. He learns to deal with the logical relationships of identity (I), negation (N), reciprocity (R), and correlation (C), which permit him to deal with problems or proportionality, probability, permutations, and combinations. The operations just referred to are called the I.N.R.C. logical group.

In summary, Piaget's theory of intellectual development is an exciting panorama of unfolding abilities of the child seen in his ontogenetic evolution from infancy to adulthood. The first stage of sensorimotor development sees the first combination of perceptual experiences, the primitive development of object performance which is implicit in the advent of notions of time, space, and causality. Conceptual thought follows an elaborate evolution starting with the development of imitative language, concrete imagery, and symbolic play activity. The concrete operational child begins to represent the world of empirical reality more symbolically rather than through action representation as seen in the preoperational stages. The formal operational child extends the world of empirical reality by representing the world not only as it is, but also as it could be. Abstract logic and mathematics are now at the child's disposal in dealing with problems. A compendium of research, both within and outside the Piagetian tradition, reveals that as children increase in age, they tend to perceive the stimulus more in general, abstract, and categorical terms and less in tangible time-bound and particularized contexts (Ausubel and Sullivan, 1970). Furthermore, they demonstrate increasing ability to comprehend and manipulate abstract verbal symbols in relationships, and to employ abstract classificatory schemas; they are better able to understand ideational relationships without the benefit of direct, tangible experience, of concrete imagery, and of empirical exposure to numerous particular examples of a given concept or proposition (Ausubel and Sullivan, 1970). Finally, with increasing age, children tend to infer the properties of objects from their class membership, rather than from the direct experience of proximate, sensory data, and are more disposed to use remote and abstract rather than immediate and concrete criteria and attributes in classifying phenomena and to use abstract symbols rather than concrete imagery to represent emergent concepts (Ausubel and Sullivan, 1970).

ISSUES AND PROBLEMS IN APPLYING A STAGE THEORY TO EDUCATION

As indicated earlier, psychological theories do not provide convenient recipes for educational innovation. It is therefore imperative to generate a variety of strategies which can potentially issue from a psychological theory and then to decide on the ones which seem to have the most heuristic value for educational purposes. In this section I would like to explore possible avenues where stage theories like Piaget's have potential educational relevance. Some of these possibilities conflict with one another and the decision for resolution must finally be made by the educator.

First of all, I would like to attempt to show how Piaget's stage theory fits into traditional pedagogy. Particularly relating to the question of individual differences across ages, traditional educational approaches have used stage theories such as Piaget's to provide differential curriculum programs for different stages of development (Sullivan, 1967b). The model or paradigm in Piaget's case, can be seen in Figure 7-2, in which changes in stage demand differential teaching programs. The pedagogical outcome of this model, in terms of differential teaching strategies for changes in stages, can lead to a justification of our present emphasis on homogeneous age grouping and critical curriculum shifts (i.e., special nursery, elementary, and secondary school curriculums). Consideration of the arguments for these types of emphasis in curriculum planning will first be considered before antithetical arguments are presented.

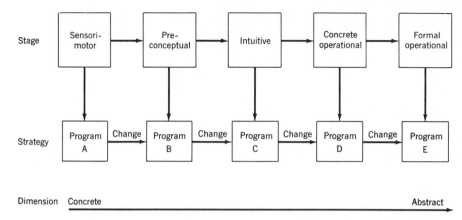

FIGURE 7-2 A Conceptual Model for Differential Teaching Strategies Relating to Piaget's Stages of Development.

Homogeneous Age Grouping

Grouping children at specific age levels is a rather recent curriculum innovation, occurring in American education at about the end of the nineteenth century. The talk about the "little red schoolhouse" where children of all ages were grouped together for the teaching-learning situation, seems strangely archaic to the present generation. Nevertheless, if we canvassed older immigrants in our own population we would find that the vast majority were educated in similar "red schoolhouses" in Europe.[3] The movement away from this type of setting was clearly designed in order to tailor the school situation to meet the obvious individual differences which occur across age spans.

Age grouping is now an institution, however, and there is something magical about grouping children according to their specific age levels. Implicitly, stage theories give a subtle justification for this type of grouping. If stages of development follow age norms, it is economical to group according to age, since there is a greater likelihood that children at the same age level will be functioning at the same stage of development. Most recently, Piaget's stage formulation has received a larger hearing because of its possible implications for the concept of *readiness* in the learning of cognitive tasks (Sullivan, 1967b). In this way, Piaget's stages of intellectual development are construed as demanding a certain age level breakdown as the roughest indicator of readiness for learning. The linkage of age with stage of development can be seen in the following quotation:

[3] Homogeneous age grouping occurred later in European than in American school systems.

Even if the child is fluent in his use of number words and can do rote counting, this does not allow us to conclude that he knows what he is talking about. There is even a danger of language becoming a substitute for thought. The wooden beads experiment, too, reveals that only at a certain stage (about 7 according to Piaget) do children realize that the part is never greater than the whole. Until they do, they are incapable of *understanding* addition or subtraction. To give the child the fullest help, we should know how far he has advanced, and what the next step will have to be. (Crawford, 1960; pp. 133–34).

Piaget's stage formulation is used and cited as a justification for critical curriculum shifts more frequently than it is used in the area of homogeneous age grouping.

Critical Curriculum Shifts

The notion of critical curriculum shifts occurring at certain times in the life cycle is a concept engrained in the American educational setup. The fact that nursery schools end at 5 years of age and elementary schools give way to secondary schools at about age 12 seems, to an American, a metaphysical reality. These critical age-sensitive curriculum changes are buttressed by the fact that the North American educational establishment is rather unified in its stress on the importance of these transition periods for major curriculum changes. Thus, one starts kindergarten and high school at approximately the same age across the United States and also in Canada. Europe, however, shows much greater diversity, possibly due to conflicting national interests. In spite of the fact that these critical curriculum shifts are idiosyncratic to our continent, it is nevertheless interesting to see how these established practices are justified in current psychological theorizing. Justification for the curriculum changes that take place between nursery and elementary schools and from there into the high schools can be seen in the following interpretation of Piaget.

Curriculum planners will have to take into account the work of Piaget on children's intellectual development. When the world is defined in terms of action linked concepts, then the child must encounter knowledge through his own actions. When he has constructed a system of concrete operations to deal with reality, the teacher must present her material in terms of specific concrete examples. When the formal stage is reached, however, theory is not only a possibility, but a necessary means of codification of experience and extending the use of the mind. (Adler, 1963; p. 35.)

These changes in teaching strategy are based on the changes that take place between Piaget's stages of preoperational, concrete operational, and formal operational thought. It is interesting to note that they take place roughly at the periods of transition from nursery to elementary and elementary to secondary schools.

The shift that occurs between Piaget's preoperational stage and concrete operational thought intuitively gives credence to the curriculum changes that take place from the nursery to the elementary school. This shift is further justified by psychological research outside of the Piagetian tradition. White (1965) has summarized numerous psychological studies which seem to indicate a fairly important psychological change occurring between the ages of five and seven. This change in the child's characteristic ways of learning appears to take place after age five; before this age the patterns of findings obtained with children resemble those obtained when animals are used in like procedures. After this age, the patterns of findings approximate that of human adults (i.e., the transition is from animal-like to human-like learning) (White, 1965). The change has frequently been attributed to a shift from perceptual to more conceptual modes of thinking (Collin, 1968; Wohlwill, 1962) and to increasing use of language mediation (Kendler and Kendler, 1962; Kendler, 1963).

Similar interpretations of the shift that occurs between Piaget's concrete operational and formal operational thought have led to differential curriculum planning between the elementary school years and adolescence. For example, in the sequencing of subject matter in science curriculums much attention has been given to Piaget's theory which centers around the question of how concrete or abstract the learning experience must be at various stages of development (Sullivan, 1967b). Piaget's potential contribution stems from his postulation of a concrete-abstract dimension in cognitive development. Each stage in Piaget's theory constitutes a progressive movement from concrete modes of thought to more abstract forms. Thus, Peel (1964) uses Piaget's stage descriptions of concrete and formal operational thought as prescriptions for the sequencing of subject matter in science education. Peel derives from Piaget's theory the conclusion that science education in the primary schools should be based on experience in the formation of concepts. The concrete operational stage should be limited to what he calls *describer thinking, propositional thinking;* scientific explanation of properties should be attempted only at the formal operational stage of thought. The achievement of formal operations allows the child to proceed to what he calls *explainer thinking* because explanation is a characteristic of propositional thought (i.e., formal operation). In a sense, this gives some credibility for our curriculum shift from the elementary to the secondary school years. The analysis thus far has focused on how Piaget's stage theory relates to current types of educational arrangements. I would now like, by means of taking a different perspective on Piaget's theory, to present some arguments which call into question the above interpretations.

Perspective

The arguments to be developed challenge the sacredness of homogeneous age grouping as well as the critical curriculum shifts that take place from nursery through secondary schools. At the same time they will not challenge the fact that as one increases age variability in the classroom, individual differences correspondingly increase. Furthermore, no challenge is made to the fact that as children grow older they deal with an increasing variety of tasks in a more abstract manner. The arguments are based upon further examination of Piaget's formulation concerning the notion of *intrinsic structure* and the role of learning vis-à-vis stage of development.

First, the use of the term "stage of development" implicitly adheres to the notion that as age is changing, the organism has at its disposal different intrinsic structures which enable him to process information in different ways. In theory, the concrete-abstract dimension that Piaget describes is attributed to these changing intrinsic structures or stages. The organism, in this dispensation, is not a mere tabula rasa but incorporates information into the system via these intrinsic structures. In order to assess the presence of a stage, Piaget has deliberately questioned children on concepts that are *spontaneously* learned rather than directly taught in the school. If there are developmental differences in the way children view the world, it is wise to tap these structural differences by using concepts in which they cannot mimic adult responses. Thus, the use of questions which probe the child's spontaneous versus learned concepts guards against the child's giving rotely learned school information and, in this sense, enables one to see if there are differences between child and adult reasoning. Even a cursory reading of Piaget will establish the fact that this strategy has been profitable.

The educational problem with a stage theory such as Piaget's involves relating the notion of intrinsic structure to the ongoing teaching-learning situation. This linking of the educational strategy to stage of development is complicated by the fact that Piaget in his research has attempted to keep them separate. One of the difficult educational dilemmas presented by Piaget's work relates to the tremendous stress that he places on spontaneous concept formation, while paying relatively minor attention to the formal concepts that are learned in school (Vygotsky, 1962). In this sense, the theory ignores the interaction between school-learned concepts and intrinsic structure (stage). With Piaget, stage of development affects the learning of school concepts but the opposite interaction does not obtain (Sullivan, 1967b). As Wohlwill (1962) points out:

Piaget, as is well known, tends to ignore the effects of antecedent conditions and the environmental variables in development, relegating them to a place definitely subsidiary in importance to the unfolding of internal structures. This does not mean that he frequently emphasized the continual interaction between external and internal forces. Nevertheless, biological orientation and interest in structure leads him to take external factors for granted and to regard the form which this interaction takes as largely predetermined from the start. The only problem, then, is that of specifying the successful stages through which the organism passes; little leeway is left for differential manifestation of external conditions. (p. 104.)

Piaget's present position, then, severely curtails the role of school learning in fostering intellectual development. If Piaget's views of the nature of school-learned concepts were valid, it would follow that such an important factor in the socialization of thought as school learning is unrelated to the development of "intrinsic structures" (Vygotsky, 1962). This is a weak spot in Piaget's position and seriously hinders practical application of his theory in education (Sullivan, 1967b). A more serious hindrance, however, is the misapplication and misunderstanding of Piaget's educational followers when they apply his stage theory to education. A misunderstanding of the stage notion enables the educational extrapolator to apply Piaget's theory to the present use of homogeneous age grouping and critical curriculum shifts.

Regarding the justification of "homogeneous age grouping", as I read Piaget, it would seem that he would not choose this type of setting as a desirable educational alternative for fostering cognitive development (Piaget, 1932). Recall that the psychological justification for homogeneous age grouping developed under this interpretation rests on the assumption that homogeneity of stage is a desirable educational alternative and that grouping by age assures greater probability that children at the same stage of development will fall within the same class. This assumption rests on a faulty and erroneous interpretation of Piaget's meaning of the term "stage", because at any given Piagetian stage the child can be at a variety of different points in his cognitive organizing. This "décalage" which Piaget describes makes it extremely difficult to postulate *a* stage as an indicator of readiness to learn a specific subject area. Thus, an assertion such as the one that it is necessary that the child have "reversible" operations before he learns addition and subtraction in mathematics (Crawford, 1960) may lead to serious problems. Piaget's "horizontal décalage" takes note of the fact that the use of reversible operations takes place at different times for different problems even within a stage of development. This is seen by the fact that the concrete operational child uses reversibility for the conservation of number first (at approximately 5 years) and for the conservation of volume much later (approximately 11 years) within this generic stage. This décalage exists because some concepts are more difficult than others and the child has more experience in some realms than others (Turiel, 1968). The fact of its presence, however, makes it exceedingly difficult for the use of generic stage notions as indicators for readiness to learn in specific subject matter areas.

More important to this question is the fact that the educational extrapolation of Piaget ignores the variability, clearly described by Piaget and his coworkers, of "intrinsic structures" within a given stage. A stage is never a static state and, as Inhelder (1962) states, each stage involves a period of formation (genesis) and a period of attainment. Thus, each structure constitutes at the same time the attainment of one stage and the starting point of the next. Piaget (1967) still holds to this interpretation when he states:

> We must, however, introduce an important distinction between two complementary aspects of the process of equilibration. This is the distinction between the variable structures that define the successive states of equilibrium and a certain constant function that assures the transition from any one state to the following one. (p. 4.)

Clearly, when he postulates an "intrinsic structure", it is always in a dynamic equilibrium which allows advancing cognitive development.

When one considers the factors which enhance the development of more advanced "intrinsic structures", there is some evidence within the Piagetian tradition which argues against excessive homogeneous age grouping. If learning could occur not simply by a teacher teaching a student but also by peer interaction, then a case could be made for having greater stage variability within one classroom. Piaget (1932) argues in the area of moral development for the necessity of peer group interaction in fostering more abstract forms of moral judgment. Recent evidence indicates that children reject moral advice which is one stage below their own, advance their development when such advice is one stage above their own, and distort advice to their own level when it is two stages above their own (Turiel, 1968). This might argue that some variability in grouping is desirable for development as long as the variability is not too extreme. Specifically, in areas such as social and moral development, it suggests that more peer group learning may be a desirable learning procedure since the teacher cannot feasibly deal with all levels or stages within a given class. At any rate, one can make a fairly good case using Piaget's theory against strictly homogeneous grouping.

Turning to the question of critical curriculum shifts (e.g., nursery school, elementary school, high school), we see how Piaget's theory becomes confounded with the particular cultural practices in education. As previously discussed, some of Piaget's critical stage transitions appear to occur at approximately the same time that there are shifts in our educational emphasis. This appears to provide credible evidence of the necessity for having these changes occur when, in fact, they do occur in practice. There is a problem, however, in the confounding of Piaget's stages with the type of education that a particular culture offers. As pointed out previously, Piaget does not sufficiently assess the effects of the educational process on his stages, but it certainly is effective since the stages occur at different rates within different cultures and are dependent on the type of schooling provided by the culture (Sullivan, 1967b). The result of this interaction leads to the familiar "chicken and egg, which came first?" problem. I shall argue that it is our culture's critical curriculum shifts that lead to the occurrence, at particular times in our culture, of Piaget's stages. This argument appears to have greater cogency than the reverse one for the following reason: If Piaget's stage transition ages were the same in all cultures, then it would probably be correct to say that our culture has intuitively broken up its curriculum in congruence with a good psychological stage theory. The fact of the matter is that Piaget's stages do vary across different cultures and it seems reasonable to say that his "stages" are partially determined (i.e., at least when they will occur) by the educational practices in our culture.

More important than the above proposition is the fact that Piaget's stages are incorrectly interpreted. He has dealt primarily with spontaneous concepts, but we do not know if the formation of spontaneous concepts follows the same course as that followed by concepts which are directly learned in a teaching-learning situation. For example, the insistence on "describer thinking" for the elementary school and "explainer thinking" for the high school in developing a physics curriculum (Peel, 1964) involves an erroneous and premature extrapolation from Piaget's stage theory. Even the development of Piaget's spontaneous concepts lacks complete transituational consistency (Stone and Ausubel, 1967; Uzgiris, 1964). Contrary to the expectations of Piagetian theory, evidence exists which indicates that formal thought, in its initial phase, is not possible in too varied subject matters. Thus, an individual may have reached the formal stage in science while not demonstrating formal thought in social studies until several years later (Stone and Ausubel, 1967). This indicates that shifts in thought processes occur at different times in different subject matter areas. There appears to be no compelling evidence from Piaget's theory that any one particular age is critical for a radical change in curriculum programming. Abstract thinking, for example, generally emerges earlier in science than in social studies because children have had more experience in manipulating ideas about mass, time, and space than about government, social institutions, and historical events. However, in some children, depending on their special abilities and their experience, the reverse may be true (Ausubel and Sullivan, 1970).

At the present time, developmental stage theory offers no clear-cut justification for critical curriculum shifts but several questions seem educationally relevant in terms of the relationship between cognitive stage theory and educational intervention. With specific reference to the change from perceptual (preoperational) modes of functioning to more conceptual (operational) modes of thought, Collin (1968) poses the following question: Does the shift in cognitive operations in one area generalize to other areas and how situation-specific are the shifts? Clearly, the answer to this question is a necessary prerequisite to further use of Piagetian theory in education. The second question centers on the role of education and its effect on "intrinsic structure". The fact that children begin elementary school at age 5 in our culture must be considered when considering the transition from preoperational to concrete operational thought. It could be at the same time a cause of the transition and the historical consequence of the potentiality for it at that age (White, 1965). More light on this interaction will probably lead to a more sophisticated use of stage theory in education.

Summary

The conclusion of this section gives no Hegelian synthesis to the issues and problems raised, but I hope that it will shed a different light on the question as originally posed. In focusing on the effects of individual differences across ages (developmental individual differences), we advanced a stage theory model and explored how this could be used to justify particular types of educational environments and teaching strategies to deal with stage changes. Initially, attempts to show how Piaget's stage theory could be used to justify certain contemporary educational practices (i.e., homogeneous age grouping and the existence of a particular nursery, elementary, and secondary school) were described. Then arguments attempting to criticize this use of Piaget's theory were advanced and a variety of alternatives which do not appear inconsistent with Piaget's stage formulation were elaborated. The main point made in this section was that there is nothing theoretically sacred about our present educational setup.

To briefly conclude, it would appear that no definitive answer can be given to the stages on particular changes in teaching strategy. A child can be at one particular developmental level in physical sciences and at a different level in the social sciences. This type of décalage should prevent the teacher from looking for, and the educational psychologist from giving, simple recipes concerning how developmental stages fit into different types of teaching strategies and different educational environments. This is probably one of the reasons why some curriculum planners have purposely side-stepped Piaget's theory. It is interesting to note that even in the area of mathematics, where Piaget's terminology appears to directly apply, there is considerable question of his immediate relevance. Kilpatrick (1964) in commenting on the Cambridge Conference on School Mathematics, takes note of this caution:

> We made no attempt to take account of recent research in cognitive psychology. It has been argued by Piaget and others that certain ideas and degrees of abstraction cannot be learned until certain ages. We regard this question as open, partly because there are cognitive psychologists on both sides of it, and partly because the investigations of Piaget, taken at face value, do not justify any conclusion relevant to our task. The point is that Piaget is not a teacher but an observer—he has tried to find out what it is that children understand, at a given age, when they have been taught in conventional ways. The essence of our enterprise is to alter the data which have formed, so far, the basis of this research. If teaching furnishes experiences which few children now have, then in the future such observers as Piaget may observe quite different things. We therefore believe that no predictions, either positive or negative, are justified, and that the only way to find out when and how various things can be taught is to try various ways of teaching them. (pp. 129–30.)

We know from Piaget in general that children usually move from concrete to more abstract modes of thinking in various subject matter areas, and this may be helpful to keep in mind when preparing programs. We also know that the child is not a "tabula rasa" but incorporates information into an actively organizing cognitive structure. This knowledge certainly represents an advance over our previous dependence on behaviorism. But the question of when developmental differences are important for educational programs and changes in teaching strategy still appears to be a practical and empirical one to be answered by teachers. It is recognized that as training environments or teaching strategies change because of developmental age differences, it becomes increasingly difficult for one teacher to span the whole panorama of developmental differences. We will never return to the "little red schoolhouse" because we have become aware that individual differences across age have important consequences for effective teaching strategies. Certainly, one teacher cannot adequately span all of these developmental differences and so we have restricted these individual differences by homogeneous age grouping. Whether it is necessary to restrict the differences by this procedure is an open question. For teachers who are unable to cope with large individual differences in their classroom it seems a likely alternative, but for the teacher who enjoys the variety it may be a restrictive bore. More will be said on the problem of variability in the concluding section of this chapter.

Contemporaneous Individual Differences

Interest in contemporaneous individual differences (i.e., types of individual differences found within a specified age or stage of development does not necessarily preclude enquiry into additional developmental dimensions as previously discussed. Nevertheless, there are individual differences that may be educationally relevant which may fall within a particular age or stage of development. Thus, there may be differences among children, who all are at the concrete operational stage, which will demand differential teaching strategies that are not derived from strictly developmental stage criteria. For example, concrete operational children may differ on other contemporaneous dimensions, such as anxiety, cognitive style, and authoritarianism. These differences may require further modifications in the types of teaching programs or strategies. The present discussion will focus on the specific question of the role of contemporaneous individual differences in the planning of differential teaching strategies. An attempt at answering this question will not suffer from a poverty of data on individual differences. The fact of the matter is that there is so much data it is difficult to know just what types of individual differences should count in planning differential teaching strategies. These types of differences are broadly defined as "aptitudes" (which, pragmatically, include whatever promotes the pupil's survival in a particular educational environment) ; they may have as much to do with styles of thought and personality variables as with abilities covered in conventional tests (Cronbach, 1967). Sex differences can also be included under this definition.

CONTEMPORANEOUS DIMENSIONS THE PSYCHOLOGISTS HAVE STUDIED

But what types of differential abilities should make a difference in our educational programming? Should we concentrate on patterns of intellectual aptitudes as exemplified in the ethnic data recently reported by Lesser and his associates (Lesser, Fifer, and Clark, 1965; Stodolsky and Lesser, 1967), or is it more important to stress the differences in information-processing abilities (Harvey, Hunt and Schroder, 1961; Hunt, 1966a; Schroder, Driver and Streufert, 1967) ? The recent studies on cognitive style (Kagan, 1966) and creativity (Wallach and Kogan, 1965) further complicate the problem of when and where to start differential teaching strategies.[4] Psychologists are by no means in common agreement as to which types of individual differences should take precedence in the educational process. Jensen (1967) maintains that the most important differences for educational purposes are intrinsic individual differences (i.e., individual differences directly related

---

[4] Recent reviews and interpretations of the effect of individual differences in the school may be found in Gagné (1967), Sears and Hilgard (1964), Thelen (1967), and Wallach and Kogan (1965).

to learning and exemplified in such tasks as memory, transfer, etc.) and that extrinsic individual differences (i.e., differences in personality traits and attitudes, etc.) should play a relatively minor role. This position contrasts with Hunt's (1966a) where the stress is clearly on extrinsic individual differences. In the latter, we see the emphasis placed on individual differences in information-processing skills which are related to certain types of personality dimensions.

Most of the studies that have taken contemporaneous individual differences into account in providing differential teaching strategies have usually centered on one or two major dimensions of individual differences. The general interaction model for contemporaneous differences is similar to the one discussed for developmental differences and is illustrated in Figure 7-3a. A concrete example of the model can be seen in a study which was designed to test the hypothesis that there would be an interaction between teaching

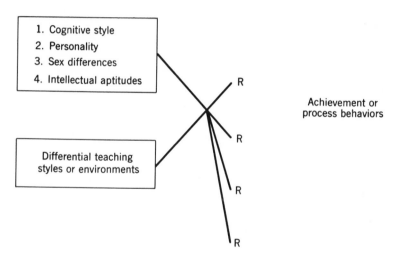

FIGURE 7-3a   General Teaching Model for Dealing with Intra-Age Individual Differences.

methods and pupils' personality characteristics in the determination of school achievement (Grimes and Allinsmith, 1961). They conjectured that elementary school children who were highly compulsive would respond to structured methods of teaching, such as teaching of reading by phonics. In line with the hypothesis, they found differences by the third grade in favor of phonics over word recognition for this type of children's population. Generally, they concluded that (1) compulsive children do better than less compulsive children under structured conditions, and (2) compulsive children are neither favored nor disfavored when teaching is unstructured.[5]

---

[5] Only a small portion of the results and design of this study are reported here.

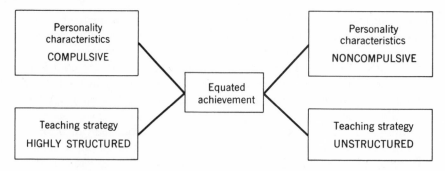

FIGURE 7-3b   Specific Application of the Model Taken from a Study Reported by Grimes and Allinsmith.

Figure 7-3b is an illustration of the hypothesis in its ideal form, but as usual, the results do not conform completely to the ideal.

Although there is nothing inherently wrong with this study or studies like it, they nevertheless defeat, to some extent, their purpose of dealing with individual differences. This occurs because most studies of this type take very few dimensions of individual differences into account. That an investigator, confronted with the plethora of individual difference dimensions that can be found in the psychological literature should take such an approach, is understandable. It is possible that in considering at any one time only a small proportion of all the existing individual differences, one would end up by projecting an infinite variety of teaching atmospheres or styles.

ISSUES AND PROBLEMS INVOLVED IN APPLYING THE CONTEMPORANEOUS APPROACH TO EDUCATION

In order to get at some of the issues and problems involved when one is planning differential teaching strategies for contemporaneous individual differences, I would like to propose a *thought experiment*. In scientific circles, a thought experiment is an attempt to derive new knowledge in an area where confusion exists (Kuhn, 1964). The thought experiment attempts to disclose a misfit between traditional conceptual apparatus and nature, and involves an imagined situation which allows the scientist to employ his usual concepts in the ways that he has employed them before. The experiment must not at the outset strain normal usage (Kuhn, 1964), however, it is presumed that the thought experiment will be directed toward pointing out the logical contradictions and confusions which the normal model produces. Thus, any situation capable of displaying such contradictions will therefore suffice. Assuming that nature and conceptual apparatus are jointly implicated in the contradiction posed by the thought experiment, it is expected that the experiment will demonstrate the need for an improved model.

The present imagined thought experiment proceeds on the hypothetical and, no doubt, erroneous assumption that there are only two major dimensions of contemporaneous individual differences that are educationally relevant. It is hoped that by combining these two major dimensions using the interaction model described above, we will be able to demonstrate the shortcomings of this model and simultaneously show the need for its change or revision. The experiment will use as illustrations two sets of data which explore the implication of differential teaching strategies stemming from the presence of demonstrated contemporaneous individual differences. The two studies which will be briefly described, and only in part, are Hunt's (1966) study on conceptual systems and Lesser, Fifer and Clark's (1965) study on individual differences in patterns of intellectual abilities. Certainly other studies could have been used as illustrations for our experiment, but the above were chosen because of the clarity of their findings and their apparent face validity as important educational findings.

Hunt's Conceptual System

The use of Hunt's (1966a) conceptual systems orientation for educational purposes is derived from a stage developmental theory propounded by Harvey, Hunt and Schroder (1961).[6] The "conceptual systems" viewpoint assumes that the normal course of development under optimal conditions leads to more flexible orientations toward the environment and the interpersonal world. This development is characterized in terms of successive developmental stages and by the specification of environmental effects in relation to specific developmental stages. Flexibility of orientation (i.e., degree of *abstractness*) or its absence in the adult is seen as a result of earlier structural progression and articulation or arrestment. We will focus on contemporaneous individual differences which are apparently due to arrestment at a particular stage, but it is first necessary to give a brief overview of the theory and some of its stage descriptions.

The basic unit of the theory is the construct "conceptual systems" which is defined as "a schema that provides the basis by which the individual relates to *the environmental events he experiences*" (Harvey, Hunt and Schroder, 1961; pp. 244–45). Like Piaget's schemas, the system is a construct for representing the mediational processes within the organism for adapting to the environment. It is similar to a computer program, in that it serves to filter and code or "read" events (Hunt, 1966a).

---

[6] Our experiment will focus on contemporaneous individual differences based on this theory. Thus, we will ignore for now the inter-age implications of the theory.

From the Conceptual Systems view, development is seen as a continuous process which, under optimal conditions, proceeds in a given order to a higher conceptual level (CL). Higher CL is associated with increased interpersonal maturity and increased conceptual complexity, and thus is a desirable state. Under optimal conditions, progression on the CL dimensions is viewed in terms of successive stages, each characterized by a specific interpersonal orientation and conceptual structure. If the environmental conditions are not optimal, then the person remains at a lower CL, and may become closed to further progression (Hunt and Dopyera, 1966; p. 48).

The first three stages and a brief description of their characteristics are given in Figure 7-4.

Stage	Self-Other Orientation	Stage Characteristics
Sub 1	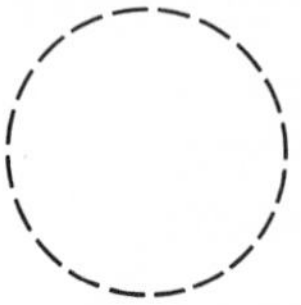	Self-centered, unorganized phase before incorporation of cultured standards
1	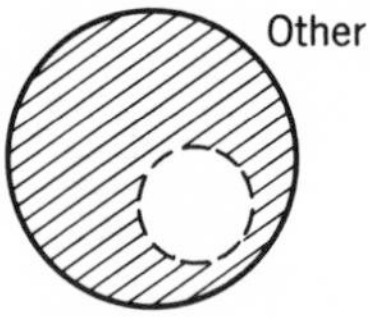 Other	Learning the ground rules or cultural standards which apply to everyone
2	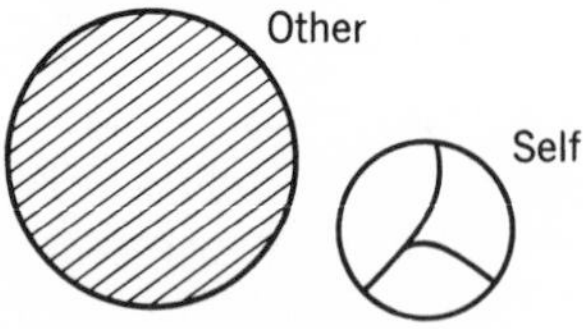 Other Self	Learning about oneself and how one is distinct from these generalized standards

FIGURE 7-4 Developmental Stages in Interpersonal Orientations (Adapted from Hunt, 1966a).

Working off the "conceptual systems" strategy in grouping a population of lower-class Negro students in a junior high school, the following findings were reported.

We have obtained evidence for the differential effectiveness of educational environments according to the student's conceptual level. With the present population of lower-class students, classroom groups were formed homogeneous in conceptual level—a Sub I-group, a Stage I group, and a Stage II group. In an exploratory study with ninth-grade students, the teachers were unaware of the nature of the groupings, but they quickly discovered that the groups were differentially receptive to specific educational procedures. The Sub I group required considerable structure and concrete experiences, and could not maintain a discussion. The Stage I group functioned most effectively when competition and debates were involved. The Stage II group seemed to function most effectively when there was considerable opportunity for independent exploration, questioning and differences of opinion (Hunt and Dopyera, 1966; p. 52).

The findings are most interesting from an educational viewpoint and warrant further discussion, but for purposes of the thought experiment let us proceed to the next set of findings.

Lesser, Fifer, and Clark's Study on Mental Abilities

The purpose of this study was the examination of the pattern of four mental abilities (i.e., verbal, reasoning, numerical, and spatial abilities) among first-grade children of four ethnic groups in which each group was further divided according to social class. The particular ethnic groups were drawn from a New York City population consisting of equal proportions of Chinese, Jews, Negroes, and Puerto Ricans. Each ethnic group was further divided according to middle-class or lower-class status. The most important finding is that ethnic background and social class have different effects. Ethnic background appears to affect the pattern of mental abilities, while social class leaves the patterns unaltered, affecting only the absolute magnitude of the specific ethnic patterns. The findings are briefly summarized as follows:

1. Verbal Ability—Jewish children rank first, being significantly better than all other groups; Negroes rank second and Chinese third (and both are significantly better than Puerto Ricans).
2. Spatial Ability—By contrast, the rank order proceeds from Chinese to Jewish, Puerto Rican, and then Negro children.
3. Reasoning Ability—The rank order proceeds from Chinese to Jewish, Negro, and then Puerto Rican children.
4. Number Ability—The rank order proceeds from Jewish to Chinese, Puerto Rican and then to Negro children.

The patterns are clearly seen in Figure 7-5. Also, when all four ethnic groups are combined, the middle-class were significantly superior to lower-class children. The most interesting results can be seen in Figures 7-6a and 7-6b. Ethnicity patterns among mental abilities maintain themselves even over social class differences for all four groups. The figures illustrate this pattern for the Chinese and Negro groups. One amazing finding is an

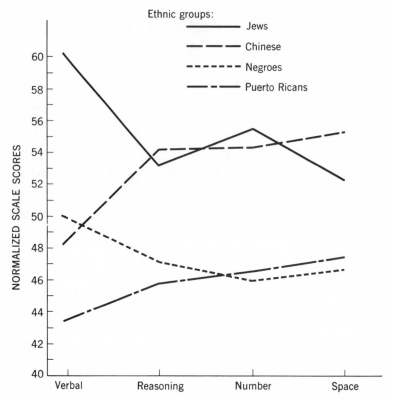

FIGURE 7-5 Pattern of Normalized Mental Ability Scores for Each Ethnic Group (from Lesser, Fifer, and Clark, 1965).

almost exact replication of this study in a Boston population (Stodolsky and Lesser, 1967). The importance of these findings for the study of individual differences stems from:

> The failure of social-class conditions to transcend patterns of mental ability associated with ethnic influences was unexpected. . . . The greater salience of social class over ethnic membership is reversed in the present findings. Ethnicity has the primary effect upon the organization of mental abilities, and the organization is not modified further by social-class influences (Stodolsky and Lesser, 1967; p. 570).

The above authors go on to discuss the educational implications of their study by asking the following questions: How can knowledge of a child's pattern of mental abilities be fitted to the content and timing of his instruction? How can instruction be adjusted to the child's particular strengths and weaknesses, or the child's abilities modified to meet the demands of instruction?

To briefly show how the authors attempt to tackle these educational questions, which incidentally clearly fit our model (see Figure 7-1), we quote them again:

> Answering these questions requires continuous, successive approximations to an analysis of the child's special combination of intellectual resources and the demands for intellectual resources placed upon him by the curriculum. We have begun two preliminary studies, one in the teaching of beginning reading, another in learning the concept of mathematical functions at the sixth grade level. One approach we have used begins with an assessment of the child's intellectual strengths to try to minimize his weaknesses. For example, in teaching mathematical functions to children strong in Space Conceptualization, but weak in Numerical facility, we use graphical presentation; in teaching the same concept to a child strong in Number facility but weak in Space Conceptualization, we rely on manipulation of numbers in a tabular form. (Stodolsky and Lesser, 1967; pp. 580–81.)

The authors discuss problems of mismatching but this is not important for our experiment, since we are not making a critique of this approach but simply using it for illustrative purposes.

The Experiment Proper

The imagined experiment proceeded on the assumption, patently erroneous, that the preceding studies demonstrated the only viable contemporaneous individual differences with educational import. Ignoring the age differences in the studies as quoted, the type of experiment I propose involves linking these two sets of data together and attempting to project programs which honor the individual differences found within them both. In effect, we are combining the *extrinsic* individual differences as exemplified in Hunt's theory with the *intrinsic* individual differences dealt with in Lesser and associates. Remember that ethnic differences override social class, so let us simply concentrate here on a group of lower-class children. Let us divide children in the lower class into ethnic groups and assume there are only four ethnic groups existing in the world (i.e., Chinese, Negroes, Puerto Ricans and Jews). If we attempt to provide differential teaching environments or strategies taking into consideration only three of the conceptual systems stages as well as ethnic patterns of abilities of the children, we could project in the ideal state at least twelve different types of teaching strategies (see Table 7-1).

It is evident that by limiting oneself to a particular social class with differential conceptual functioning and by assuming that there are only four relevant ethnic groups with patterns of abilities centering around four major factors, the problem of planning for individual student differences by projecting differential teaching strategies presents already a rather formidable

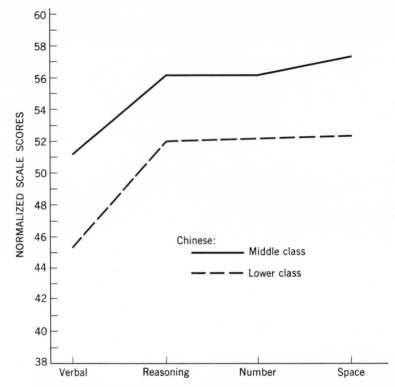

FIGURE 7-6a Patterns of Normalized Mental Ability Scores for Middle- and Lower-Class Chinese Children (From Lesser, Fifer, and Clark, 1965).

TABLE 7-1 An Ideal Projection of Differential Teaching Strategies for Children at Three Different Conceptual Levels

	Ethnic Patterns			
	Negro	*Puerto Rican*	*Jewish*	*Chinese*
Hunt's	1. SUB 1	4. SUB 1	7. SUB 1	10. SUB 1
Conceptual	2. Stage 1	5. Stage 1	8. Stage 1	11. Stage 1
Stages	3. Stage 2	6. Stage 2	9. Stage 2	12. Stage 2

task using the normal model. The problem would become more complicated if we added only a small number of the other contemporaneous individual differences for consideration. Cognitive styles, modes of creativity, personality characteristics, and intrinsic individual differences in tasks, could well lead to an infinite variety of teaching strategies or atmospheres. Reflecting on our original question, it is probable that one could demonstrate

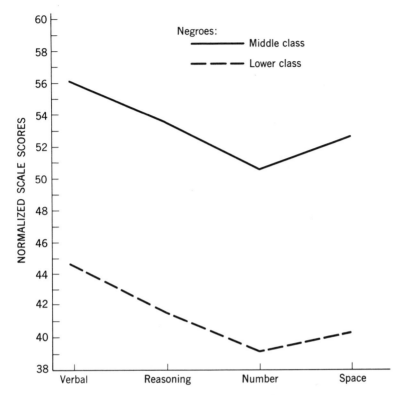

FIGURE 7-6b   Patterns of Normalized Mental Ability Scores for Middle- and Lower-Class Negro Children (From Lesser, Fifer, and Clark, 1965).

that a vast portion of the individual differences reported will show differential educational results as a result of differential teaching strategies. It is very easy for the armchair psychologist to propose that we should plan differential teaching strategies for individual student characteristics. The problem for the teacher and curriculum planner lies in choosing from the vast array of individual differences those characteristics which are educationally relevant. The complexity of the enterprise, no doubt, discourages many from even attacking the task in practical educational settings and as a result it is largely left in the realm of theory for educational psychologists. Thus:

> Individual differences are given much lip service and even more drawer space in the form of filed test results, yet educational planners and decision makers continue to work from models for "students-in-general". Teachers may know quite a lot about how students differ in educationally relevant ways, yet they continue to use a "lockstep" curriculum plan. (Hunt, 1968; p. 1.)

No one will deny that many teachers and educational planners are prone to taking the easier and less complicated educational route of ignoring individual variation and directing their focus to the middle of the class while providing special remedies for the extremes. Nevertheless, one must be sympathetic to the fact that the knowledge of the presence of a large variety of individual differences in a classroom gives no indication as to where to start with differential strategies or as to which types of individual differences should be focused upon. In all honesty, the recently edited review of individual differences in learning is of little help in answering these practical educational questions (Gagné, 1967). The platitudes expressed by many educational psychologists illustrate their scientific bias rather than their educational depth. For example, the following quote is taken from a well-known educational psychology textbook:

> The writer looks forward to the day when the teacher will begin the school year by spending perhaps two days collecting data systematically about the pupils, feeding the data into an electronic computer, and receiving back from the computer conclusions about possible sources of difficulty children may encounter in learning. It can be anticipated that these two days of systematic enquiry, together with the one the electronic computer will perform on the data, will provide a much more thorough understanding of the individual child than the teacher can at present during a full year of work with the same children. . . . What is being pointed out is that there is no substitute for the systematic, careful collection of data and processing and the processing of that data by up-to-date methods (Travers, 1963; p. 33).

The fact is, however, that we have plenty of data already and this mania for collecting reflects the empiricist bias of many educational psychologists. The assumption that this data will somehow become integrated in the absence of theory has been aptly termed "super-optimism" (Olson, 1967). Commenting on this fad for data collection, Miller (1962) notes:

> A great scientist, Lord Kelvin, once said, 'When you cannot measure. . . your knowledge is of a meagre and unsatisfactory kind'. He was, of course, a physicist. . . . It is a bit ironic that Kelvin's proclamation is better known amongst social scientists than natural scientists. Social science has always been a little defensive about its status, a little sensitive about its claim to be scientific. So, when a great physicist announces that measurement is to keep to scientific knowledge, he is apt to receive more attention than he deserves. In truth, a good case can be made that if knowledge is meagre and unsatisfactory, the last thing in the world you should do is to make measurements. The chance is negligible that you will measure the right things accidentally. Nevertheless, many social and behavioral scientists, assured that measurement is the touchstone of scientific respectability, have rushed out to seek numbers before they knew what the numbers would mean (p. 79).

It would seem that this is one of the problems with which the teacher and the curriculum planner is faced when psychologists present him with the infinite variety of data on individual differences. In most cases, the data is rarely couched within an adequate theoretical framework for him to make the bridge between the data on individual differences and practical classroom strategies. It may well be that we will need the use of a computer to cut down the data to sizeable proportions. At present, this computer strategy is only at the talking stage, as is seen in Cronbach's (1967) suggestion:

> It seems likely to me that even with this sort of multivariate testing a computer can provide, we will have to build up adaptations slowly, on the basis of only a few differential variables. While in principle a unique instructional diet could be matched to the students' idiosyncratic intellectual metabolism, nothing is to be gained by introducing unvalidated modifications. And it will be a long time before we have adequately validated rules of adaptation that take into account even a half-dozen differential variables. As I see it, our greatest hope for fitting the school to the individual lies in the development of theory that finally marries the differential and experimental approaches to learning.

If we wait for psychologists to develop the theory and have their matching procedures validated, we will probably start our work on individual differences in heaven (or hell). Moreover, prescriptions such as the one proposed in the above quote rests on the assumption that the social order is a fixed entity which does not change. If this assumption is not valid, we can expect many old individual difference configurations to dissolve and a host of new configurations to emerge. It may be that by the time we have the psychological theory and its educational validation completed, it will be geared to a set of individual differences which have become obsolete.

A more realistic approach would involve setting the educational task of dealing with individual differences within a clearly delineated philosophical perspective. As I stated previously, psychology is a descriptive science and education is a moral enterprise. Moral statements are not descriptive as are scientific statements, but are prescriptions which are accompanied by such words as "ought," "right," "wrong," "good," and "bad" (Hare, 1952). It is in this sense that educational objectives are stated in moral evaluative terms (e.g., in a democratic society we ought to take into consideration student individual differences in fostering their educational growth). In approaching the problem of individual differences and differential teaching strategies, it might be helpful first of all to articulate the moral necessity of even entertaining this problem. If it turns out to be a justifiable problem, which I think it will in our society, it will pose several other relevant questions which will help to eliminate some of the confusions precipitated by the almost infinite variety of individual differences which the educator gleans from psychological data.

For example, Stodolsky and Lesser (1967) raise very basic questions for teachers and curriculum planners who are interested in the problem of matching the curriculum to the student's individual characteristics when they ask:

> Should schools provide equal opportunities to promote the *equal* devel-
> opment of all groups and individuals or equal opportunities for the *maximum*
> development of each group or individual? Can the schools aim to do both?
> (p. 583).

Questions such as the above are not asking for *descriptive* statements but for moral imperatives. The fact that these questions are not entertained is probably one of the reasons that many of the existing compensatory education programs proceed by attempting to deal with individual differences by eliminating them. The differential teaching strategies for the culturally deprived are designed to obliterate the individual differences that exist between social classes. While certain aspects of this strategy may be desirable, the program in toto may be a contradiction for a society that preaches democratic principles. Focusing on these questions may aid us in determining which contemporaneous individual differences are relevant and commensurate with our educational objectives when planning differential teaching strategies or environments. The seemingly laudatory strategy of grouping *critically deprived* children together for maximum educational change may prove in the long run a means of proliferating the *de facto* segregation that exists in our society. If it turns out that certain aspects of our objectives are centered on the maximum development of each group or individual's idiosyncratic individual differences, it may be that:

> Rather than adapting to or reducing individual differences, they may
> actually have the effect of accentuating or increasing individual differences.
> This could be much more than a 'sleeper' effect—one that would show up
> only after the passage of time. It might actually have immediate effects.
> Using verbal, spatial, or symbolic teaching methods might have the effect of
> making some children highly verbal, others highly spatial, and others highly
> symbolic in their thinking (Carroll, 1967; p. 43).

Certainly many other questions about educational objectives will come to mind which will be helpful in focusing on relevant individual differences for educational programming. For instance, if we are stressing *achievement* outcomes as our objectives, we will probably do well to concentrate on

Jensen's (1967) *intrinsic individual differences,* whereas if we are stressing *information processing abilities* (e.g., Hunt, 1966a; Schroder, Driver and Streufert, 1967), it may be wiser to focus on *extrinsic individual differences.*

Summary

The thought experiment was designed to point out the shortcomings of the normal interaction model for dealing with contemporaneous individual differences and procedures for differential teaching strategies or environments. It was evident that the staggering variety of contemporaneous individual differences with which the strategists are confronted presents enormous problems for planning educational programs. In attempting to answer the question of whether or not the plethora of contemporaneous individual differences would make it impossible for a single person to teach, it became apparent that there was no metaphysical necessity for differential strategies or teachers, but rather a moral necessity. Dealing with this moral problem, however, demands more information than the present interaction model offers. It was suggested that focusing on our educational objectives might constitute a fruitful approach for determining which individual differences should determine our differential programming.

Retrospect and Prospect: Future Directions

In our analysis thus far, we treated the questions of developmental and contemporaneous individual differences separately and yet the complexity of the problem of dealing with individual differences was clearly illustrated. If we combine these questions (i.e., consider individual stage differences and individual differences within stage concomitantly) the problem becomes further compounded. Such a combined analysis would further add to the conclusion that the present ways of conceptualizing the problem of individual differences and differential educational programming are inadequate and in need of revision.

The general spirit of this chapter has, in some ways, given the impression that the poor formulation of this problem is by and large the fault of educational psychologists. This is difficult to ascertain, and it would not be difficult to build an alternative case which states that the psychologist rarely suffers from being confronted with the right educational questions concerning the problem of individual differences.

In theory, the question of individual differences and differential educational environments stems from a society with a professed *democratic* ideology in contrast to a society, such as Russia, where Marxian ideology underplays the role of individual differences. But in everyday practice, there is some evidence to indicate that democratic attitudes of teachers and prospective teachers are inadequate and distorted vis-à-vis the meaning of democracy as stated by the bill of rights (Weiser and Haynes, 1966). The problem is further complicated by the *social structure* in America which by and large gives lip service to democratic ideals while applying them in a few select places. Thus, even if psychologists were able to come up with a sufficient set of conclusions about individual differences, the cost of differentiating instruction may appear too high to suit practical administrators (Carroll, 1967). But this is simply trying to couch the problem in a larger social perspective which bears a more elaborate analysis in and of itself. Even from a more limited psychological perspective one can assume that American society, during the latter part of the 20th century, will undergo further rapid social and technological change. If this assumption is borne out, the difficulty of predicting the types of individual differences that might become educationally relevant and the available resources in teaching strategies, content area, and types of environments that will exist, becomes apparent. An important question centering on this projection into the future is raised by Joyce (1967).

> What do we do, however, when we wish to create a program to prepare teachers who will not only be able to perform tasks we are able to envision, but who will be able to create future educational forms and develop unique solutions to problems we are unable even to imagine? Can we develop systems that give teachers the power to create as well as perform? (p. 12).

One possible approach to these questions involves the development of skills which give the teacher practice or training in dealing with individual differences (Hunt, 1966b; Hunt and Joyce, 1967). This training involves the development of three subskills (Hunt, 1966b). First, it is necessary to have the teacher develop skills for discriminating individual differences. Second, the skill of discrimination must be coupled with skills for radiating different training environments for these discriminated differences. Finally, the teacher requires a capacity for shifting from one type of environmental radiation to another when the teaching situation demands it (Hunt, 1966b).

In a sense, this approach rests on the assumption of nonspecific transfer of skills. Thus, the skills that the teacher trainee practices now may prove to be irrelevant by the time he commences teaching, but this mode of attack still remains and can be utilized again. Also, this *moratorium* for the practice of these skills may be the stimulus for the exploration of new strategies which are geared toward anticipated social or technological changes. McDonald (1968) emphasizes this training for change when he states:

If you agree with me that substantial changes will be wrought in the nature of schooling by the development of technological systems, then it becomes clear that we, as psychologists interested in the training of teachers, ought to commit ourselves to the development of new teaching styles. We ought to commit ourselves to finding the ways in which human beings as teachers can influence learning. Obviously, many of us will continue to work on the correlative task, finding ways of instructing that do not require human beings except in ancillary roles, or where the human being is the designer of this system but is not a functional component in it (p. 5).

The problem of handling individual differences in classrooms, however, will not be alleviated simply by advancing technological resources. For the future, it may be worthwhile to examine the time at which teacher training should commence. If we really believe in modulating the teaching environment to the individual, it appears necessary to have a greater work force to deal with this student variability. It seems reasonable to commence teacher training programs much earlier than the present schedule, by having peers teach other peers. Earlier in this chapter we discussed the possible undesirable effects of homogeneous age grouping and indicated some of the advantages of having older peers present in the classroom for enhancing cognitive development (Piaget, 1932, 1951). Here, I would like to advance the notion that *peer teaching* may be a very effective way for handling the individual variation in a classroom. his potential source of teacher manpower is normally ignored in educational planning.

In our society, today, the major responsibility for helping children acquire their skills, attitudes and values necessary to function successfully as adults has been placed in the hands of parents and educators. This model of a few adults and teachers working with, and being responsible for, such a complex learning program presents serious difficulties. There are limits to the amount of individualized attention that the learner can receive when the major weight of all learning transactions is placed on the relationship between adults and a large group of youngsters.

We may not be making the best use of the powerful potential educational resource represented by cross-age relationships among children. It is an observed fact that children, with proper training and support from adults, are able to function effectively in the roles of helpers, and teachers of younger children—and that the older children find this type of experience meaningful, productive, and a source of valuable learning themselves (Lippitt and Lohman, 1965; p. 113).

A similar advantage of peer learning and teaching can be found in the adolescent years. As Elder (1967) points out, the lack of interest in this potential resource of teachers stems from our history of age-graded education. This history has contributed to an incapacity on the part of educators to envision the potential educational values of adult-youth relationships in the classroom. Segregation by age, for most American high schools, sharply reduces such learning experiences, maintains negative stereotypes of age groups, and appears to contribute to the discontinuity between adolescents and adults. Peer learning and teaching does not necessitate the image of a highly permissive classroom with highly unstructured interactions. Certainly, the above type of atmosphere, especially with certain types of groups, has a deleterious effect on the child's cognitive development (Kohlberg, 1968). If clearly defined situations are prepared, in which peers are set in a teaching role (e.g., older with younger peers), this prevents peer interaction from being simply a play situation.

These speculative suggestions are attempts to further explore and possibly improve the present models for dealing with individual differences in an educational context. It is very difficult to spell out the importance of these suggestions, since we know that the future holds new technologies and new sources of individual differences. "We see all these things, but through a glass darkly" (St. Paul).

References

ADLER, M., Some implications of the theories of Jean Piaget and J. S. Bruner for education. Toronto: Board of Education for the City of Toronto Research Service, 1963.

AUSUBEL, D. P., and E. V. SULLIVAN, *Theory and Problems of Child Development.* 2nd ed., New York: Grune and Stratton, 1970.

CARROLL, J.B., Instructional methods and individual differences. Discussion of Dr. Cronbach's paper. In R. N. Gagné, ed., *Learning and Individual Differences.* Columbus, Ohio: Charles E. Merrill, 1967, 40–44.

CRAWFORD, D. H., The work of Piaget as it relates to school mathematics. *Alberta Journal of Educational Research, 6* (1960), 125–36.

CRONBACH, L. J., The two disciplines of scientific psychology. *American Psychologist, 12* (1957), 671–84.

CRONBACH, L. J., How can instruction be adapted to individual differences? In R. N. Gagné, ed., *Learning and Individual Differences.* Columbus, Ohio: Charles E. Merrill, 1967, 23–39.

ELDER, T. H., Age integration and socialization in an educational setting. *Educational Review, 37,* No. 4 (1967), 594–619.

FLAVELL, J. H., *The Development Psychology of Jean Piaget.* New York: Van Nostrand Reinhold, 1963.

GAGNÉ, R. N. ed., Learning and individual differences: A symposium of the Learning Research and Development Center, University of Pittsburg. Columbus, Ohio: Charles E. Merrill, 1967.

GESELL, A., and F. L. ILG, *Infant and Child in the Culture of Today.* New York: Harper and Row, 1943.

GOLLIN, E. S., Conditions that facilitate or impede cognitive functioning: Implications for developmental theory and for education. In R. D. Hess and R. N.

Bear, eds., *Early education: A Comprehensive Evaluation of Current Theory, Research, and Practice.* Chicago: Aldine, 1968, 53–62.

GRIMES, J. W., and W. ALLINSMITH, Compulsivity, anxiety, and school achievement. *Merrill-Palmer Quarterly of Behavior and Development, 8* (1961), 247–72.

HARTUP, W. W., and N. L. SMOTHERGILL, eds., *The Young Child: Reviews of Research.* National Association for the Education of Young Children, Washington, 1967.

HARVEY O. J., D. E. HUNT, and H. N. SCHRODER, *Conceptual Systems and Personality Organization.* New York: Wiley, 1961.

HUNT, D. E., A conceptual systems change model and its application to education. In O. J. Harvey, ed., *Experience, Structure, and Adaptability.* New York: Springer, 1966 *a*, 277–302.

HUNT, D. E., A model for analyzing the training of training agents. *Merrill-Palmer Quarterly of Behavior and Development, 12,* No. 2 (1966 *b*), 137–56.

HUNT, D. E., Matching models and moral training. Paper prepared for the conference on "Ethics, Psychology and Moral Education". Toronto: Ontario Institute for Studies in Education, June 20–22, 1968.

HUNT, D. E., and J. DOPYERA, Personality variation in lower-class children. *The Journal of Psychology, 62* (1966), 47–54.

HUNT, D. E., and B. R. JOYCE, Teacher trainee personality and initial teaching style. *American Educational Research Journal, 4,* No. 3 (1967), 253–59.

HUNT, J. McV., *Intelligence and Experience.* New York: Ronald Press, 1961.

INHELDER, B., Some aspects of Piaget's genetic approach to cognition. In W. Kessen and C. Kuhlman, eds., Thought in the young child. *Monograph of the Society for Research in Child Development, 27,* No. 2 (Whole No. 83), 1962, 19–33.

JENSEN, A. R., Varieties of individual differences. In R. N. Gagné, ed., *Learning and Individual Differences.* Columbus, Ohio: Charles E. Merrill, 1967, 117–35.

JENSEN, A. R., Social class, race, and genetics: Implications for education. *American Educational Research Journal, 5,* No. 1 (1968), 1–42.

JOYCE, B., Method in teacher education: Geist, Substance and Form. Paper prepared for the University of Alberta Conference on teacher education. Alberta: October, 1967.

KAGAN, J., Developmental studies in reflection and analysis. In A. H. Kidd and J. L. Rivoire, eds., *Perceptual Development in Children.* New York: International Universities Press, 1966, 487–522.

KENDLER, H. H., and T. S. KENDLER, Vertical and horizontal processes in problem solving. *Psychological Review, 69* (1962), 1–16.

KENDLER, T. S., Development of mediating responses in children. In J. C. Wright and J. Kagan, eds., Basic cognitive processes in children. *Monograph of the Society of Research in Child Development, 28,* No. 2 (Whole No. 86), 1963, 33–48.

KESSEN, W., Stage and structure in the study of children. In W. P. Kessen and C. Kuhlman, eds., Thought in the young child. *Monograph of the Society for Research in Child Development, 27* (Whole No. 83), 1962, 65–82.

KILPATRICK, J., Cognitive theory and SNSC program. In R. E. Ripple and V. N. Rockcastle, eds., Piaget rediscovered: A report of the Conference on Cognitive

Studies and Curriculum Development, March, 1964. Ithaca, N.Y.: School of Education, Cornell University, 128–33.

KOHLBERG, L., Development of moral character and moral ideology. In M. Hoffman and L. Hoffman, eds., *Review of Child Development Research*. New York: Russell Sage, *1* (1964), 383–431.

KOHLBERG, L., Montessori with the culturally disadvantaged: A cognitive-developmental interpretation and some research findings. In R. D. Hess and R. N. Bear, eds., Early education: A Comprehensive Evaluation of Current Theory, Research, and Practice. Chicago: Aldine, 1968, 105–18.

KUHN, T. S., A function for thought experiments. L'aventure de l'esprit. In A. Kogré, ed., *Histoire de la pensée XIII*. Ecôle Practique de hautes études. Sorbonne, Paris: Hermann, 1964, 307–34.

LESSER, G. S., J. FIFER, and D. H. CLARK, Mental abilities of children from different social-class and cultural groups. *Monograph of the Society for Research in Child Development, 30,* No. 4 (1965).

LIPPITT, T., and J. E. LOHMAN, Cross-age relationships—an educational resource. *Children, 12* (1965), 113–17.

MCDONALD, F. J., The relevance of psychology to teaching conceptualization as information processing. Paper prepared for a conference on psychology in a teacher preparation curriculum. Toronto: April, 1968.

MILLER, G. A., *Psychology: The Science of Mental Life*. New York: Harper and Row, 1962.

OLSON, D. R., Super-optimism and the science of education. Invited address to the Canadian Council of Research and Education (CCRE). Winnipeg: June, 1967.

PEEL, E. A., Learning and thinking in the school situation. In R. E. Ripple and D. N. Rockcastle, eds., Piaget rediscovered: A report of the conference on Cognitive Studies and Curriculum Development, March, 1964. Ithaca, N.Y.: School of Education, Cornell University, 101–4.

PIAGET, J., *The Moral Judgment of the Child*. New York: Harcourt   Brace Jovanovich, 1932. (Republished: New York: Free Press, 1948).

PIAGET, J., *The right to education in the modern world*. In UNESCO Freedom and Culture. New York: Columbia University Press, 1951, 67–116.

PIAGET, J., *The Psychology of Intelligence*. Totowa, N. J.: Littlefield, Adams, 1960.

PIAGET, J., Psychology and philosophy. In B. B. Wolman and E. Nagel, eds., *Scientific Psychology*. New York: Basic Books, 1965.

PIAGET, J., *Six Psychological Studies*. New York: Random House, 1967.

SCHRODER, H. M., N. J. DRIVER, and S. STREUFERT, Human information processing: Individuals and groups functioning in complex social situations. New York: Holt, Rinehart and Winston, 1967.

SEARS, P. S., and E. R. HILGARD, The teacher's role in the motivation of the learner. In E. R. Hilgard, ed., National Society for the Study of Education. Part I. *Theories of Learning and Instruction*. Chicago: University of Chicago Press, 1964, 182–209.

STODOLKY, S. S., and G. S. LESSER, Learning patterns in the disadvantaged. *Harvard Educational Review, 37,* No. 4 (1967), 546–93.

STONE, M. A., and D. P. AUSUBEL, The inter-situational generality of formal thought. (Unpublished.) Ontario Institute for Studies in Education. Toronto, 1967.

SULLIVAN, E. V., Experiments in the acquisition of conservation of substance—an overview. In D. W. Brison and E. V. Sullivan, eds., Recent research on the acquisition of conservation of substance. *Educational Research Series No. 2* Toronto: The Ontario Institute for Studies in Education, 1967 *a*, 1–10.

SULLIVAN, E. V., Piaget and the school curriculum: A critical appraisal. Bulletin No. 2. Toronto: The Ontario Institute for Studies in Education, 1967 *b*.

THELEN, H. A., *Classroom groupings and teachability.*   New York: Wiley, 1967.

TRAVERS, R. M. W., *Essentials of Learning: An Overview for Students of Education.* New York: Macmillan, 1963.

TURLEL, E., Developmental processes in the child's moral thinking. To appear in P. Mussen, J. Langer and M. Covington, eds., *New Directions in Developmental Psychology.* New York: Holt, Rinehart and Winston, 1968.

UZGIRIS, I. T., Situational generality of conservation. *Child Development, 35* (1964), 831–41.

VYGOTSKY, L. S., *Thought and Language.* New York: M. I. T. Press, 1962.

WALLACH, M. A., and N. KOGAN, *Modes of Thinking in Young Children: A Study of Creativity-Intelligence Distinction.* New York, Holt, Rinehart and Winston, 1965.

WATSON, J. V., Psychology from the standpoint of a behaviorist. Philadelphia: Lippincott, 1919.

WEISER, J. C., and J. E. HAYES, Democratic attitudes of teachers and prospective teachers. *Phi Delta Kappa,* May 1966, 476–81.

WHITE, S. H., Evidence for a hierarchical arrangement of learning processes. In L. P. Lipsitt and C. C. Spiker, eds., *Advances in Child Development and Behavior.* New York: Academic, 2 (1965), 187–220.

WOHLWILL, J. F., From perception to inference: A dimension of cognitive development. In W. Kessen and C. Kuhlman, eds., Thought in the young child. *Monographs for the Study of Research in Child Development, 27,* No. 2 (Whole No. 82), 1962, 87–106.

8

Variations on a Systems Theme: Comprehensive Reform in Teacher Education

BRUCE JOYCE

On March 1, 1968, ten institutions in the United States, several as coordinators of consortia, commenced an attempt to build system models from which teacher education programs could be constructed. This was done as part of a program (sponsored by the United States Office of Education) designed to apply systems planning techniques to the reconstruction of teacher education curriculums in the United States. The participating institutions were:

1. Florida State University
2. University of Georgia
3. University of Massachusetts
4. Michigan State University
5. Northwest Regional Educational Laboratory
6. University of Pittsburgh
7. Syracuse University
8. Teachers College, Columbia University
9. The University of Toledo
10. The University of Wisconsin

The institutions completed their final reports within eight months and a program of feasibility studies has been completed shortly thereafter.

To a curriculum theorist, the product of the U.S. Office of Education study represents a first generation effort to make an application of broad systems planning principles to a major area in education. Although the work was concluded within a very short period of time, and is flawed as a result, we have never had, in the history of education, ten strong teams approaching the same area simultaneously, employing similar and conscious program-planning principles but otherwise under no constraints to do similar work. A massive increase in the literature of teacher education has resulted, the substance of which is being used to plan some very different programs of teacher education. The products are a base on which some major attempts at comprehensive reform in teacher education will be based. In addition, the result of the effort is exceedingly instructive in terms of the technologies of curriculum development. It is especially interesting to look at the resulting products in terms of the similarities and differences with which the teams of planners completed the tasks of systematic program construction and the tasks which now need to be engaged to implement the program models which emerged from the early effort.

This paper will begin to make an analysis of the commonality and variety with which six program planning tasks were completed. Although systems procedures have by no means been standardized, the six tasks generally appear in any paradigm for systematic program construction, although they sometimes exist under different names than the ones which will be employed here, and the order in which they are accomplished varies quite widely. However, there is a certain logic in the following order:

1. The development of the performance model. A major task is the conceptualization of the goal of the training program, and this task must be accomplished in terms of a working model of the product of the program. The working performance model should be as complete as possible and describe aspects of performance and interrelationships among the aspects. In the case of a teacher education program, the fulfillment of this task requires the development of a working model of a functioning teacher. This model is described as an imput-output system. Furthermore, the teacher must be conceptualized in terms of the system within which he is operating. Classrooms and schools need to be described at a minimum, as well as teams of teachers if he is to be a member of a team, and it would be desirable for the conceptualization to include also the wider systems of the community within which the educational institution functions.

2. The analysis of the performance model into sets of behavioral objectives. The model has to be broken down into specific domains of functioning (if these are not already available within the model) and these in turn have to be broken down into sets of behaviors, sequentially organized wherever that is possible, so that programs can be built to achieve those objectives, and to provide the trainee with the devices for integrating them into the overall performance system. This task is exceedingly complicated when one is dealing with a complex functionary like a teacher; cognitive behaviors, affective behaviors, and skills interrelate and overlap, and yet, must be perceived distinctly and in relationship to each other if rational program planning is to proceed.

3. The specification of training subsystems (the development of components and component strategies). The next task consists of the development of program components to accomplish distinct sets of behaviors. Within each set component, distinct curricular or teaching strategies need to be constructed, and sometimes many need to be developed for a particular component. Components need not be homogeneous with respect to teaching strategies. For example, the same component may use sensitivity training techniques to achieve certain kinds of behavior, and behavior modification strategies within simulators for yet other sets of behaviors. However, the training subsystems need to be clarified in a modular organization. One of the interesting features of the ten developed models is the wide range of curricular strategies which are recommended within and between components. The development of components needs to be accompanied by the development of specifications for needed support systems (as closed-circuit television laboratories, etc.).

4. The development of the overall training system (the creation of interlocking relationships among components). It is always tempting for a program planner to develop discrete components having their own distinctive strategies, their own instructional materials, and their own special procedures for staff training. However, for the sake of the student, whose life should not be fragmented unnecessarily, and in order to achieve an integrated performance at the end of the program, components need to be related to one another systematically, then modules cast in reconcilable terms. In addition, support systems need to be developed and integrated into the training components, and the performances and training of training agents must be specified.

5. The development of management systems to monitor a large program. To enable a large program to adjust to the individual differences among students (in terms of goals, achievement, and learning style), to build in provisions for program revision, to insure continuous feedback and evaluation for managers, faculty, and students, and to integrate components and support systems smoothly, comprehensive management systems need to be developed.

6. The reconciliation of the program and product with the client and the field. A young person entering the field of education has personal needs and conceptions of teaching which he needs to explore and to relate to the training opportunities which are presented to him. He has to explore himself as a person as well as explore himself as a professional-in-training. Whether he is learning to be a teacher aide in a hierarchical team, or preparing to be a specialist in a subject discipline, he needs to learn frames of reference which will enable him to apprehend alternative careers, ways of following them, ways of reconciling his personal needs for marriage and family with the demands of career, and ways of making a training program work for him, so that he does not become an artifact of a machine. Hence, specific procedures for humanistic guidance have to be developed for the client of the program.

Similarly, the teacher education program must be related to the field which it serves. Teacher education has to supply the institutions with competent and humanistic personnel; these institutions must share in the identification of competencies and the development of training procedures. A smooth transition needs to be provided between any training institution and the educational institution in which the teacher will work. In fact, the creation of the setting for teacher education is a joint problem for universities, training institutions, and elementary and secondary schools. The problems of reconciliation with the field become particularly acute when the training program is designed to produce a teacher who is in any way different from the typical functionary in the existing schools, and whoever designs the training program, it is almost always a major hope that they *will* be different.

The completion of these six tasks results in a program model which is ready for field trials to test model elements and for the development of implementation stages (that is, the creation of instructional materials, program and management systems, support systems, staff training procedures, and the like). The program models become the guidelines of these activities. The immediate task is to maximize the feasibility of the models—to rectify their defects and capitalize on their strengths while developing and implementing them.

This paper is devoted to a survey of the program goals—the performance conception of the teacher who is to be the product of the programs. The range and type of performance models reveal the complexity of systematic program procedures and the extraordinary variety which emerges when different frames of reference are permitted wide latitude as they apply systematic planning procedures to a major training area. This variety is particularly striking because of the common belief that systematic program planning necessarily results in program homogeneity. This distinctly has not been the case with respect to teacher education. Hence the title "Variations on a Systems Theme" is used for this chapter.

Common Assumptions

The teams worked separately and completed their reports within a very short time. In addition to their use of systematic planning procedures, the ten teams operated on certain implicit but common working hypotheses about teacher and training programs, although they differed considerably in application of these assumptions to teacher education program development. These common hypotheses are manifested through the program reports and represent basic but tentative assumptions which either implicitly formed a common frame of reference about teaching and training which could be used to make decisions concurrently with the testing of the assumptions themselves.

1. All of the teams viewed the teacher as a clinician in much the sense that physicians are clinicians. The teacher was seen as the possessor of strategies for making instructional decisions, and as the possessor of the needed repertoire of knowledge and clinical skills for carrying out his decision. It was assumed that decision-making competence and interactive teaching competence could be defined with precision and both played prominent roles in the performance models. (For examples, see the Michigan State, Comfield, and Florida State models described later in the chapter.)

2. Teachers were generally thought of as members of clinical teams, and frequently as specialists on those teams. Several of the models provided "career ladders" with places for many kinds of specialists in a career hierarchy. This should not be interpreted to mean that "team teaching," as presently practiced, was seen as a panacea for the ills of education. Rather, it reflects the belief that colleague relationships are necessary to that teachers check one another's opinions, examine one another's teaching, coach one another, and specialize in order to increase competence.[1] (For descriptions of teams of specialists, see the Georgia, Toledo, Wisconsin, and Massachusetts models.)

3. All of them assumed that it was possible to define the needed competencies of the teacher in terms of specific behaviors and to match those behaviors with specific learning experiences, especially short instructional modules calculated to achieve those objectives. Furthermore, it was assumed that large sets of instructional modules could be combined into curricular systems which could be entered at many points in the teacher training process and could be prescribed to match the personal characteristics of the future teachers. It was assumed that the objectives and the specifications of modules

---

[1] The conception of the teacher articulated by Robert Schaefer in *The School as a Center of Inquiry* (New York: Harper and Row, 1967).

could be stored in automated data banks so that they could be retrieved on the basis of diagnoses shared in or even made by the teacher trainee himself.[2]

4. It was assumed that management and control systems could be developed to monitor teacher training programs and to provide them with flexibility, especially adaptability to the student. In several cases, the models included the specifications for computerized systems for managing programs including several thousand behavioral objectives matched with an equally large number of instructional modules. (For succinct descriptions, see the Florida, Syracuse, and Comfield models.)

5. All of the models assumed that any teacher who could take major responsibility in a classroom would need a long period of training and that a consortium of colleges and school districts was necessary to provide the conditions for academic training, preservice training, internship or practice teaching, and continuing inservice education. They also assume that an educational team will contain personnel of more limited functions whose training could be relatively brief.

6. All of the teams made a heavy use of simulation laboratories—situations which were somewhat less complex than the "real world of the teacher" in order to teach clinical skills. The "real world of the classroom" is thought to be entirely too chaotic a place to function as a setting for learning complex teaching skills. The simulation laboratory, by simplifying the training situation, permits teaching skills to be acquired sequentially until the teacher has a range and depth of competency to cope with and learn in the complex school situation. The models tended to prescribe a sequence of activities which proceed from an identification of a clinical skill, its practice under simulated conditions or with small groups of students, and then its practice in a field situation. This kind of pattern, replete with systematic feedback and assessment, occurred again and again in all ten of the models. (See the Comfield model, whose plan centers about the use of teaching laboratories.)

7. All of the teams hoped to make available to the teacher knowledge from the behavioral sciences which he could use to make and carry out educational decisions. They saw the teacher as an applied scientist in a basic sense of the word, using behavioristic techniques to plan for students and select appropriate experiences for them. At the same time they were acutely conscious of the limits of our knowledge both about teaching and about the preparation of teachers. Hence, most of the models included a large variety of strategies for preparing the teacher; all of them were designed to equip him with a large repertoire of teaching strategies he could select from and use with his students as well as techniques he could use to study the effects of his teaching. (See the Teachers College model for explicit positions in this area.)

8. Last, it was assumed that a model should contain provisions for revision and redevelopment as a fundamental feature—not as a subsidiary element or aftergrowth. Replanning and reimplementation are assumed to be basic— as basic as training components themselves. Also, all of these models were

2 The Michigan State Model, for example, contained more than 2,300 behavioral objectives matched with instructional modules, all organized within an automated retrieval system. Toledo selected over 1,400 objectives from an list of over 2,100.

created within a very short period of time, and each of the teams was acutely conscious of the need to build a structure that could be revised and further developed. Consequently, various aspects of each model are better developed than other aspects. In some cases, the behavioral objectives were elaborately specified, but much work remains to be done in the development of instruction systems to achieve those objectives, although the basic strategies were laid out. In other cases, a great deal of attention was paid to the development of management systems, although much remains to be done to build satisfactory behavioral objectives and instructional modules to complement the well-developed management systems. A fortunate result of this is that there presently exists for the field of teacher education a set of exemplary components—elaborate performance models of teachers, intricate instructional systems, comprehensive management systems, and well-developed procedures for creating and administering consortia for teacher education, but none of these is fully present in any model and all of the models contain integral provision for redevelopment. (For statements of the revisionary role of management systems, see the Syracuse, Florida, Toledo, and Georgia models.)

The Assumptive World of Systems Planning in Teacher Education

The set of common aspects of the program models reflect an assumptive world which is partly made up of a commitment to the application of systematic, future-related planning procedures to education; partly of a commitment to bring educational training to bear directly on the revision of public education; but even more to an awareness of the possibilities of contemporary management technology. An individualized (let alone a personalized) program can not really be conceived of for a large student body without the capacity to obtain and store vast amounts of information about students and to maintain and deliver a wide variety of alternative instructional experiences as appropriate.

Thus, although educators have talked about individualized curriculums for decades, they have not lived in a technological world which would enable a really thorough form of it. Nearly all successful forms of individualized instruction have depended on a very favorable instructor-student ratio and even then the instructors have to be highly competent and committed to individualization and personalization.

Quality control has been similarly limited. Although curriculum theory has postulated for many years that these should be direct linkages between behaviorally stated objectives, instructional alternatives, and evaluation processes, the actualization of this paradigm has not really been possible. For example, even a committed instructor teaching a course to twenty students simply cannot manufacture enough tests by himself to track progress adequately and adjust instruction to the varying rates of progress of his students.

With the advent of technologies for developing large and complex information storage and retrieval systems, there arrived also the capacity to develop management systems which could coordinate student characteristics and achievement with instructional alternatives and maintain reasonable levels of quality control. Very few educators have as yet become familiar to these technologies, partly because they are new and not yet disseminated throughout the education community and partly because many educators have reacted adversely and equate "management systems" with "dehumanization."

It is safe to say that all the program model teams are comfortable with the idea of management systems and believe that when we learn how to them, we will make education much more flexible and human. Thus, they live in an assumptive world in which one looks for ways of developing "support systems," "choice points," and "feedback systems," they develop training in "simulators" with "recycling to a more appropriate alternative" and "increasing complexity of instructional tasks." In other words, they attempt a massive task analysis of the problem of preparing a teacher, confident that the task analysis can be made and that management systems can be created to implement the results. They recognize that enormous quantities of jargon will be needed to symbolize the concepts of objectives, modular curricular alternatives, evaluation, and support systems necessary to such an effort. They believe that such a technology will eventually not only permit instruction to be tailored to individuals but also will enable many instructional goals and means to be shaped by the student himself.

Hence, the "model developers" live in an assumptive world comprised of management systems theory, a concern with efficiency and systematic training (cybernetic psychology), and the belief that applying these to teacher education will mean a more personal environment for the student, a more effective teacher product, and a university in which desirable innovation can be made (cycled into the system) much more easily than with the present organization.

The Nature of the Performance Models

A performance model is an integrated set of behaviors which are coherently related to each other. This system of behaviors constitutes the product which the educational program is designed to achieve. When the desired end product of a program has been described as a functioning system of performance—a working model of a teacher in this case—it is possible to begin the substantive development of the means of the program.

There are great difficulties in developing a "system" description of a complex functionary like a teacher. We can underline these difficulties by identifying the conventional ways of developing conceptions of complex jobs and the obstacles to applying these to the description of the teacher. There are four general ways of developing performance or working models of complex functionaries. One of these is by the empirical study of a functionary. To develop a model of a salesman, for example, we might study the most successful salesman of a given product (the one whose dollar sales were the highest) and determine his behavior. A second method is to obtain a consensus by members of a field about the characteristic or optimal behavior of functionaries within the field. Again, using the case of a salesman, one might ask outstanding salesmen what behaviors were responsible for their success, or ask regional sales supervisors what makes the best salesmen so effective. A third is to derive the model from the application of a theory, either an empirically verified theory or a deductive construction. With respect to salesmanship, one might study social psychological theories about reasons for increased sales with the object of training salesmen to bring about those conditions. Selecting a theory, one would deduce the properties of the salesman from it. Hence we would have (*do* have) theories of salesmanship based on rapport-building activity (make friends with the client), on behavior modification (*shape* the client!), on status-linked behavior (make the client feel he will lose face if he doesn't buy), and so on. The fourth method is to make a comprehensive analysis of all the processes engaged in by the functionary. Such an analysis draws on theories, consensus, and the application of empirical studies where appropriate. To develop a model of an airline stewardess, for example, we might analyze the aircraft and the equipment, work out a description of services which might be offered during flight, check customer and supervisor opinion, and build, from those data, a simulator in which we could try alternative patterns of behavior until a satisfactory combination emerged.

Ultimately, the application of systems procedures to the development of a training program requires the fourth course of action. We are not ready for this course as yet. There are, as yet, relatively few comprehensive empirical studies of what teachers do, and there is still little knowledge about the kinds of procedures which are followed by the most able teachers. (In fact, how to identify effective teachers is a question which has by no means been resolved!) There is, in fact, considerable controversy about *what* criteria of performance to use. Complicating the situation is the position taken by many educational leaders, such as Arthur Combs[3], that the

---

[3] Arthur Combs, *The Professional Education of Teachers: A Perceptual View of Teacher Preparation* (Boston: Allyn and Bacon, 1965).

to employ in individualizing instruction. In other words, the same specifications are used for the teacher performance model as for the teacher education system model, except for the obvious adjustments for client differences.)

To make an operational definition, the description of individualized instruction was expanded and made more specific, although the Pittsburgh Model is still unfinished and much work will be done before we can assess it. As pointed out elsewhere, the Pittsburgh conception of the teacher assumes a particular type of school with special support systems—there is no attempt to train a teacher of classes. The Pittsburgh teacher is a teacher of individuals and is thus seen as a system within a system, which increases the likelihood that their working model will be feasible.

The Pittsburgh approach contrasts interestingly with the one developed by the Northwest Laboratory team.

THE COMFIELD APPROACH:
A TEACHER WHO CAN PRODUCE LEARNING

The performance model developed by the team representing the consortium gathered together by the Northwest Regional Education Laboratory describes the teacher in terms of instructional and noninstructional competencies. We shall give attention only to the instructional aspect. The description of instructional competency begins with the teacher as a "person who can bring about learning in children," or stated differently, "who can bring about appropriate changes in pupil behavior."[6] In order to make this specific, they had to develop a descriptive taxonomy of the kinds of learning that are desirable for elementary school children and determine the kinds of teaching which would be likely to achieve those objectives.

> Having established the prime objective of a teacher education program, the next step is to determine how this objective is to be brought about. In terms of a systematic analysis, this requires four interrelated steps:
>
> 1. specification of the pupil outcomes desired,
> 2. specification of the conditions by which each outcome can be realized,
> 3. specification of the competencies needed by teachers to provide the conditions that are needed for the realization of each outcome, and
> 4. specification of the conditions by which the needed teacher competencies can be realized.[7]

In order to make a full development of such a statement of performance, the Comfield team needed to go through four steps. The first three

[6] Northwest Regional Educational Laboratory, *A Competency Based, Field Centered, Systems Approach to Elementary Education,* OE 58020 (Washington, D.C.: U.S. Office of Education, 1968), p. 6.

[7] *Ibid.,* p. 7.

defined the performance model, or the goals of teacher education, and the fourth developed the teacher education program itself.

TABLE 8-1   Steps in Developing a Program[8]

Step One	*Step Two*	*Step Three*	*Step Four*
Pupil outcomes that are desired.	Conditions that bring about the pupil outcomes that are desired.	Competencies needed by teachers to provide the conditions that bring about the pupil outcomes that are desired.	Conditions that bring about the competencies teachers need to provide the conditions that bring about the pupil outcomes that are desired.
The goals of education.	The instructional program within the schools.	The goals of teacher education.	The teacher education program.

Put another way, it was necessary for the Comfield team to develop a taxonomy of pupil outcomes, to make postulates about the kinds of environmental conditions that would be likely to bring about those outcomes, and to make a further specification of the behavior of the teacher which would produce those environmental conditions.

This approach involves the specification of theoretical or empirically derived positions about learning. It thus can take advantage of the behavioral sciences, but must also operate under the limitations that exist in our present knowledge about how to bring about various kinds of learning outcomes.

It is worth noting that both the Pittsburgh and the Comfield approaches conceptualize the teacher as a behaviorist (all the models do, in fact). The behaviorist conception requires the teacher to specify learning outcome in terms of pupil behaviors, and to tailor the environment to the characteristics of the student and the particular kinds of outcomes desired. Whereas the Pittsburgh model emphasizes the specification of means for producing outcomes for particular learners, the Comfield model includes individualization as a general aspect of educational method.

The Comfield conception raises a number of complex questions which have to be resolved before their performance model can be fully comprehended. Two of these stand out. First of all, it is not clear whether every teacher is to be responsible for bringing about *any* learning outcome with an appropriate strategy for *every* learner. This is a crucial question, for there are myriad types of learning and a vast number of potential strategies

[8] *Ibid.,* p. 6.

for bringing these about. The model seems to lead to an unmanageably complex functionary. The partial answer to this is found in Comfield's expectations of the future.

> In order to plan an instructional program meaningfully, some prediction as to the nature and purpose of education in the 1970's and beyond has to be made. Two predictions have been agreed to by the planners of Comfield.
>
> 1. A functional science and technology of education will evolve, and it will bring with it an educational program that is markedly different from that which is now found in most schools. Two differences are anticipated: 1) the widespread use of pupil-materials instruction, and 2) the application of systems technology in the design of instructional experiences. Out of both will grow the application of "instructional systems" to the education of children.
> 2. Three major classes of educational specialists are anticipated: 1) instructional analysts, 2) instructional designers or engineers, and 3) instructional managers. As presently conceived the instructional analyst will be the member of the instructional team primarily responsible for identifying the classes of pupil outcomes for which the school should be responsible, and the instructional conditions that bring them about; the *instructional designer-engineer* will have the task of developing instructional systems to bring these outcomes about; and the instructional manager (IM), will bring the effort of the first two members to bear upon the educative process. The task of the IM is viewed as one of creating and/or maintaining an instructional environment that brings about learning in children. The IM's specific function within the school is likely to be primarily a *supervisor* of the instructional process rather than the prime *manipulator* of it. Operationally this means that while the IM of the future must be able to diagnose learner readiness, prescribe appropriate learning experiences, evaluate their effectiveness and prescribe next learning steps, he must also be able to apply the instructional systems developed by the other members of the educational team, supervise instructional assistants, use electronic and computer media, etc.[9]

Thus, Comfield's teacher is an instructional manager who works in an environment which increasingly consists of student-material relationships with a presumed vast storehouse of instructional possibilities which are mediated through instructional systems. This greatly reduces the burden on the teacher, but it also greatly changes our view of him. Thus, the second question which has to be resolved involves determining the nature of responsibility when a teacher *supervises* rather than *manipulates* instruction. Is not the *system* the primary agent? *Can* the technician be held responsible?

As these questions are resolved, the model of the teacher will be in sharper focus and programs to achieve the model will be more clearly feasible.

[9] *Ibid.,* p. 18.

THE GEORGIA APPROACH:
WORKING FROM THE OBJECTIVES OF ELEMENTARY EDUCATION

The Georgia model was developed by conceptualizing a desirable kind of elementary education and identifying the teacher performance which would be necessary to bring that kind of elementary education into existence.

To do this, the Georgia team began with the identification of seven broad objectives of elementary schools. These in turn were used to determine the kinds of conditions that would be likely to lead students toward those objectives. From those conditions the teacher job analysis was made. "What should the teacher do to produce those conditions?" was the question asked. Then the job analysis was broken down into specific teaching behaviors. The following chart gives an example of the working procedures used to develop this performance analysis.[10]

Objective: To learn to solve problems.

Pupil Learning Behaviors
1. The child identifies problems.
2. The child formulates hypotheses.
3. The child gathers information.
4. The child analyzes lata.
5. The child evaluates alternative solutions.
6. The child generalizes solutions.

Teaching Behaviors
1. The teacher organizes problem situations.
2. The teacher interests pupils in problem and observes its formulation.
3. The teacher observes information gathering and processing.
4. The teacher assists, as required, in developing a solution to the problem.

Suggested Specifications for a
Teacher Education Program
A teacher education program will provide the student with:
1. Knowledge of and skill in developing problem situations.
2. Knowledge of and skill in techniques of presenting problem solutions methods.
3. Knowledge of and skill in critiquing problem solutions.

Consensus of experts was used by the Georgia team to identify the elementary school objectives and the pupil learning behaviors from which the job analysis was derived.

---

[10] University of Georgia, *Georgia Educational Model Specifications for the Preparation of Elementary Teachers,* OE 58019 (Washington, D.C.: U.S. Office of Education, 1968), p. 37.

The overall method for developing the specifications is clear enough—teams of specialists identify school objectives; from those, desirable pupil behaviors are generated and then, in turn, teacher behaviors and competencies are developed. The result is that the substantive conception of the teacher grows in small pieces. This has advantages and disadvantages. An advantage is that the job can go on in manageable pieces. A team can identify one goal and go straight through until the competencies related to it are identified and matched with performance modules that constitute the substance of the program. This produces a "vertical" consistency of all modules and the overall goals.

There are several problems with this method which can be overcome. First, the selection of the content areas greatly affects the nature of the competencies which result. What should the areas be? If one weighs philosophy and the arts heavily, the competencies will be weighted on that side. The possible content areas are very large. *The process of selection of the content teams should be fully rationalized and transparent. In addition, potential relationships among the areas should be made clear and a system for relating the work of the teams to each other should be employed so that needless duplication is avoided and the languages of the teams can be related to each other.* The Georgia program as it stands does not provide a rationalization for the selection of the content areas nor a system for relating the work of the teams (except for a system to make the concepts used to describe specifications relatively uniform).

As a consequence, the Georgia conception of the teacher is constructed of sequences of small units within separate content areas. There is no clear plan for sequencing—the relationship among the units must be inferred from examining them.

In the course of implementation, these problems should be faced directly and solved. Before performance modules are developed, an integrated conception of the teacher should be developed (quite possibly by developing an integrated conception of the goals of the elementary school). The content areas should be rationalized in terms of this unified conception and a system for relating the specifications to each other in the several content areas should be developed. In addition, systematic plans for sequencing within the content areas would ensure that the units of behavior add up to a solid performance in each area.

In the course of making this analysis, the Georgia team decided that no one kind of personnel could engage in all the behaviors that were being identified, and they were divided into four major categories for elementary school personnel: aid, teaching assistance, certified elementary teacher, and specialist. Each of the levels implied competency at the previous levels, and the four categories provided a career hierarchy for instructional personnel within the elementary school. The education-career combination can be seen in Figure 8-1.

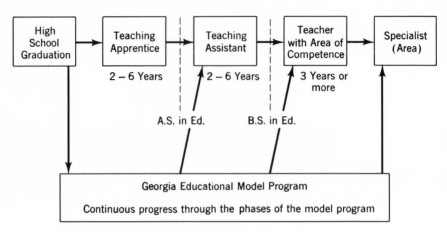

FIGURE 8-1   Paths in the Teacher Career Field (From the University of Georgia, *Model Specification,* p. II-5)

THE UNIVERSITY OF TOLEDO MODEL: THE TEACHER AS A TEAM MEMBER

The Toledo group developed their performance model by describing a clinical team of teachers in action and by analyzing the functions of a team member:

> *A New Role for the Elementary Teacher.* Simply stated, the prime functions of the teacher are the transmission of knowledge and the transmission of values. As previously mentioned, both cognitive knowledge and societal values and norms are becoming increasingly complex. When attempting to fulfill his task as a transmitter of values and norms, the teacher must not only mediate between the child's world and the adult in an effort to close the ever widening generation gap, but he must also deal with a serious cultural gap. The cultural gap is especially important when the student's cultural background is markedly different from the teacher's. When norms are in a state of flux, as in our attitudes toward sex and drugs, the teacher may not feel competent to force his values upon the pupils. When the teacher attempts to fulfill his function as a transmitter of knowledge, he is again caught in the web of rapid change. It seems clear that if the teacher is to fulfill these two functions successfully, he will need help.[11]
>
> *The Teacher as a Team Member.* If the elementary teacher is to maximize his effectiveness in the transmission of cognitive knowledge, he will need to be a member of a team—a team made up of specialists. The purpose of

[11] University of Toledo, *Educational Specifications for a Comprehensive Elementary Teacher Education Program,* OE 89026 (Washington D.C.: U.S. Office of Education, 1968), pp. 61–62.

the team would be to design instructional systems. An instructional system is a strategic complex of human and nonhuman components which are dynamically interdependent and interrelated and work together to attain a particular instructional goal or set of goals. The instructional system receives inputs from the external environment, processes these inputs in a prescribed instructional environment according to strategies derived from research and expert opinion, so that the output generated will have a high probability of achieving the prescribed goal or goals. The instructional system components may include some or all of the following: learner(s), teacher(s), mediated instructional materials, assessment and feedback instruments, information processing and displaying machines, support technician(s).

The key to this arrangement is the *team*. Instructional decisions are made cooperatively by a team of specialists with a master teacher serving in the role of instructional specialist throughout the entire instructional system design process. Each team could serve a number of master teachers. For example, in a building of thirty teachers and nine hundred pupils there could be six master teachers all of whom were served by the same Instructional System Design team.

The membership of the ISD team would vary depending upon the needs and background of the pupils, e.g., a slum school would probably need the services of at least one sociologist or an elementary school near Cape Kennedy might require a specialist in space technology in order to take advantage of the children's knowledge of space science which they learned at home. Some of the specialists that would very likely serve if all instructional systems design would be:

1. *Subject matter specialist:* To update the subject matter.
2. *Curriculum specialist:* To determine the mix of what to teach to whom.
3. *Research specialist:* To evaluate the instructional systems efficiency in terms of the output produced and to collect and feed back data needed to redesign the system; to calculate cost/effectiveness estimates of alternative instructional strategies and systems.
4. *Educational sociologist:* To interpret the social and cultural milieu of the child.
5. *Educational psychologist:* To study the child's growth and development and his individual learning patterns.
6. *Instructional technologist:* To design, develop, and test modules of mediated instruction.
7. *Administrative specialist:* To meet the administrative managerial needs of the team.
8. *Information management specialist:* To develop information storage and retrieval systems, computer based information management system, and computer simulation techniques.
9. *Counseling and guidance specialist:* To fill the guidance and counseling needs of the students through and with the help of the teachers.
10. *Pupil evaluation specialist:* To specify in behavioral terms the goals for each pupil, to assess the progress of each individual pupil, and to make recommendations to the ISD team for modifications of the pupil's program.

The next step was to develop complete models of each of these roles and to fit them together again in a model of a smoothly functioning team.

Toledo imagined, as did Comfield and Pittsburgh, a school which is organized in sets of instructional systems and staffed by teams of developers who constantly evaluate and improve the system and work with teachers to tailor learning environments to children.

THE MICHIGAN STATE MODEL:
THE APPLICATION OF THE BEHAVIORAL SCIENCES TO TEACHING

The Michigan State model gave the greatest emphasis to the teacher as an applied behavioral scientist in the classroom, creating and testing hypotheses. The Michigan State team's description is directly to the point:

> A key concept of the BSTEP model is *clinical behavior style*. The major function of this concept is to regularize the behavior of teachers. Clinical behavior style denotes those particular and stylized sets of activities and mental processes which a practitioner possesses. Such a practitioner of education will be specifically trained to utilize his client-related experience as the basis for continuous learning and improvement of his skills as a teacher. The clinical behavior style which is appropriate for a professional teacher consists of six phases: describing, analyzing, hypothesizing, prescribing, testing, and observing consequences. The last phase, observing consequences of the treatment administered, leads in turn to the first by a process of recycling in order to describe the changed situation.
>
> The progressional foundations of the program are centered on the behavioral sciences for two reasons: (a) The dominant task of all educational activity is to develop pupil behavior within various settings. The behavioral sciences provide the systems of knowledge and inquiry most relatable to this task. (b) A distinctive feature of empirical science as a way of acquiring knowledge is that it is self-corrective.[12]

The teacher was seen within this concept in terms of three processes: proposing, doing, and reflecting. He would identify problems, propose solutions to them and reflect on the situation. Starting from this view of performance, the Michigan State team proceeded to identify the competencies needed to apply the behavioral sciences to the solution of educational problems. The total number of competencies reached more than 2300 by the time the team had completed the work.

The behaviorism and the clinical view of teaching found in the Michigan State model were common to various models as was the range of concepts used. The other model builders—Syracuse, Massachusetts,

[12] Michigan State University, *Behavioral Science Elementary Teacher Education Program,* OE 58024, two volumes, (Washington D.C.: U.S. Office of Education, 1968), p. 6.

Florida State, and Wisconsin—shared many elements with this conception. The Wisconsin model described teacher "role orientations," one of which is in terms of decision-making; the Wisconsin model is especially detailed with respect to competency within curriculum areas, as in reading, science, mathematics, etc. Table 8-2 is drawn from the reading sequence. The several volumes of the Wisconsin model are filled with detailed analyses like the above, describing decision-making behavior and interactive teaching behavior. The philosophical tone of the above example is typical—the teacher is seen as a reflective, philosophically aware behaviorist. It is interesting that Wisconsin, like Georgia, used the *Taxonomy of Educational Objectives* to guide the teams which developed the objectives for which instructional modules would be developed.

THE MASSACHUSETTS APPROACH: HUMAN RELATIONS, TEACHING SKILLS, AND CONTENT

The Massachusetts approach describes teaching in terms of three components: human relations, behavioral (teaching skills), and content. In itself, this tri-partite conception is imaginative, and all three aspects can be defended as important to teaching. Giving such prominence to human relations represents an important contribution to conceptions of the teacher. However, the selection of the three components is not explained, nor are they related to each other. Some philosophical and psychological underpinnings are provided in the human relations area, but not in the others. Thus, a promising idea does not result in a real working model of the teacher, although we believe this problem could be remedied.

The Massachusetts conception makes a strong contribution in another direction. It is structured so that the program can be adjusted to persons seeking a wide variety of specialties in differentiated teaching staffs. Several types of competency and a profile of performance are identified for each specialist. Each type of competency is organized in terms of a sequence of competencies so that students can enter each type at their level of achievement. Figure 8-2 (from the Massachusetts report) is used for a profile analysis.[14]

In the Massachusetts profile analysis, profiles are constructed in several areas for each of several positions within differentiated teaching staffs. The entering student is matched with the desired profile for the particular specialty for which he is aiming, and the diagnosis that results can be used in planning his curriculum. As in the case of the other modular curricular

[14] University of Massachusetts, *Model Elementary Teacher Education Program,* OE 58024, two volumes (Washington D.C.: U.S. Office of Education, 1968), p. 84.

TABLE 8-2 Supplement II: Is Knowledgeable about Aspects of Developmental Programs in Communication[13]

Knowledge	Comprehension	Application	Analysis	Synthesis	Evaluation
A. Knows the scope and varied sequence of behavioral outcomes desired when teaching each of the language processes to elementary pupils.	Comprehends the scope and varied sequence of behavioral outcomes desired when teaching each of the language processes to elementary pupils.	Lists and can define the scope and varied sequence of behavioral outcomes desired when teaching each of the communication processes to elementary pupils.	Classifies elements in the scope and varied sequence of behavioral outcomes desired when teaching each of the communication processes to elementary pupils.	Formulates the scope and varied sequence of behavioral outcomes desired when teaching each of the communication processes to elementary pupils.	Evaluates the appropriateness of scope and behavioral objectives in communication processes.

13 University of Wisconsin, Madison, *Wisconsin Elementary Teacher Education Project*, OE 58025, 3 volumes (Washington D.C.: U.S. Office of Education, 1968), 3, 26.

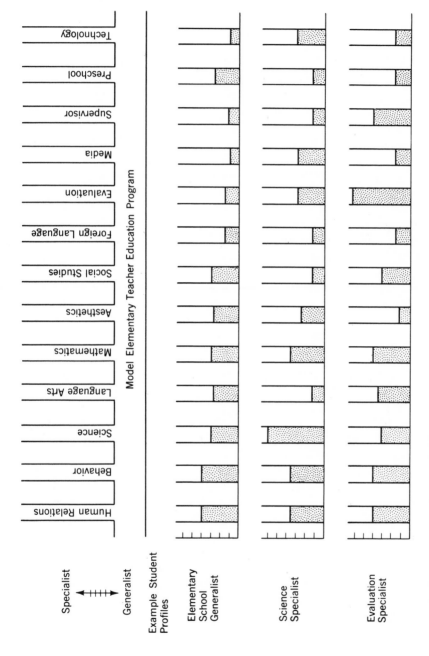

FIGURE 8-2 University of Massachusetts Profile Analysis.

225

designs, the Massachusetts model links specific learning objectives with instructional alternatives, and the selection of these can be made in relation to the specialties for which the candidate is preparing.

THE SYRACUSE APPROACH: INTENT, ACTION, AND FEEDBACK

The Syracuse program is structured around a conception of teaching which is to characterize both the teacher who emerges and the school in which he is to work. This conception is an "intent-action-feedback-process" model.

The model program is seen as functioning according to the following patterns. The demands of a changing world will make demands on the program for some kind of relevant response. In the pluralistic situation, we believe there will be a diversity of proposed responses relevant to the situation. This diversity of possible responses will lead to confrontations in an open, inquiring climate. The better alternatives should ultimately prevail. These alternatives will be translated into what have been defined as responsible behaviors, and are characterized as:

A.	Intending	Intent
B.	Acting on the basis of the intention	Action
C.	Accounting for the consequences of the action	Feedback
D.	Using the results of the accounting to modfiy future intents and actions[15]	Process

The substantive conception of the teacher within the framework of this model is described in terms of seven components, one "liberal" and six "professional."

The components of the model program

The model program is designed as a five year program. The first two years are devoted to liberal studies. The junior year begins exploratory professional study and continues liberal studies. The senior year is devoted to full time professional study. The final year, including the summers preceding and following, is seen as a resident year and a period for developing and refining: (a) skills and knowledge learned in previous years, and (b) a specialization that is unique for each student.

The seven components of the program are integrated into the basic design of the total program. These components are: (a) Liberal Education, (b) Methods and Curriculum, (c) Child Development, (d) Teaching Theory and Practice, (e) Professional Sensitivity Training, (f) Social-Cultural Foundations, and (g) a Self-Directed Component. The staff

15 *Ibid.,* p. 18.

developing the model composed of these components provided an excellent test for the workability of the pluralistic assumption about the nature of reality in teacher education. The components are diverse in nature and character. The full range of their diversity will be more apparent in subsequent chapters of this report which spell out each component more fully.[16]

Nearly all the models employed behavioral performance analysis to affective as well as cognitive and skill domains. An example from the Syracuse program shows a statement of educational objectives for a module relating to affective behavior.[17]

TTP-7: Educational Objectives for Affective Behavior

I. *Prerequisites:* Completion of TTP-5. Concurrent with tutorial experience in the public schools.

II. *Placement of Module:* Junior, preprofessional year.

III. *Estimated Time:* Student time—4 hours. University faculty time—0 hours. Clinical Professor and Clinical Teacher time—0 hours.

IV. *Operational Objectives:* The purpose of this module is to develop the ability to discriminate between statements of personal involvement, attitudes, motivations, values, etc., and to write objectives for lessons and curricula which include these types of outcomes. The general objectives of this module should prepare the student to do the following:

A. Recognize and discriminate between statements of educational goals describing the affective characteristics of children (as distinct from the other objectives already studied) as inferred from watching specific types of behaviors.

B. Write and justify the appropriateness of statements concerning the affective outcomes of lessons and curricula.

If these broad objectives are achieved, the student should, for example, be able to do the following:

A. When given a list of educational objectives, including the types of objectives studied in preceding modules and the different types and levels of affective behavior, be able to identify each and state the criteria for discriminating between them.

B. Given a case study description of an elementary classroom, including the characteristics of the pupils, be able to prepare a set of educational objectives for the class and individual pupils for at least three levels of affective involvement, such as:

1. Being willing to attend to the stimuli of the situation.
2. Responding when directed.
3. Consistency of self-initiated responses, at least within the limited regions of activity, etc.

[16] *Ibid.,* p. 19.
[17] Syracuse University, *Specifications for a Comprehensive Undergraduate Pre-Service Teacher Education Program for Elementary Education,* OE 58016 (Washington D.C.: U.S. Office of Education, 1968), pp. 245–46.

C. Be able to relate a taxonomy of affective behavior to the various types and levels of attitudes, (towards self, others, objects, and activities), motivations (affiliation, achievement, power, avoidance of failure) interests, and values.

D. When asked to prepare a set of affective objectives for the child with whom he is working in a tutorial relationship, prepare objectives for at least three levels of pupil involvement. Justify the importance of these objectives for the child, school, and society.

This example shows not only a specie of behavioral analyses in the affective domain, but the emphasis on reflective thinking by the teacher that characterized most of the models. The behavioristic description of the teacher did not ordinarily imply a mechanistic behaving teacher, but one with fluid, adaptable capability.

Syracuse also described the teacher as a member of a team, working with support teams and with a great variety of instructional systems and specialists available to him. This matrix is not fully described, but again we find the teacher in a very different role than in the average present day elementary school.

The complexity of the model required a complexity of component strategies which had to be integrated with the behaviors specified within the components.

THE FLORIDA APPROACH: THE INSTRUCTIONAL MANAGER

The Florida State University conception of the teacher was arrived at in an attempt to break down the tasks of teaching into identifiable parts which could serve as the unifying goal of the program.

Five categories of teacher behaviors were identified as basic to all elementary teaching. They are stated here in their most abstract form. The first four are:
1. The teacher will plan for instruction by formulating objectives in terms of behavior which is observable and measurable.
2. The teacher will select and organize content appropriate to specified objectives in a manner consistent with both the logic of the content itself and the psychological demands of the learner.
3. The teacher will employ appropriate strategies for the attainment of desired behavioral objectives.
4. The teacher will evaluate learning outcomes on the basis of changes in behavior.
These four behavior categories are integral parts of a regenerative or cybernetic conception of teaching in which both long range and immediate knowledge of results serves constantly to modify the direction and shape of the teaching act. (See Figure 8-3.)
The fifth category of behaviors was of a somewhat different order:

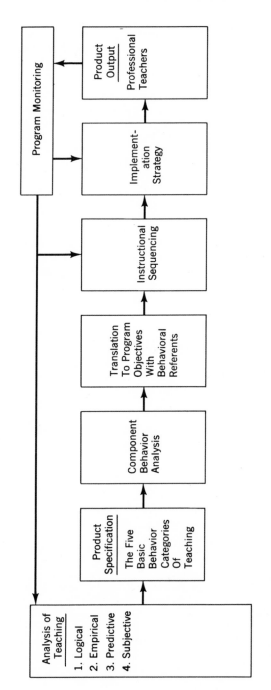

FIGURE 8-3 A Model for Rational Program Development.

5. The teacher will demonstrate an acceptance of leadership and professional responsibilities and demonstrate the ability to serve as a professional leader.

. . .

The statement of objectives in behavioral terms facilitates elements of other basic tasks, such as the systematic selection of content for learning. A teacher who has learned to apply principles of selection will carefully diagnose learner characteristics and will consider the logic of specific content. He can apply these principles in such a way that learner interaction with that content will be enhanced. Teachers have traditionally played a significant role in structuring content for particular learners. The teacher of the future is likely to play a somewhat different role with respect to the selection and organization of content. A trend toward use of multimedia, including pre-packaged programs for individual learners, suggests a teacher role which is less that of a developer of instructional programs, and more that of an assessor and adaptor of pre-packaged programs. Either role demands that selection and organization skills be highly developed, and that considerable practice in examining, selecting, and utilizing a wide range of available content material be provided.

At some point, the teacher must decide on a strategy for arranging and controlling the conditions of the contact of learner with content, and then implement whatever strategic interaction he has selected. The model program treats factors underlying both the preactive behaviors needed for strategy selection and the interactive behaviors involved in strategy implementation under the single behavior category of "strategy."

Strategy selection requires the teacher to make decisions about what kind of learning is involved, what environmental arrangements are most likely to promote that kind of learning, and what kinds of interactions will promote the most productive involvement of a given learner with selected content. These preactive decisions must be made if teaching is to be performed scientifically rather than haphazardly. Thus, the model program provides specifications for a sound theoretical decision base and for practice at reaching such decisions.

The ability to execute strategies, once selected, is a major goal of the model program and is considered a key to the successful performance of all types of teaching. Teachers must be able to arrange two basic kinds of strategic interactions: (1) non-personal interactions, and (2) interpersonal interactions, including both content-oriented and functional interactions.

. . .

To the same extent that a teacher performs certain tasks preactively and interactively as he seeks to influence learning systematically, he must also consider post-actively the results of his efforts. A conceptualization of evaluation which includes a formative (regenerative) function is fully compatible with the classic summative function which furnishes information in the form of grades and ranking. Teachers must evaluate the outcomes of instruction for the purpose of modifying the course of instruction, as well as to provide information relative to learner status and progress (Wilhelm, 1967). The instructional objective, considered first as the *sine qua non* of planning, serves also as the basis for evaluation since it has been precisely stated in terms which facilitate observation and measurement. A wide range of skills must be acquired in order to evaluate the outcomes of instruction for the full range of purposes.

The fifth major dimension of teacher behavior, involving professional responsibilities and leadership, cuts across all other tasks and adds to the performance of teaching that quality which sets it apart from more inert activities. The component behaviors of this fifth behavior dimension receive somewhat less emphasis during the pre-service phase than in the in-service phase of training because of the more urgent priority of instructional and management skills and because of a readiness factor which cannot be assumed until there is input from experiences gained while carrying out full teaching responsibility.

In this category are skills related to handling of one's emotional behavior and development of a personal teaching style; skills in handling interpersonal relationships with colleagues within the profession and with persons and agencies outside of the profession; and with skill in interpreting, assessing, and applying results of educational research. All three of these areas are intimately interrelated and are necessary for a teacher who is to be an agent of change, and who will be able to adapt to changing conditions.[18]

The extent of rationalization of the Florida conception of the teacher was unusual—the development team clearly was making a serious effort to develop a model of a functioning teacher and relate the parts of that model to one another.

In the Florida model, sixteen types of student activities, or training experiences are combined in various ways in relation to particular objectives. Table 8-3 shows the code chart for the fourteen activities; throughout the program the fourteen activities are related in various ways in the sub-elements designed to produce particular types of competence.[19]

The range of activities is worth noting, and the number of them which are self-administering or in which the student is involved prominently is instructive. The high degree of student involvement is related to the desire to involve the teacher actively in his education and to link his preparation to the creation of the future.

Summary

Hence, both the activities and the performance criteria of all the models manifest a concern with an emerging future. The documents so frequently refer to the inadequacy of our present knowledge about how to educate children that you might suppose the teams to be obsessed with feelings of ignorance as they prepared the models. There was a determina-

[18] From Florida State University, *A Model for the Preparation of Elementary Education Teachers,* OE 58018 (Washington, D.C.: U.S. Office of Education, 1968).
[19] *Ibid.,* p. 18.

TABLE 8-3 Experience Codes (From The Florida Model)

Individual Activities

Cmp	Computer Interaction
Int	Interview and Consultation
IS	Independent Study
LAV	Laboratory and Audio-Visual
Wr	Writing

Group Activities

Dsc	Discussion Group
Lct	Lecture
Prj	Project
Prs	Presentation

Field Observation

Ocl	Observation in Class
OO	Observation in Other Site

Simulation

SmO	Observing Simulated Situations
Smp	Producing Simulation

Teaching

Tcl	Classroom
Tsg	Small Group
Tt	Tutorial (one student)

tion to develop a teacher who would join in the battle against ignorance. He would act as a hypothesis tester, as one who would propose objectives for students, who would define the conditions likely to achieve those objectives, who would bring about those conditions and evaluate the outcome, and then would set to work again on the basis of what he observed. Although the styles of specification varied greatly, the teacher was seen in all cases as a member of a clinical team which would use the tools of the behavioral sciences to clarify objectives and to generate theses about the kinds of conditions that would achieve them. As an evaluator, also, he was seen as a behaviorist, using the techniques of social science to attempt to determine the results of his efforts.

In the affective and human relations domains, the behavioral sciences were also very prominent. The teacher was seen as relating to other professionals; it was assumed that it would be possible for him to be clinically trained to help him relate to others productively and that he would use knowledge from the behavioral sciences to guide his work with peers, community members, and students.

The teacher, then, was conceived as an applied scientist who would help create his field as well as practice on the basis of its present knowledge.

Implications for Teacher Education:
Commonality and Variability in Models of Teachers

The developed performance models reflect an implicit consensus about the most productive roles for the teacher today:

1. As an applied scientist (one who helps find the answers) and a behaviorist.
2. As a team member (a colleague and a specialist).
3. As a decision-maker and clinician (a strategist with a range of competencies).
4. As a change agent (whose personality can cope with change).
5. As a manager of instruction, orchestrating vast amounts of instructional material and support systems.
6. As a behaviorist—a "systems" man in his own right, setting behavioral objectives, breaking down learning tasks into their elements, and selecting learning activities and evaluation devices tailored to a range of students and differing kinds of learning.

In other words, no one developed a fixed performance model of the teacher —he was seen as one emerging and growing with the times and his own development. All saw behavioristic modes of planning and training as compatible with humanistic, affective goals. In fact, all saw behaviorism as the best avenue to a more humanistic as well as a more efficient education for children and teachers alike.

Hence, all of these systems planning teams denied the familiar assertion that systems planning techniques and humanistic education are incompatible.

The wide range of approaches to the development of the performance models included:

1. Conceptions of individualized and personalized education (several models, with Pittsburgh giving this conception a major focus).
2. Conceptions of teachers as people who make educational decisions, implement them, and get results. (Comfield is most direct with this conception, but it is shared by all models to some extent, and the "clinical style" from the Michigan State Model focuses an enormous array of modules.)
3. Conceptions of teachers as changers of educational institutions. (Especially heavy emphasis by Syracuse and Massachusetts, with Teachers College giving its entire conception to an innovator, and Florida and Comfield providing linkages to schools through schools especially committed to innovation.)

4. Conceptions of interpersonal and affective behavior (Syracuse and Massachusetts were most explicit here).

This wide range (which appears wide upon close examination) belies the notion that systems planners tend to produce homogeneous conceptions of goals and means. The products represent an especially wide range of alternative goals that can be used by second generation planners to make available, within training problems, different conceptions of education and teacher education. A second generation effort in this field can capitalize on the diversity represented here and a map of alternative performance models should gradually emerge.

Nearly all of the conceptions of the teacher need a fuller systematic description as the program models are refined and implemented. As much as is possible, the performance models need to be:

1. Dynamic models which can unify vast, complex programs and give clear guidance to developers. (The Pittsburgh Model is very strong here.)
2. Rationalized conceptualizations which relate the components of teaching to one another and, thus, lead naturally to related program components. (Florida State's conception is heuristic.)
3. Clearly related to the systems which surround the teacher—material, personal, support, and decision-making. (The Comfield Model is heuristic in this regard.)
4. Provide some guidance for the task analysts who will break down the major elements of teaching behavior into a clarified system of objectives. (Toledo provides a useful example here. Its description of the teacher provides clues for analyzing and sequencing behaviors. Georgia does also, but to a lesser extent.)

Living in an Assessment Environment

Although systematic planning of teacher education programs is promising and the modular designs in particular offer a high level of individualization, a very serious and fascinating problem which needs to be faced while the programs are being developed is one which inheres in any extensive modular curriculum plan. The problem is that of arranging the program so that the student does not live in an "assessment environment"—a kind of hell of pre-tests, post-tests, and continuous and abrasive feedback about his performance and the way that his performance relates to his capabilities. The problem is a fairly obvious one, but it is a serious one, and its solution is essential if the programs are to become feasible. We believe that it is possible to solve the problem, that it is not a problem which will solve itself and unless the systems development of the program is thoughtfully done, the very advantages of the program can exacerbate the problem to the point where the program environments could be really horrendous. The problem develops quite simply and logically. Imagine:

1. A teacher education program of about two thousand modules all organized under a management system which provides for the diagnosis of student development and needs and the prescription of the appropriate modules along certain streams of development. In addition, the system encourages the student to develop his own instructional alternatives to those already provided and, in fact, to participate in the development of objectives in some domains and the generation of experiences for achieving those objectives.

2. Each of the modules consists of a pre-test, a statement of objectives, a system for providing remedial experiences prior to the module if they are needed, a series of instructional alternatives, a post-test, provision for recycling, and for further post-tests and provision for exit from the module, for contact either with a guidance system or to another module.

3. In order to humanize this, we arrange that the student will have frequent appointments with a guidance counselor or with the "self-development component" and all relevant guidance information will be shared openly with him to help him make his own decisions and so that he will know why certain kinds of decisions are being made for him. This means that if a student progressed optimally through a program, there would be at least five thousand assessments. In the average four year college program there are about six hundred days during which a student is instructed, (about 150 days a year) and, in a 2500 unit modular curriculum, he would be assessed approximately four times each day. In that same average day, he might receive the information from the previous day's test, again four in number, and he would be working through modules preparing for tomorrow's four tests so that altogether he could be living in twelve test environments in one day. In fact, he surely would on the average if these programs are carried out as they are specified.

We hasten to warn those who would quickly dismiss systems models and turn the above statistics in rhetoric against systems planning. In the present college curriculum, a student may go for fifteen weeks and then take four tests all in one day or within one week and those four single assessments determine his success for an entire semester—that is an absurdity and a cruelty as well. It is far better to have too much assessment and have a person know where he stands than to have him wander through idyllic weeks and a pleasant college campus and then get the ax unexpectedly.

To make the "systems" models feasible, we feel that it is imperative that solutions be developed to this problem. Perhaps sampling techniques could be used so that a student would not be assessed with respect to each module but at regular intervals with the progress in between those intervals estimated on a probabilistic basis. This does not guarantee the efficiency of each module for each student to anything like the extent that the regular assessment system does, but human beings are not so erratic that it might not be quite serviceable.

Also as Hunt (Chapter 3) has pointed out, some students prefer to give themselves feedback, others prefer to have it from their peers, and yet others prefer to have it from persons who are in authority or in a position of an expert. This might be capitalized on to develop a differential feedback model in which students would receive feedback from various modes at various times with respect to particular kinds of learning outcomes. With greater variety of sources of feedback and more modes of feedback, the environment might be made more gentle and less abrasive.

Another potential direction for solution is to make large portions of the assessment process rather informal (with only some of the parts being formal) and related to the information retrieval system on the student. For example, much of the evaluation in seminars might be informal peer evaluation through the discussion of issues and problems or students who are trying a new teaching strategy could give each other feedback about how well they were doing and provide some coaching for one another with the tougher, more unyielding checkpoints being spaced at fairly good intervals.

Yet another potential direction lies in the gradual accrual of knowledge about the effectiveness of modules. For example, once it has been established that a certain proportion of the modules in a program have a particular efficiency ratio (let us suppose that they are 95 per cent efficient with 95 per cent of the students), then regular assessment of every student does not become necessary. We can assume, on a probabilistic basis, that those modules will be effective and use sampling devices to find out for which students they are not effective and which ones of them lose their effectiveness over time.

A combination of sampling procedures, intermingling of formal and informal feedback, utilization of a variety of modes of feedback and the testing of modules could result in patterns quite different from those toward which all the modules appear to be heading at this writing.

9

Behaviorism and Conservatism: The Educational Views in Four of the "Systems" Models of Teacher Education

MICHAEL APPLE

Michael Apple combines interests in philosophy and curriculum. He has been a member of the innovative team in teacher education at Teachers College and is presently a professor of curriculum at the University of Wisconsin in Madison. He was part of a team which contracted with the United States Office of Education to make an analysis of the products of the Bureau of Research Project to apply systematic planning procedures to the reconstruction of teacher education. During the project, Apple became interested in the apparent conservatism of the "systems" models and began to speculate on the possible relationship between the use of behavioristic techniques to define program goals and training procedures and conservatism in the view of the teacher and his training. The result of his curiosity is a fascinating essay on the potential difficulties involved in behavioristic planning and issues which have to be resolved if systems approaches to education are to fulfill their promise for modernizing education and relating it to contemporary and future social needs. Apple argues that thus far behaviorism has been conservative—has not been forward-looking either in the conceptions of the school or the roles of the teacher which have resulted from its use. He presents his arguments in such a way that they can guide those of us who will redesign and implement systems models in the coming decade.

What are the implicitly held value stances and particular educational conceptions found within the teacher education models and what problems are latent in those stances and conceptions? I believe that on the whole the merits of the proposals may outweigh their negative attributes; however, there are certain fundamental problmes that have to be examined if the effectiveness of the models is not to be merely verbal.

The behavioristic view of teaching found in these models carries with it certain assumptions regarding varying aspects of education—the teacher, the teaching process, the mind, the student, and the curriculum. These assumptions appear to embody latent elements of conservatism which play upon each dimension in a different way. The conservative elements include restrictions of scope (such as with curriculum), a ceiling on the provisions for change in both the educational environment and the larger societal context, limitations on the opportunity for creativity in both learning and teaching, and finally, a commitment to a philosophy of external control and regulation of human behavior. Some of the manifestations of these assumptions present political and practical difficulties; others are problems of logic associated with a behavioristic view of teacher training and teaching. The question that must be asked as we examine these assumptions is which elements are inherent in the behavioristic view of teaching and which simply reflect the limitations of our own visions, imagination, technology, and choice? Only then can we fairly and intelligently face the decision of commitment.

There are basic differences here between the four models. One is quite conservative and offers little hope of change since its methodology posits a fairly rigid structure. Another envisions teachers who specialize in one of four academic disciplines and who will be trained to function in a multi-unit school, but with so little attention paid to the very real political problems of instituting its reforms that it holds little hope of change. One has a forward-looking conception *and* a structure which makes implementation seem less than impossible.

Purpose

The tone of the analysis may seem negative at times. This has been a result of a deliberate choice to subject the models to serious criticism. The models, with their competency-based and behavioral orientation, offer what is essentially a new paradigm for educational practice and research. Such a break with the past must be examined quite carefully. There has not been a tradition in the literature in teacher education of honest, searching criticism of proposals, much to the detriment of the field. This decided lack of a critical perspective has led to periods of either stagnation or rapid but surface change so similar to the "bandwagon" phenomenon that has had such a long career in other areas of educational thought and practice. Also, the models are disturbing intellectually in some crucial ways. These deficiencies will be pointed out, not merely to engage in nihilistic activity but because of a commitment to the opening of a perspective on the need for continuing dialogue among concerned educators of a variety of persuasions. This is best thought of in dialectical terms. A field becomes vital when its members present well thought-out proposals, are open to rebuttal, and engage in argumentation and counter-rebuttal, and hence progress to a more sophisticated understanding of its complex problems. Thus, while my tone is critical, it is in the spirit of developing a dialogue over complex issues.

One task of this analysis, then, is essentially to raise significant questions concerning the models of elementary teacher education. It is hoped that the next step of the necessary "debate" will be continued by the model proponents. The issue is not whether the competency-based proposals will produce a *relatively* better skilled and more articulate teacher than is now usually being trained. *There is really little doubt that they will at least produce more technically competent teachers.* The more important questions are: "Competent to do what?" "Competent by whose standards?" And above all, "Can the models be made better if certain basic issues are dealt with more cogently?"

Another task is to examine the realities behind the goals as stated in the models of elementary teacher education. For it is a quality of educational slogans (here not meant in a pejorative sense, but in a descriptive and analytic way) that they do not imply their particulars. That is, they are broad categories under which one can place many programmatic suggestions, even to the extent where the same slogan can refer to two or more disparate educational ends or programs. The current watchword of "relevance" is a case in point. It serves as an umbrella for many types of educational concerns and ideologies, from the romantic anarchism of Paul Goodman to the social and economic reconstructionism of the spokesman of the ghetto. Their programs are often contradictory, yet they do fall under the all-embracing call for a more relevant education.[1]

The models of elementary teacher education use terms similar to the

---

[1] Michael W. Apple, "Relevance—Slogan and Meanings," *The Educational Forum* (May 1971).

slogan of relevance. Each proposes a program which will prepare teachers who, to paraphrase, "will be able to adapt to the changing environment, will be effective and skillful in dealing with school situations involving teaching and learning, and who will act as potential leaders in the continual rejuvenation of society." Yet behind these worthwhile goals and slogans lie different views of the teacher, of the best modes of preparing these teachers, and implicit value stances which can serve to enhance or detract from the attainment of the goal. We shall have to go behind such initial statements and explicit program intentions in order to get a more accurate perspective on the actual substance of the models and to examine possible implications of their differences.

A Conservative View of the Teacher

As mentioned in the previous selection, all of the model-builders agreed to base their program on the behavioristic view of teaching and to use a systems approach in designing them. The conception of the teacher found in the models is often closely related to the systems design methodology used in determining the characteristics of the teacher they wish to produce.

Although a behavioristic view of teaching and systems design methodology are not synonymous, they are highly compatible, perhaps, even interdependent. The concept of systems design used by most educators seems to have originated in industry's concern for efficiency in developing a standard product. It is geared to similarity of output and provides a means of quality control. By specifying the product one wants and then working backwards to analyze the inputs and processes which make up that predetermined product, efficient production and quality control can be maintained. This is the logic of industrial production and the logic applied to the processes of education in the application of systems design. It is thought that such a model (some might wish to call it a factory model) is useful in establishing means for minimum satisfactory performance of teachers and for bringing about minimum levels of competency in students.

THE TEACHER AS DETERMINED BY JOB ANALYSIS

Following the industrial production analogy and logic, Georgia attempted to develop a behavioral model of the teacher using *job analysis*.[2] In their naive use of the approach, Georgia's proponents seem unaware of the fact that there is a significant history in the curriculum field of the use of job or activity analysis. The historical criticisms of the method are

---

[2] *Georgia Educational Model Specifications for the Preparation of Elementary School Teachers* (Washington, D.C.: U.S. Department of Health Education, and Welfare, 1968), p. 5.

quite pertinent today for examining significant problems in their job conceptions of the role of the teacher.

Georgia states that its task is to prepare a program "in relation to the job the teacher is required to perform in the classroom. By defining what the job actually is, the competencies necessary to perform specific tasks may be adequately determined."[3] They then go on to state that "it would *logically* follow that the content of a teacher education program should be based on the teaching act itself."[4] Discounting the fact that the logic used here is essentially tautological, there are a number of issues that need to be raised.

A major difficulty is a problem which they do not squarely face—that is, what constitutes a "good teacher?" Is one to assume that their working definition is that a "good teacher" is that individual who can cope with the activities which currently go on in schools? If so, this is rather conservative. The knowledgeable criticisms of current educational practices are too potent to be ignored. While the method of activity or job analysis gives us data on what "is," it can tell us nothing about what "should be." When it is relied on heavily, it is more suited to a static society than one which is obviously changing as rapidly as our own. Georgia attempts to deal with the problems inherent in job analysis by including in its model plan goals for the schools as stated by experienced educators, philosophers, and others. However, an analysis of the stated activities of teachers and the roles which they actually play in the Georgia model shows convincingly that what "is" *has*, in fact, been used to legitimate and give extreme weight to what "should be." We shall examine these activities in detail later in the analysis.

Part of the difficulty inherent in their failure to deal adequately with the important issue of what constitutes a "good teacher" is the significant amount of argumentation in the field of teacher education as to what teaching effectiveness actually entails. There is little difficulty in locating, say, a good plumber whose activities can be analyzed, but even an in-depth examination of the literature reveals no such agreement on the characteristics of teacher quality. What it does reveal, however, is that there is agreement that much of what occurs in schools is less than adequate and much teaching activity must be *changed* from what is found today to a more knowledgeable ideal. That there are other quite conservative elements in the models, and in Georgia, especially, can be shown.

The process-product rationality fosters an orientation toward efficiency in teaching based on a standardized product. By itself, the efficiency rationality presents few problems. What is disturbing is its apparent propensity for generalizing itself into nearly all major aspects of the educative environ-

3 *Ibid.*, p. 35.
4 *Ibid.*, p. 35 (italics added).

ment. Thus, while such criteria are not necessarily antithetical to diversity, there is apparently a strong tendency, simply by following the logical structure of the system itself, for efficiency rationales to dominate. The result is that those elements which can be best produced and reproduced, which can be identified and are easily quantifiable, will tend to be given more consideration. Also, orderliness and very rational (often suprarational) procedures are apt to be given currency over less manifestly orderly and somewhat more ambiguous procedures, thus acting to place pressure for clear cut directives and answers where the ambiguity and complexity need much further investigation. It generates pressure to be able to give clearly stated cause and effect relationships' in a quasi-scientific fashion when, in fact, such relationships are logically unsound.

THE TEACHER AS CLINICIAN

The conception of the teacher developed by Syracuse, Massachusetts, and Michigan State is somewhat different than that developed by Georgia, perhaps, due to a different point of origin. They perceive the teacher as one who can become, *through training,* increasingly aware of the elements involved in making decisions, who consciously tests and revises hypotheses, and who approaches the classroom in a fairly sophisticated fashion. Michigan State, for instance, views its teacher as someone who is rather similar to an action researcher, with, however, some strongly worded qualifications differentiating between a teacher with a clinical behavior style, as they call it, and an action research style.[5]

> The key rallying cry within the action research movement was, "Research is easy, and it's fun! Anyone can do it, and those who do discover more enjoyment in teaching." Most practitioners who engaged in easy, fun projects obtained a misleading view of research and scientific inquiry as a game having a few simple rules that could be played by anyone with a little intelligence and initiative. In contrast, experiences of the training programs described in this report are designed to help trainees view behavioral science not as a simple game played by amateurs for their self amusement but as a complex activity conducted by skilled professionals for the benefit of mankind.

The model continues in its attempt to distinguish between clinical behavior style and action research.

> ...Action research experience tended to obscure the importance of doubt and uncertainty and error and changing conceptual structures; science as the

---

[5] *Michigan State University Behavioral Science Elementary Teacher Education Program, Vol. I* (Washington, D.C.: U.S. Department of Health, Education, and Welfare, 1968), p. III 14–15.

construction and reconstruction of abstract conceptual structures linked to empirically observable phenomena was hidden from view. In contrast, the training programs outlined in this report attempt to reveal in honest but manageable form the complexity and diversity of conceptual structures and methods of inquiry in behavioral science. Within a clinical behavior style of teaching, various modes of inquiry and conceptual structures will be used to look at an instructional problem from alternative points of view, subject to empirical testing of actions derived from those points of view and *restructuring the problem in accord with observed consequences.*[6]

The clinical behavior style has three components which, as we shall see, are quite similar to those proposed by Massachusetts. The "reflecting phase" involves describing and analyzing a problem within one or more theoretical frameworks[7] and producing a diagnosis. Second is the "proposing phase" which involves constructing alternative solutions to the problem and determining proper "treatment" or "prescription." Obviously, the third component of the clinical behavior cycle is the "doing phase" which "involves treating the client and observing what happens subsequent to treatment. Seeking evidence on the consequences of treatment, and then viewing the treated client in his situation as a new problem to be investigated by reapplication of the cycle, is the activity which allows the practitioner to 'learn from experience'."

The similarity of the language used here to that of the medical profession is important. The possible consequence of it will be dealt with in detail shortly, as will those consequences associated with a strong professional and clinical view of teaching.

In nearly all of the other models chosen for analysis, the orientation is also toward viewing the teacher as an expert clinician who consciously (and self-consciously) diagnoses situations and can act appropriately. Perhaps the best statement of this perspective on the teacher is made in the Massachusetts endeavor. Their object is to bring the teacher's processes of decision-making to increased awareness so that he may consider alternative procedures based on the wide selection of professional skills, strategies, and data that he possesses. The "thinking and behaving" is divided into three

6 This may be a rather limited conception of relevant conceptual structures. See, for example, the discussion of divergent frameworks of valuing in Dwayne Huebner, "Curricular Language and Classroom Meaning." in James B. Macdonald and Robert R. Leeper, eds., *Language and Meaning* (Washington, D.C.: ASCD, 1966), and the well-written analysis of the many "modes of knowing" we have in Philip Phenix, *Realms of Meaning* (New York: McGraw-Hill, 1964). These important pieces offer an interesting alternative way of critiquing the perspective on teaching in the models.

7 This use of different theoretical frameworks to illuminate the problem and see it from another perspective is a very important point in its favor.

stages which are shown in this schematic presentation reproduced from the model.[8]

Stage I: Problem Definition

  A. Consideration of alternative definitions of the problem (Divergent Thinking).

  B. Tentative commitment to one definition of the problem (Convergent Thinking).

Stage II: Consideration of Alternative Solutions

  A. Development of as many possible alternative solutions to the problem as possible (Divergent Thinking).

  B. It may be noted that the decision to include a thought as a possible alternative solution or reject it as irrelevant is convergent thinking.

  C. If it is difficult to discover alternatives, a redefinition of the problem and a return to Stage I may be necessary (Feedback).

Stage III: Decision for Action

  A. Consideration of the possible implications for action of each alternative (Divergent Thinking).

  B. A tentative commitment is made to a course of action (Convergent Thinking).

  C. If none of the alternatives seem suitable or the decision proves inadequate, return to Stage III A to examine other alternatives, or Stage II to develop new alternatives or Stage I to reconceptualize the problem (Feedback).

There are two latent problems with this conceptualization of the teacher as conscious decision-maker that are not limited to this particular statement by Massachusetts. While it is crucial to recognize the importance of producing a teacher who is in fact conscious of the types of decisions he must make and who is given concrete skills in making these decisions, it is also imperative to point to the density of the reality which this teacher must face in schools. It may be that the immediacy and complexity of dealing with twenty-five (or thirty or twenty) human beings and with an established institution with the usual bureaucratic conditions will not allow for the process of conscious articulation of decisions and alternative structures *during* activity.[9] What may be happening here, in effect, is the equipping

---

[8] *Massachusetts Model Elementary Teacher Education Program: Appendix I* (Washington, D.C.: U.S. Department of Health, Education, and Welfare, 1968), p. 26.

[9] Cf. Philip Jackson, *Life in Classrooms* (New York: Holt, Rinehart and Winston, 1968), pp. 111–77.

of teachers with both a vocabulary and ideology of conscious decision making and the skills to do this in *limited* representations of educational reality, but with no rationality which can deal with the *political* problems of actually changing school structures so that these conscious properties can be useful. This is a major problem with the models and one which will be pointed to in greater depth in our discussion of the possibility of ideological conflict between competing interest groups.

What should be noted before temporarily leaving this topic is that historically one of the primary causes of disenchantment and feelings of normlessness and anomie is the conflict engendered when a personal ideology does not match a political reality. It is quite possible that the models of teacher education must develop a much stronger critical perspective and newer vision of the school as an institution not limited to a building divided into boxes, no doubt better equipped boxes, but boxes nevertheless. A changing view of the teacher requires concomitant attention to the structure of the institution *and more concrete and sophisticated* analyses of how these institutions either totally or partially are to be restructured. To divorce one's view of teaching from one's view of the milieu in which this teaching is to be carried on, or to link one's new perspective on teaching to a possibly outmoded and, perhaps, alien institutional structure is to deal but superficially with what we all know is a supremely complex problem. There needs to be a closer examination of the impact by environmental and architectural systems upon the interpersonal ones, not "merely" the articulation of alternative organizational plans on which the models concentrate much of their attention.

It should be obvious by now that the achievement of any educational goal is a result not "merely" of the teacher's behavior, but also myriad other factors in the environment and how these are perceived and manipulated by the individual actors *in situ*. Attempting to determine effective teaching in isolation as *the* variable neglects the density of the situation.[10]

A second, and equally significant problem, especially in urban areas, is that with the envisioned development of a corps of teacher/clinicians organized around a sense of professional expertise, there will no doubt be a commitment by these teachers to a professional ideology similar to that found in medicine. Part of this ideology will be based on a belief that the members possess what sociologists of knowledge like to call "expert knowledge." The holders of this expert knowledge form a definite community, an in-group, so to speak, which often resents incursion into its defined territory by nonmembers. This is quite the case in medicine as it is in other

[10] Marvin Taylor, "Educational Goals and Teacher Effectiveness," in Ronald T. Hyman, ed., *Contemporary Thought on Teaching* (Englewood Cliffs, N.J.: Prentice-Hall, 1971), p. 227.

areas of knowledge and professional competence such as astronomy and historical biology where the Velikovsky case caused quite a stir.[11] The development of such an ideology may lead to confrontations with some of the people who are served by the public schools.

Over the past few years, a hard-fought battle has been waged in urban areas of the country for community involvement in, even control of, the schools. Often teachers must work closely in these areas with community leaders, sometimes treading carefully, and often filling what may be only an advisory capacity in the actual making of many decisions which affect what goes on in the schools. The conflict between teachers who hold an ideology which disallows nonprofessional encroachment on what are deemed to be professional matters and parents whose growing ideological position concerns the necessity of literally controlling their own destiny, with the schools as a prime medium of this control, could be bitter. One of the most difficult tasks that the teacher educators who are developing the models must face (and one which very few of them, in fact, have given more than perfunctory attention to) is the possibility of this type of conflict over the control of schools.[12]

A basic reason for the lack of insight in the models into the more than likely discord between "clinicians" and citizen groups is their failure to follow the logic of systems thought to its completion. One of the primary prerequisites of systems analytical procedure and systems design is to conceptualize all of the relevant subsystems interacting with the functional whole. To neglect this is to lose much of the potency of systems thought. A significant area, which is not dealt with or is treated in only a very cursory fashion by the models, is that of conceiving the teacher as a member of a political system, that is, one who is involved in the distribution and possible redistribution of power to make decisions. In fact, this question is begged.

A Conservative View of Teaching

CHANGING THE LEARNER'S BEHAVIOR

Like the design methodology, the behavioristic view of teaching to which all the models subscribed, contains conservative elements which need to be examined and recognized. To quote the Michigan State Model, "In general *teaching* is defined as human behavior which results in a change in

---

[11] Michael Mulkay, "Some Aspects of Cultural Growth in the Natural Sciences," *Social Research,* **XXXV** (Spring 1969), pp. 22–52.

[12] It should be mentioned that there is an attempt to place some degree of emphasis upon understanding inner-city cultural patterns in the more astute models. Yet to intellectually comprehend cultural patterns is not the same as coping with the potential political conflict.

human (learner) behavior."[13] A close examination of this view of teaching leads to some basic difficulties, especially those concerned with the connection between teaching and learning.

Now, obviously "teaching is a change in learner behavior" is a slogan under which is subsumed certain goals. These are probably something like the following: (1) We must focus on students not on subjects, or as it is often put, we teach students not subject matter. (2) Look, for teaching to be better, we really have to focus more on competencies and actual effectiveness. And in order to focus on how effective we are, we must specify the actual behaviors that students will engage so that we can refine our teaching and be better next time.

We should remember that ideally this is an attempt to humanize teaching by making the teacher more effective and more conscious of the behaviors that he can employ to bring about the best results. Yet, while no one would quarrel with the ideal, one can question its conceptual simplicity.

In essence, the relationship can be indicated by a rather simple equation.[14]

$$\underset{\text{Pupils}}{\text{Behavior}} = f \; \underset{\text{Teacher}}{(\text{Behavior})}$$

This serves to indicate that the behavior of the pupil is a function of the behavior of the teacher.

The linkage of teaching with learning is perhaps helpful on some (but not all) practical grounds, but is a bit too superficial if one is to base a lasting view of the teacher upon it. Scheffler's discussion of teaching illuminates certain problems. There are, in essence, two uses of teaching viewed as activity. These are logically separate and involve the distinction between a success sense and an intentional sense of teaching.[15]

By its very nature, teaching is in some way an act of influence. In its usual usage, it aims at establishing or intends certain goals[16] and aims at designing environments which can best achieve them. The intentional nature of teaching lies in this attempt to create humane environments for reaching these goals. If these goals are, in fact, reached, then the teaching has, ob-

---

13 *Michigan State,* p. I 21.

14 William Rabinowitz and Robert M. W. Travers, "Problems of Defining and Assessing Teacher Effectiveness," in Ronald T. Hyman, ed., *Contemporary Thought on Teaching* (Englewood Cliffs, N.J.: Prentice-Hall, 1971), p. 217.

15 Israel Scheffler, *The Language of Education* (Springfield, Ill: Charles C Thomas, 1960), pp. 41–44.

16 That this is not accepted by all educators should be noted. See, for example, Dwayne Huebner, "Curriculum as a Field of Study," in Helen F. Robinson, ed., *Precedents and Promise in the Curriculum Field* (New York: Basic Books, 1965).

viously, been successful. Yet to link the two permanently would be less than accurate.

Let us take as an example an attempt (intention) to teach a student to draw. Using all the resources at his disposal, the teacher is basically and continually unsuccessful even though he is strikingly creative in his attempts. Would we then say that the teacher has not been teaching? As one more example, we might examine the teacher teaching by being a model for the propensity to behave in accordance with democratic principles. Since there are usually very few opportunities for the student in school to demonstrate this in other than rather trite and unimportant ways, are we to assume that it is unimportant to teach them because success cannot really be demonstrated? This temporal dimension of the linkage between teaching and learning is crucial and will be raised again.

There are other logical difficulties with a definition of teaching like that implied in the models (i.e., teaching is bringing about a change in behavior). I am wary of pushing the more "academic" problems too far (after all, our job is educating teachers in the best possible way we can). However, the view of teaching embodied in the models is founded strongly upon this definition, and what may be more important to gaining an intellectual sophistication so necessary in teacher education, it points to the continued neglect by teacher educators of analytic perspectives. Teaching viewed as changing of behavior of students does not enable distinctions to be made concerning the very *moral* nature of the teaching act itself. It ignores the important differences between, say, teaching and training or teaching and indoctrination. I may brainwash an individual and definitely change his behavior; however, most would agree, I am certain, that this could not be labeled as teaching. It also runs the quite realistic risk of substituting a technological slogan for what should be a reasoned moral choice.

Linked to this is the fact that learning here is also seen as a change in behavior. A very real problem that *must* be dealt with much more cogently than has been the case in the models is what is to count as *behavior*. It is a word that is remarkably ambiguous. For a group attempting to develop a more rational and sophisticated (if not scientific) view of the act of teaching, it is surprising that the sophistication does not extend to this problem, except to substitute further ambiguity such as using the word "action" instead. To define learning as a change in behavior (and this reflects heavily on the view of teaching posited by the models) does not differentiate learning from other processes which result in changes in behavior. It should be obvious that not all changes in behavior are learned and that to view *all* learning as resulting in changes in behavior merely begs the question as to the constitutive rules or criteria for defining behavior itself. This leads to a circularity of thought that is in no way helpful to solving the very practical problems of getting evidence of one's teaching success.

While it is not always logically defensible, a case can be made by the model developers for linking teaching with learning on political grounds. This may be rather important. By defining teaching as "behavior which results in changes in learner behavior," then the teacher can and should be held *accountable* for the learning of his students. This eliminates many of the socio-psychological explanations that have been used to account for the failure of schools in the past (in urban areas in particular) and centers responsibility once more squarely upon the schools themselves. The notion of teacher accountability is revolutionary in that teaching *must* succeed if it is to be considered teaching at all. Learners' behaviors must be changed to show that teaching has been successful. The political dimensions of this area of the models are intriguing. Whose idea of what constitutes effective teaching will they use to legitimate their activity? Perhaps the last question can be more clearly stated—*to whom* and to what criteria will the teacher be accountable? The lack of political (broadly conceived) insight and rationality in the models detracts from their possible potency here.

A CONTROL-ORIENTED CLASSROOM SOCIAL CLIMATE

Another question that must be asked is whether the behavioristic view of teaching leads to a "teacher-dominated" social climate? The Michigan State Model, for instance, has a somewhat conservative view of teacher functions. It is rather control oriented in its outlook with an emphasis upon the teacher as the central figure who dominates a great deal of classroom activity. The patterns of influence are unidimensional. That is, if one were to mentally construct a matrix of strength of influence, it would emanate from teacher to student with little or no mutuality. In itself this is merely realistic since enough research has been done to give us information that this is how most classrooms operate. When coupled with the other more control-oriented perspectives and aspects of many elements of the various models, however, it makes one pause.[17] For instance, one might conjecture

---

[17] Perhaps the best example of the overemphasis on the behaviorist-as-controller orientation (and here it must be noted that the two need not necessarily go together) is found in one of the models not being treated in this analysis. However, it is useful as an example of the extremes to which this may be taken. In the Comfield model, behavioral expectations are to be noted for parent-teacher conferences. The teacher is to conceive of what he wants as his outcomes of the conferences in behavioral terms. This can lead to a manipulative set toward interpersonal relations and may bring about an assumption that openness is of less importance than, say, turning the parent's views into "proper channels" so to speak. Cf. Joel L. Burdin and Kaliopee Lanzillotti, *A Reader's Guide to the Comprehensive Model for Preparing Elementary Teachers* (Washington, D.C.: ERIC Clearinghouse on Teacher Education, 1969), p. 59.

on the significance of the following element of teaching behavior which considers the "environmental dimensions" of the classroom. A function of the teacher is "deciding on classroom rules necessary for maintaining an efficient and orderly classroom—permissions and prohibitions, rules and regulations."[18] That this differs in its basic orientation to teaching from, say, that posited by the English Infant School movement which is beginning to have an impact in the United States needs to be stated. The models view classroom activity as essentially centered about the teacher who determines objectives and teaches according to the primary criterion of efficiency in learning.

A Conservative View of the Curriculum

BEHAVIORAL OBJECTIVES

Coupled with the behavioral change view of teaching is the emphasis on behavioral objectives. The two go hand in hand, as it were. Strengths and weaknesses in one affect the relative strengths and weaknesses in the other.

Let me reiterate here that while the weaknesses of the behavioral perspective on teaching have been and will be stressed, the possible positive features of the use of the behavioral paradigms *must* be given their due as a major aspect of teacher education. They can serve to focus on the student; they can enable the development of a relatively more skillful teacher in some areas; they are first steps in the articulation of a more comprehensive perspective on the teaching act; and, of great importance, the models attempt to use behaviorism to establish a sense of teacher responsibility and accountability which goes beyond any previous usage. Yet, with all this said (and most of it has been said by its proponents time and again), it should be noted that much of the emphasis on behavioral modes may stem from the fact that this is where funds are to be found and where support lies. As in the physical sciences, research and development often follows the lead of government support.[19]

The models almost totally neglect the vital intellectual controversy over the use of behavioral objectives in education. They give the impression that there is no significant body of scholarship critiquing the behavioral orientation.[20]

The argument for behavioral objectives has been thoroughly articulated in the Michigan State Model. Let us examine this closely.

[18] *Michigan State,* p. III 56.
[19] Cf. Warren O. Hagstrom, *The Scientific Community* (New York: Basic Books, 1965).
[20] Whether this is due to the fact that funding might not have been forthcoming is interesting and serves to illuminate the final point of the previous paragraph.

Basing BSTEP on precisely written, performance-based behavioral objectives clearly has the support of leading thinkers in education today. Ojemann emphasizes the importance of overt performance as the base for evaluation, saying, "The only way one can learn whether a child has mastered a skill, a bit of knowledge, or a feeling pattern is by observing his behavior in specified situations." The need for specificity has been cited by Bloom, who says, "For the educational technologists and evaluators, the clearer the specifications are in terms of both content and behaviors, the better."

The use of such behavioral objectives has a number of strengths. Most important, behavioral objectives communicate clearly. Criterion measures let the student know at once the behavior he is expected to exhibit in the course of study and specify for the instructor the precise behavior he must develop in his students. Once instruction begins, the criterion measures become even more useful in providing feedback to the student concerning his progress in the component and in providing diagnostic data for the instructor's use in providing special help for those who need it.

Secondly, the use of behavioral objectives enhances the evaluation of the program itself. Once the intended learnings are identified, collection of objective data about the system becomes easy. Decisions concerning the effectiveness of instructional techniques and materials are made not on the basis of subjective judgments, but by comparing results against the specific criterion outcomes specified in the objectives. Hence, program modification and evaluation is enhanced.

Third, explicitly stated behavioral objectives guard against alteration in the program by various pressures and whims. As Bloom stated:

"If the purposes and specifications for education are not explicit, then it is possible for them to be altered by social pressures, by fads and fashion, and by new schemes and devices which may come and go with momentary shifts on the educational scene. Implicit purposes are difficult to defend, and the seeming vacuum in purpose invites attack and substitution of explicit purposes by a constant stream of pressure and pressure groups."

While continual evaluation and modification in the program is certainly desirable, such modifications must be based on specific data rather than on whim. Behavioral objectives, by their specificity, insure that such will be the case.

Fourth, the use of performance criteria and behavioral objectives makes it possible to determine clearly whether or not the student meets the minimum level of performance deemed necessary for beginning teachers...

Finally, by examining behavioral objectives, persons outside the university community can tell exactly what it is a student can do. Currently, student competency is defined by a letter grade or number grade received in a course. Such measurement is haphazard, since it provides no insights concerning what the student knows, or what he can do, or how well he can perform.... Behavioral objectives, on the other hand, aid communication because they cite in detail the performance to be expected and the level of competence of a graduate from such a program.[21]

[21] *Michigan State Behavioral Science Teacher Education Program: Feasibility Study* (Washington, D.C.: U.S. Department of Health, Education, and Welfare, 1969), pp. 91–92.

While this is essentially an argument for behavioral objectives on a university level in a competency-based program, much of the argument is also used to legitimate the behavioral orientation on the elementary school level. The fundamentally deterministic foundation is evident here. But what is really disturbing is the rather conservative political outlook most apparent in the third listed "strength" of behavioral objectives—that behavioral objectives help guard against pressures from social groups. It is definitely the case that safeguards must be constructed to protect schools from the all too prevalent whims of society's manifold groups. However, also behind the statement seems to be presupposition that such conflict is necessarily bad and is not just as often (and perhaps more so today) a positive force for needed educational change. It would be naive and less than accurate, though, to strongly correlate a behavioral orientation to teaching with political conservatism. There are other elements that correlate with a conservative educational viewpoint, however.

Looking behind many of the comments on behavioral competencies, one finds such statements as, "If *intent* to teach is presumed to be an essential feature of the act of teaching, then competence in teaching is primarily effective transmission of knowledge."[22] The critical question to be asked here is, "How is this effectiveness to be ascertained?" Knowledge, here, is used in such an open way that it includes more than what is usually grouped under the cognitive label.

As educators, we are concerned with not only "knowledge" and skills, we are also vitally interested in less immediate concerns such as states of appreciation and self-awareness, which occur over longer periods of time and are not necessarily evident in changes in behavior at the time a student is in school. An appreciation of diverse forms of music or positive attitudes toward one's own or other races are examples. By limiting ourselves to behaviors which can be seen here and now or over a fairly limited amount of time, we run the risk of severely curtailing what may be just as important activities in the long run.

It is quite true that aimlessness is lessened by such a procedure and that we can often obtain evidence of the success or failure of our teaching, but the evidence (behavior) that learning has taken place may not be manifest until a substantial period of time after the occurrence of the learning itself. Even when the learning is manifest, it may come in a totally dissimilar form than what was anticipated.[23] In actuality this should be looked upon as a boon, not a problem. If a principle or, maybe more important, a disposition toward, say, intellectual openmindedness is truly made

22 *Ibid.,* p. 139.
23 Donald Arnstine, *Philosophy of Education: Learning and Schooling* (New York: Harper and Row, 1967), p. 17.

one's own, it is generalized to different situations. What is more, the meaning that we as observers may give to it may be totally different than that given to it by the actor himself.[24]

The program developers were apparently aware of the problem, but rather than attempting to develop patterns of evaluation to deal with extremely subtle types of growth, the programs themselves seem to be written with ease of evaluation in mind. This is evident in the statement quoted earlier arguing for behavioral objectives. With the emphasis upon concrete observation of change and probable evaluation through the use of instruments, the focus of the programs tends to be upon those elements for which the teacher can be most easily prepared—areas of clear, easily measured objectives and well-known, efficient means. That is, those goals about which we have less knowledge and less skill in reaching have a tendency to become marginal. This is a serious problem of conceptions of teacher effectiveness gauged through behavior change in the learner. The problem does not disappear by recognizing it and not expanding conceptions of the teacher to include the less obvious goals and means.

Given the total number of people in a classroom, how is one to determine when an *individual* teacher has satisfied performance criteria? The most likely result, even with the differentiated staffing plans used in the models, will be some sort of the usual test or standard *group* criteria. In only a small way does this add significantly to the possibilities of individualizing instruction. Given institutional pressure, it is quite possible that we shall see the establishment of a system similar to the Regents Examinations found in New York; it is also possible that the National Assessment Program will serve in this role. What is more, to quote Rabinowitz and Travers:

> Though available tests are almost all in the field of subject matter achievement, a broad concept of effectiveness includes the teacher's influence on emotional adjustment in pupils' social attitudes, creative expression and the like. There are eminently commendable goals toward which a teacher might aspire, but we have, sad to say, few acceptable methods of measuring progress toward these goals.[25]

The behavioral orientation also has severe practical difficulties in dealing with the dialectic of group interaction (as, to be truthful, do the other accepted orientations that have been used historically in education). The behavioral orientation finds its basis in an experimental psychology which

[24] Cf. The distinction between act and action meaning, in Abraham Kaplan, *The Conduct of Inquiry* (San Francisco: Chandler, 1964), pp. 358–63.
[25] Rabinowitz and Travers, "Teacher Effectiveness," p. 219.

is itself founded upon research on singular events and research on individuals or rather small groups of organisms. It provides much less basis for training the teacher to help groups work together or practice group inquiry. The models are, not surprisingly, most effective when they see the teacher as a tutor or a manager of instructional systems. That they do not conceive of him as a group leader reflects in the basis of this individual-oriented technology.

There is also an assumption in the models that specific "atomized" behavioral elements or knowledge are additive. That is, by merely presenting elements in "bite-sized pieces" the task of mastery of higher order operations is simplified. Not all of the models neglect this very real problem. Massachusetts, for one, recognizes that there is a distinction between knowing the component parts of a skill and the artful performance of the skill itself. They refer to Polanyi's significant work, pointing to his view that "human experiences and feelings are more than the sum of their several components."[26] In more common sense terms, I may be able to successfully fulfill all the subroutines of bicycle riding—steering, pedaling, balancing correctly on a seat, etc.—yet the coherence of all these component parts into a working "gestalt" is not guaranteed. I may, in fact, not be able to put them all together and may fail miserably at riding a bicycle every time I gather up enough courage to try. Anyone who has spent years learning how to play a musical instrument *artistically* can multiply this example tenfold. The models specify bite-sized behaviors, but deal much less effectively with the integration of these into significant clusters of behavior.

Since the schools also serve to develop important attitudes (and remember that Massachusetts and the others include this in their "sets of learnings"), it is quite legitimate to ask how these are broken down. How, for instance, does one behaviorally reduce such global responsibilities as those involved in moral education?[27]

Let us consider another example of deficiencies associated with behaviorally specified objectives. There is little doubt that most educators would agree on the necessity of having students engage in what we broadly call problem solving. Now teachers could and do encourage their students to actively search for solutions to problems, to independently conduct research and experiments. However, difficulties arise for a number of reasons if this objective is to be reduced to specific behaviors: (1) Psychologists have not as yet identified many of the most important behavioral elements of problem

---

[26] *Massachusetts Model*, p. 78. That they note but still actually ignore it will be shown in the section on "sensitivity."

[27] Cf. the excellent analysis by R. S. Peters in "The Concept of Character," in B. Paul Komisar and C. B. J. Macmillan, eds., *Psychological Concepts in Education* (Skokie, Ill.: Rand McNally, 1967).

solving; (2) Behaviors involving search and exploration can and do entail a greater range of behaviors than is usually recognized, and also "lead to such a multiplicity of achievements that, even if a list of specific behaviors could be produced, it would be of such an unmanageable length as to be worthless."[28]

The more mundane the activity and the goal, the easier it is to operationalize. This is evident in the list of instructional and noninstructional activities for the four job classifications. The examples of behavioral goals used by Georgia are of this rather mundane variety. It is easy to specify actions relating to, say, collecting milk money or checking mastery of spelling or arithmetic, but one cannot be as facile with activities related to the emotional and artistic development of the child or, to use one of their own goals, assisting the student in developing a personal value system that will enable him to make rational choices.[29] Examples of these are nowhere to be found and one is forced to conclude that there seems to be little relation between the worthwhile goals and philosophy of the Georgia program and its abstract view of the teacher, and its operationalizing of these goals and views. The same basic criticism can be leveled against much of the substance of the other models examined.

Furthermore, the danger of this type of reductionism *in practice* is that the lists of activities are obviously geared to making a more efficient present. Where are the activities, so essential to the continual rejuvenation of schools, such as questioning institutional arrangements? Also missing is the sense of the creativeness involved in teaching, not just in methodology but, for example, in a realization of the necessity to examine new media for what they do for and with consciousness, such as film art and the grammar of film itself.

One of the more interesting proposals of the Massachusetts Model concerns itself with the attempt to overcome the lack of familiarity with the grammar of media both as communication equipment and as significant art form. They propose that still and movie cameras and film, for instance, should be provided for *each* candidate.[30] This is significant in three major ways. First, and what may prove to be increasingly important, is the fact that organizing an educational environment for children (in effect, teaching) is a *design problem* requiring both a high degree of skill and an artistic sense for the relations of parts to the whole. By using film, the prospective teacher is introduced, through concrete means, to the problem of designing, say, an artistic creation, a social statement, or a communicative experience.

28 Robert M. W. Travers, "Models of Education and Their Implications for the Conduct of Evaluation Studies," (Western Michigan University, 1968), mimeo, p. 4.
29 *Georgia Model*, p. 256.
30 *Massachusetts Model*, p. 147.

Like microteaching, it acts to give the trainee a sense of the elements involved in designing meaningful experiences. It also introduces the trainee to the need for and the possibilities inherent in expression by both the student and the teacher in nondiscursive as well as discursive forms.[31] Three of the four models chosen for analysis show a signal neglect of the importance of nondiscursive logics and grammars in teaching. The continuation of a totally linear and discursive approach does not do justice to the psychological principles upon which much of the various programs are based.

Secondly, it is becoming obvious that film art is a primary channel of increased awareness. One need not totally accept the assertions of McLuhan to realize the potential for involving elementary school students in film for perceiving familiar facets of their environment in new ways.

Thirdly, there has been a tendency among educators to use the terminology of "the teacher as artist" as merely a ceremonial slogan. The focus upon film grammar, or the grammar of other media, can be an attempt to avoid the dichotomization of the teacher as artist (but a *highly* skilled one) who has had experience in the concrete creation of personally significant art forms through film and the teacher as reinforcer and instructor. Not only is the dichotomy naive, it may be dysfunctional to the view of a teacher as one who can make decisions based on a sense of the *totality* of the influences within an educational environment. Here Massachusetts seems particularly strong.

A Conservative View of the Mind

Any view of learning must in some way account for the human mind. Some views attribute to it an active, leading role while others demote its contribution to a passive, service function. The behavioral orientation falls into the latter category. With its emphasis and criterion for learning on the specification and enactment of behavioral objectives, the implied conception of the mind is that it is merely a container, a receptacle whose content is externally determined.

Consider, for instance, the following description as it appears in one of the models:

> Behaviors are determined by educational specialists who are thoroughly familiar with both the area of learning and with the characteristics of the learner. They are based on the assumption that the learner can demonstrate through his performance that he has *acquired* the *prescribed* element of knowledge, thought processes, skill or attitude.[32]

[31] *Massachusetts Model: Appendix II,* p. 42n. See also Suzanne K. Langer, *Philosophy in a New Key* (New York: Mentor, 1951).
[32] *Georgia Model,* p. 14 (italics added).

and

> Instruction [is] the act of attempting to change the learner's behavior in the direction of preselected objectives.[33]

The teacher is essentially viewed as a presenter and controller. This is true to varying degrees in all the models. Without getting into the long standing debate concerning the advocacy of discovery vs. other approaches, it would seem as if this view tacitly accepts as a fundamental premise that the teacher is to preselect content which is set out to be "acquired" by the students. Content seems to include not only "cognitive" knowledge (or learnings, as they often put it, which is quite a cannibalization of a phrase), but also thought processes, skills, attitudes, propensities, dispositions, etc. This has as its basis a model of the human mind as a container. That is, knowledge is reified into things which are known before acts are engaged in. These things can then be appropriated by the student, and he will demonstrate that he now has these things inside him by behaving according to preestablished criteria.

This view of teaching is close to what historically has been called the "impression model." Its one important defect is that it fails to provide adequate room for radical innovation by the student. Also, to quote Scheffler, "We do not, after all, feed into the learner's mind all that we hope he will have as an end result of our teaching. Nor can we construe the critical surplus as generated in standard ways out of the materials we supply."[34] This attribution by the models of a causal relationship does not do justice to the facts of the matter or to the extent of the knowledge we possess concerning the relationship between teaching and learning.

A Conservative View of the Student

It is also possible to critique the conception of the pupil found in the models, which stems from their strongly behavioral orientation. We have already noted the implicit use of the container metaphor in the models, one which envisions education as "filling the student's brain" with data such as skills, facts, and emotions. There is an implicit model of the elementary school student in the teacher education models, one which fits extremely well into an industrial-production type of logic. Here the pupil is seen as a "plastic mass of raw material" that can be slowly and effectively shaped.[35] The criticism to be offered here is not to say that teachers are not already

[33] *Ibid.*, p. 15.
[34] Israel Scheffler, "Philosophical Models of Teaching," in R. S. Peters, ed., *The Concept of Education* (New York: Humanities Press, 1967), p. 124.
[35] Travers, "Evaluation Studies," p. 5.

shaping children's behavior; obviously, this is the case. What is more to the point is, however, that as a model of the pupil it is a very limited representation of reality, and is woefully inadequate. The underlying assumptions of a position determine to a very large extent the logical and programmatic structure built upon them. Continuing the implicit factory metaphor, with the student as a product who is shaped, ignores a significant amount of philosophical and psychological progress made in the last decades. It posits an ideological and moral position which needs to be questioned strongly and rethought.

One of the more crucial problems with a high degree of specificity of objectives is that, in the language of systems analysis, it tends to produce a *closed loop system* which provides little possibility for fundamental change or advancement. What is more, systems that are built around highly specified objectives are nearly inevitably culture bound and seem to turn to the immediately available social order to determine the specific activities in which pupils will engage in school.[36]

Let us be very specific here. The emphasis on immediately observable behavior is most evident in the statement by Georgia that "behaviors of the pupils were found necessary to completely and accurately define those necessary for the teacher."[37] That is, the behaviors of elementary school students must be known *beforehand* so that we can then delimit the teacher's own behaviors. The problems involving the issue of creative behavior and the extreme difficulty in ascertaining a complete taxonomy of pupil behavior are clearly not met here. Yet, even if we were to hold such criticisms temporarily in abeyance, our doubts about the problems of taking such an orientation to extremes are not allayed by the following.

In the Georgia model, for example, at no time is an adequate example given of statements of behavior which are of a higher order than memory or a low level of psychomotor operation. After stating that the student should demonstrate through his performance that he has acquired not only the requisite knowledge (here meant to be "thats" or factual data) but also such complex items as thought processes and attitudes, the examples given to legitimate this concern are rather limited. "The child writes his name correctly in manuscript form" and "The pupil spells 90 percent of the words in the level four list correctly" are the illustrations used.[38] While these might initially suffice, the basic premise of the model of basing *everything* on behavioral change must be questioned if examples of the usefulness of this mode of orientation applied to what many consider to be the most crucial aspects of schooling, such as higher order thought processes and complex skills and appreciations, are not forthcoming.

36 *Ibid.,* p. 5.
37 *Georgia* Model, p. 7.
38 *Ibid.,* p. 14.

Choice and Sensitivity—A Counterbalance

While this analysis has focused primarily on issues with which the models do not adequately deal—most importantly, the restricted scope, the limitation on change and creativity, the strong control orientation, and their lack of logical and political sophistication—there are facets in Syracuse, Michigan State, and Massachusetts which attempt to counterbalance the possible conservatism.

In the Syracuse model there is a self-directed component in which the student is given concrete experience in being responsible for structuring at least a portion of his own program.[39] The feeling is that to do otherwise functions to maintain a view of society which, in their words, is *non-open*. The self-directed component ideally implies "a critical examination and resynthesizing of the ideas and understandings" that the student is asked to deal with. On a political level, this view of teaching assumes that it will lead to a greater degree of institutional innovation in society.[40] Such a proposal cannot help but give the student experience in the possibilities for teaching in a relatively less structured environment and designing such an environment for partial use in his own classroom.

One of the more promising aspects of the models, especially those of Massachusetts and Michigan State, is the specification of alternative activities leading to the same objective. The view of trainee as chooser among various alternatives can, no doubt, serve to reinforce the commitment of the trainee to making concrete decisions in his own teaching based on a consideration of other possible modes of reaching a particular goal and the structuring of alternative paths *among which his students may choose*. This is one of the strongest points of the models and realistically may lead to a more humanized rather than control-oriented school.

Also serving to counterbalance the control orientation is the emphasis by two of the models on inter- and intrapersonal awareness. Not only is teaching characterized as a "continuous process of problem resolution,"[41] and as a decision-making process,[42] but both Massachusetts and Syracuse place a good deal of weight on sensitivity training, believing that teacher effectiveness is enhanced by personal sensitivity to self and others.

Massachusetts focuses on a teacher who is a person with a high degree of self-awareness of interpersonal relationships and the component mechanisms which make these relations fruitful, such as empathy, respect, and

---

[39] *Syracuse University Specifications for a Comprehensive Undergraduate and Inservice Teacher Education Program for Elementary Teachers* (Washington, D.C.: U.S. Department of Health, Education, and Welfare, 1968), p. 54.

[40] *Ibid.*, p. 411.

[41] *Ibid.*, p. 90.

[42] *Ibid.*, p. 219.

spontaneity. These constructs are broken down into behavioral parts which are practiced in the hope that by overtly focusing on these specific behaviors, the student will be more likely to engage in more genuine interpersonal relationships than he would have without the training.

For example, empathy is defined in terms of the following types of specific behaviors: (1) attending behavior (maintaining eye contact, physical attentiveness, verbal following behavior in which the individual stays on the other's topic of conversation), (2) reflection of feeling (trainee attends primarily to the feeling or emotional statements of the others), and (3) physical empathy (simply assuming the physical posture of the other in an attempt to feel more closely what the other is feeling). It is believed by the model builders that, if these skills are practiced in sensitivity training exercises similar to gestalt therapy and esalen techniques, that "true empathy" becomes a heightened possibility since a tacit understanding of the complex phenomenon of empathy can evolve.[43] In their words, "This is a first step toward a true acquisition of these human relations skills."[44] Much of the model focuses on human relations "skills" such as these or on various nonverbal and physiological skills, awareness of sexual and racial relations, group interaction, etc. through the various training exercises. The vision of the teacher as open and sensitive to new modes of perception and bringing to the level of awareness usually hidden modes of interacting with one's environment is also evident in their emphasis upon increased sensory awareness through sensory experiences in aesthetics.[45]

The outlook on the teacher as one who is able to experience much more by freeing his often culturally constricted modes of perception is powerful. One must question some of its operationalization, though.

Polanyi's and others' point that there is a gap between the conscious reduction of feeling states, of artistic modes and perceptions, and even of much scientific activity, to concrete skills and the activity or mode of perception itself[46] is noted; but, in essence, it is ignored. This is not to say that the reduction practiced by, say, Massachusetts is not perhaps somewhat better than the lack of attempts at sensitivity today. It is to say that it very well may be a false search in the long run and may cover up the ambiguity of what it is really like to confront another person. The conscious articulation of the "skills" of empathy, etc. may open people to the

43 *Massachusetts Model,* pp. 82–84.
44 *Ibid.,* p. 84.
45 *Ibid.,* pp. 98–100.
46 Michael Polanyi, *The Tacit Dimension* (Garden City, N.Y.: Doubleday, 1966); Thomas F. Green, "Teaching, Acting, and Behaving," in Israel Scheffler, ed., *Philosophy and Education* (Boston: Allyn and Bacon, 1966); and Ira Steinberg, *Educational Myths and Realities* (Reading, Mass.: Addison-Wesley, 1968) are but a few of the references that treat the subject.

possibility of greater interpersonal involvement but, at the same time, it may destroy the very qualities of humaneness that make such encounters worthwhile. Rather than join the increasing, but all too familiar band-wagon, it might be preferable to give some thought to the "latent dysfunc-tions" as well as the possibly very real positive aspects of the endeavor. The rebuilding of the atomized skills of human relations to the gestalt of unself-conscious activity where one (here a teacher) dwells in the intersubjective situation is not done in as facile a fashion as one might think from a reading of the Massachusetts model. While the view that the teacher qua sensitive individual (in the most pregnant sense of the term) can be engineered by reducing these qualities to skills may be intuitively pleasing, it requires an act of faith that needs more of a warrant than is presented. While human relations teaching is one of the more forward-looking aspects of these models and is, no doubt, worthwhile, a genuine warrant is essential if we are to meet the goals espoused by the models.

Summary

The tone of this analysis has been one of caution. The models of ele-mentary teacher education offer perspectives on teaching which is quite different from those of the past. Due to this, we have tried to present issues that are raised by the models' behavioral conception of teaching which are disconcerting on a practical level and somehow disturbing on an intellectual one.

Throughout this analysis one of the things we have pointed to repeatedly is the need for the builders of the models of elementary teacher education to go further than they have done in developing their perspective. This is not merely a matter of the limited time to write the models. They have limited themselves to the development of a scientific and technical rationality and neglected the political and ethical dimensions of their acts and the political elements of the systems designs they have articulated.

We have also noted in our discussion of the behavioral orientation that effectiveness and quality are different concepts and do not necessarily entail each other. While effectiveness may be one measure of quality, it is not the boundary measure. Our discussion has often centered around the con-trol modality which is prevalent in the models and the "mind as a container" metaphor that seems to cohere with this position. Control becomes a sig-nificant issue that should be given further examination. Many individuals and groups in schools are becoming increasingly disaffected with schools, not only because the schools are "irrelevant" (whichever meaning one gives that ambiguous word) but even more because they are disturbed by at-tempts by some educators to control the minds of the young in the name of efficiency. This can have profound consequences for the basic perspective on the teacher espoused by the models. Are they prepared to face this issue? If their conception of the teacher is confined to an efficient achiever of the easier educational objectives, they buy a conservatism of a disturbing sort.

Finally, one cannot but wonder if the implicit search for total surety in the models does not mirror a false quest for unambiguous meanings. It may be more an attempt to construct a science of education based on the impressiveness of scientific language and explanation than on a respect for the complexity of the data. The reality of children's lives and the complexity of their search for meaning in a difficult world require a far more radical conception of teaching than the behaviorism of the models has provided us.